Richard Porson

Letters to Mr. Archdeacon Travis

In Answer to His Defence of the Three Heavenly Witnesses

Richard Porson

Letters to Mr. Archdeacon Travis
In Answer to His Defence of the Three Heavenly Witnesses

ISBN/EAN: 9783337212216

Printed in Europe, USA, Canada, Australia, Japan

Cover: Foto ©ninafisch / pixelio.de

More available books at **www.hansebooks.com**

LETTERS

TO

MR. ARCHDEACON TRAVIS.

LETTERS

TO

Mr. ARCHDEACON TRAVIS,

IN ANSWER TO HIS

DEFENCE

OF THE

THREE HEAVENLY WITNESSES,

1 JOHN V. 7.

By R. PORSON.

Tun' ut omnes in omni doctrinæ liberalis genere principes adlatres, et censeas fore, ut offam laudis tibi objiciamus, quæ te nobis tranquilliorem faciat, potius quam rationibus te verberemus, et si opus fuerit, etiam de CANINA TUA FACUNDIA *mutuemur aliquid, quo tanquam fuste probe dedolatus, incipias velle mussare, et moderationis, modestiæ, verecundiæ limites non migrare?*

MUSAMBERTIUS *Commonitorio ad* RAMIRESIUM DE PRADO.

LONDON:

Printed for T. and J. EGERTON, *Whitehall.*

M DCC XC.

PREFACE.

IT is scarcely necessary to tell the reader, that in the years 1516 and 1519 Erasmus published his first and second editions of the Greek Testament, both which omitted the three heavenly witnesses. That having promised Lee to insert them in his text, if they were found in a single Greek MS. he was soon informed of the existence of such a MS. in England, and consequently inserted 1 John V. 7. in his third edition, 1522. That this MS. after a profound sleep of two centuries, has at last been found in the library of Trinity-college, Dublin. That the Complutensian edition, which was not published till 1522, though it professes to be printed in 1514,

1514, has the seventh and eighth verses patched up from the modern Latin MSS. and the final clause of the eighth verse, which is omitted in its proper place, transferred to the end of the seventh. That Colinæus in 1534 omitted the verse, on the faith of MSS. That R. Stephens, in his famous edition of 1550, inserted the verse, and marked the words ἐν τῶι οὐρανῶι as wanting in seven MSS. That Beza, suspecting no mistake, concluded that these seven MSS. contained the rest of the seventh verse, and the eighth with the words ἐν τῆι γῆι. All these circumstances are either so well known, or mentioned so fully in the following Letters, that it would be a tedious repetition to dwell longer upon them at present.

In the year 1670, the Arian Sandius made a formidable attack upon the verse, which was followed by a more formidable attack from Simon in his Critical History of the N. T. and other works pertaining to the same subject. Soon after the appearance of Simon's book, between the years 1690 and 1700, Sir Isaac Newton wrote a dissertation upon 1 John V. 7. in which he collected, arranged,

PREFACE.

arranged, and strengthened Simon's arguments, and gave a clear, exact, and comprehensive view of the whole question. This differtation, which was not publifhed till 1754, and then imperfectly, has been lately reftored by Dr. Horfley in the laft edition of Newton's works from an original MS. In the mean time Kettner anfwered Simon in three publications, in which he has produced moft of the arguments ufually alledged on his fide, but mixed with fo many abfurd and trifling obfervations, that to read through them is no moderate exercife of patience. He reckons in the fecond century twenty-feven, in the third twenty-nine, in the fourth forty-two reafons, which might hinder the Fathers from appealing to the heavenly witneffes. Of the third fet of reafons, his eighteenth is, left that text might feem to favour Sabellianifm; his twenty-fourth, left Conftantine the Great, being then a catechumen, fhould be fcandalized! At the end of his differtation he burfts out into the following rapturous expreffions, which I fhall copy, without attempting to transfufe their elegance into Englifh.

" Nihil

PREFACE.

" Nihil enim mihi gratius quam bene mereri de hoc illustri dicto, quod est Theologia Johannea in nuce, est instar stellæ primæ magnitudinis in Scriptura, est margarita Biblica pretiosissima, & flos Novi Testamenti pulcherrimus, est compendium analogiæ fidei de Trinitate, ut alia elogia in dedicatione adducta taceamus,

" Latet inexhaustus scientiarum thesaurus in hoc excellentissimo dicto. Hic enim Theologi tres articulos fidei, Jurisconsulti tres advocatos cœlestes et testes summos, Medici tres animarum medicos inveniunt. Sistitur nobis in hoc dicto Philosophia et Pansophia quædam sublimior. Metaphysici ens unum verum, bonum, Logici prædicationes inusitatas contemplari possunt. Ethicus cernit in hoc loco summum Bonum, Physicus Iridem trium colorum, et Astrologus concursum trium planetarum sive tres soles observat. Mathematicus discit, quomodo tres sint unum in Arithmetica Divina. Musicus Musicam suavissimam trium vocum in textu concentumque harmonicum audire potest. Opticus, si quid videt, videt speculum Deitatis et in suo intellectu ob hujus mysterii altitudinem in-

PREFACE.

venit Cameram quandam obscuram. Pneumatici spiritualitatem Dei cognoscere possunt. Rhetores hoc dictum considerantes, affectum admirationis movere coguntur et exclamare, O profunditas sapientiæ Dei! Aulici tres gratiosissimos Monarchas cœlestes erga subditos in regno gratiæ venerari possunt."

At last Mill's long-expected edition of the N. T. was published. Still more and more evidence produced against the verse! Mill, after fairly summing up the evidence on both sides, just as we should expect him to declare the verse spurious, is unaccountably transformed into a defender. Abbe L. Roger, Dean of Bourges, published, Par. 1715, two dissertations, in the first of which he defends 1 John V. 7. It ought to be mentioned to his credit, that, having examined the MSS. in the royal library at Paris, he subscribed to the opinion of Lucas Brugensis, Simon, and Le Long, and ingenuously confessed that the semicircle in Stephens's edition, which now follows the words ἐν τῷ οὐρανῷ in the seventh verse, ought to be placed after the words ἐν τῇ γῇ in the eighth.

But Martin, Paſtor of the French church at the Hague, thought ſuch moderation as this a baſe deſertion of the cauſe. In his Treatiſe on Revealed Religion he ſpends a great part upon the ſingle queſtion of 1 John V. 7. He afterwards defended the genuineneſs of the verſe in three books againſt Emlyn's Full Enquiry, Anſwer and Reply. In all theſe performances he manfully aſſerted the right poſition of Stephens's ſemicircle. This he did by a ſlight aſſumption, that Stephens and all his aſſiſtants, compoſitors, &c. were infallible; an aſſumption which Mr. Travis has ſince borrowed. Emlyn, it muſt be owned, left Martin in poſſeſſion of the field; and yet, I know not how, the opinion of Emlyn made many converts; and Biſhop Smallbrooke* ſeems not to have been ſatisfied with Martin's defence; for he ſays, that little has been ſaid againſt Mr. Emlyn, except what has been offered by the ingenious Mr. Martin,

---

* In a letter to Dr. *Bentley* concerning the Complutenſian edition. See the beginning of *De Miſſy*'s firſt letter, Journ. Brit. Vol. VIII. and *Felton*'s Moyer's Lectures, p. 368.

PREFACE.

The Greek-English editor of the N. T. in 1729 threw the verse out of his text, and subjoined a long note to the place, which, though it is apparently written with great labour, does not deserve the praises bestowed upon it by Sosipater*. Twells refuted this editor after his manner; but he scarcely quits Martin, except in giving up the spurious Prologue, and appealing to the new-found testimony of Cassiodorus.

Bengelius, whose edition was published in 1734, allows, in his note on this passage, that it is in no genuine MS.; that the Complutensian editors interpolated it from the Latin version; that the Codex Britannicus is good for nothing; that Stephens's semicircle is misplaced; that no ancient Greek writer cites the heavenly witnesses; that many Latins omit them; and that they were neither erased by the Arians, nor absorbed by the *homœoteleuton*. Surely then the verse is spurious. No; this learned man finds out a way of escape; the passage was of so sublime

---

* Commentaries and Essays, Vol. I. p. 145.

and mysterious a nature, that the *secret discipline* of the church withdrew it from the public books, till it was gradually lost. Under what a want of evidence must a critic labour, who resorts to such an argument! Wetstein and Mr. Griesbach have in their respective editions given judicious abridgements of the authorities and arguments on both sides; but from the necessary brevity of notes, some previous information is requisite, before they can be perfectly understood.

Such was the state of the controversy, and all the learned * had abandoned the defence of the verse. Mr. Gibbon expressed the general opinion with great exactness and impartiality in a passage of the third volume of his History. Perhaps the historian, who must have foreseen many attacks upon other parts of his work, apprehended none on this passage. Perhaps he thought, that an opinion

---

* *Bentley* read a public lecture, which is still extant, and Abbe *Longuerue* wrote a dissertation, which perhaps is still extant, to prove this verse spurious. *Semler* too has written a Critical History of the text, in German, which I have not been able to procure.

PREFACE.

which he possessed in common with many orthodox critics, might be suffered to pass without molestation.

But if these were his hopes, he was disappointed.

The Rev. Mr. Travis published three short letters against him in the Gentleman's Magazine, 1782. These letters he afterwards reprinted (4to. 1784), with two others, much longer, addressed to Mr. Gibbon, in which he professed to discuss the whole question, and vindicate the authenticity of 1 John V. 7. Afterwards having learned that Sir Isaac Newton, Mr. Griesbach, and others, had written upon the subject, he published a second edition (8vo. 1786), with some alterations, and a considerable increase of bulk.

I had read, though without examining every minute particle of their reasoning, Mill, Wetstein, Newton, and I was fully satisfied of the spuriousness of the verse from my general recollection of their arguments. But I must thus far confess my obligations to Mr. Travis, that the appearance of his book induced me to reconsider the subject with a little more attention. In the course of of this enquiry, I found such astonishing instances of error, such intrepid assertions contrary to fact, that I almost doubted whether I were awake while I read them. But at last I discovered that Mr. Travis was a stranger to all criticism, sacred and profane; and that he had read scarcely any thing even on the subject of the contested verse, except Martin's publications. This discovery opened my eyes, and made me see why Mr. Travis was, as Professor Michaelis rightly says, *half a century behind-hand in his information.*

The reader will hardly thank me for repeating my own opinion of Mr. Travis; but it may amuse him to know the sentiments of learned foreigners. I shall therefore give some extracts, communicated to me by a friend, from Michaelis's *Neue Orientalische und Exegetische Bibliothek*, Gottingen, 1786, p. 144. He says, that " Mr. Travis is indisputably half a century behind-hand in critical knowledge; and, consequently, unacquainted with matters universally known; a proof this, that the verse 1 John V. 7. has more and warmer friends in England than in Germany." He declares that he shall not honour Mr. Travis

PREFACE.

with a particular review, to the loss of his own time, and of his reader's money and patience; that most of Mr. Travis's arguments have been already answered, or given up by the very defenders of the verse; that if he were disposed to re-examine the question, he should be obliged to transcribe his own *introduction*, which Mr. Travis quotes in the English translation of the first edition; but though he has not seen the last edition of 1777, he might have found the particulars in other authors. He proceeds to remark how shamefully Mr. Travis treats Dr. Benson, while he himself betrays a more blameable ignorance concerning the Slavonic version. After quoting Mr. Travis's words on that subject, " Now," says the Professor, " let any one compare my 88th section, and the note from Mr. Poletika's letter *, and judge.

I do

---

* The sum of Mr. Poletika's note is, that he believes 1 John V. 7. to have been inserted in the Slavonic version during the life-time of the patriarch Nicon; for it is in the edition of 1653, but not in the preceding editions printed at Moscow and Kiow. All these editions Mr. Poletika possesses; he likewise possesses some MSS. of the

Acts

I do not here complain of diffimulation, but of extreme ignorance."

"Againſt Mr. Griesbach, Mr. Travis writes with incredible ignorance. If Mr. Griesbach chuſes to defend himſelf, he may; but I ſhould judge it perfectly needleſs. Why is there not a word for or againſt Matthæi, an orthodox Athanaſian rejecter of the verſe? He wrote too in Latin, and might have been read by Mr. Travis, who ſeems to underſtand no living languages but French and Engliſh. But perhaps" (and I firmly believe the Profeſſor in the right) " Mr. Travis did not know that there was ſuch a man or ſuch a book in the world."

Acts and Epiſtles written before the æra of printing; but neither in them, nor in any copies that ever came into his hands, could he find the paſſage.

" Michaelis adds, that it is not in the Oſtrow edition, nor in ancient MSS. He doubts whether the edition of 1653 has it in the text or margin. I am almoſt perſuaded that it is in the margin, becauſe elſe I ſee no reaſon why the overſeers of the edition of 1663 ſhould not have taken it at once into the text, if they borrowed it from an edition where it was already in full poſſeſſion. See the latter part of my eighth letter.

Mr.

PREFACE.

Mr. Zoellner loudly complains that Mr. Travis has not only disfigured his letter by errors of the press, but also mutilated it in such a manner, as to make him appear the defender of a bad cause*. He then adds that part of his letter which Mr. Travis had suppressed after the second break in his Appendix, p. 59. It consists of two paragraphs, which together would have made, as I calculate, about thirty lines of Mr. Travis's book. These are some of his words; " Omnia hæc accuratius perpendenti, mihi quidem videtur, codicem Ravianum *adhuc non satis certo* pro apographo polyglottorum Complutensium haberi." Mr. Travis, by the *prudent* omission of this hesitating sentence, has made Mr. Zoellner seem to give a final opinion in favour of the genuineness of the MS. There is no mark of defect in the letter, as it is printed in the Appendix; so that the reader cannot help taking it for the whole that Mr. Zoellner wrote. Being curious therefore to know how Mr. Travis had expressed his promise to print

---

* I had myself observed, that Mr. Zoellner was rather an advocate than a judge, Letter V. p. 123.

the

the letter, I turned to p. 304, and found this cautious note. "Appendix, No. XXIII. where this letter is given *more at large*." But who would believe that in Mr. Zoellner's letter the following sentence originally existed? *Extra omnem dubitationis aleam, si nihil aliud, id quidem positum est,* codicem Ravianum in re critica vix ullius momenti esse; *non tam quod non vana suspicione prematur, sed quod valde recens sit, Stoschio aliisque judicibus,* certe post annum 1453 *scriptus*. Let any man believe Mr. Travis hereafter, when he talks of his own truth, candour, charity, and upright intentions, or when he is angry with others for their deficiency in those qualities. Whenever I hear such zealous sticklers for truth, they bring to my mind those undetected females who rail with all the bitterness and insolence of conscious virtue against the frailties of their less prudent sisters. Mr. Pappelbaum also wrote a letter to Mr. Travis on the subject of his book; but, as Mr. Travis has not thought fit to publish it, Michaelis promises to print it, if he can obtain the author's leave.

Messrs.

Messrs. *Henke* and *Bruns*, in their *Annales Literarii* (Helmstadt, May 1786, p. 385—394), have given a short review of the same work. After quoting Mr. Gibbon's note, they proceed in this manner: " These few words of Mr. Gibbon, who perhaps never uttered more truth in his life, have so vexed the writer of these letters, that he has resumed the whole dispute, as if it were still undecided, and has brought forth this child of his diligence, or rather this abortion, with a vast body, but no brain.——The singular good fortune of this work, to be twice published in a short space of time, has inspired our artist with a wonderful confidence, which he himself professes; others perhaps may call it impudence." They then give a brief sketch of the work, with some proper remarks: they make themselves very merry with Mr. Travis's suspicions of Erasmus and the argument drawn from his Paraphrases, together with the accurate chronology of making Erasmus publish his Paraphrases in 1541, five years after he was dead, and twenty-one years after they were written. They laugh at Mr. Travis's credulity in relying upon Stephens's

Stephens's accuracy, and Beza's ocular inspection of the 15, not 16 MSS.; at his repetition of Martin's miserable reasons; at his appeal to L. Valla, and *the only edition extant in Europe;* at his implicit trust in the later Latins, Lyranus, Aquinas, Durandus, Lombard, &c.; at his *infallible method of arguing* to prove that Walafrid Strabus found the heavenly witnesses in Greek MSS. With equal contempt they pass over his preference of the interpolated edition of Eucherius to the genuine; his security in the prologue of Pseudo-Jerome addressed to Damasus (read Eustochium); his confidence in the testimony of Cyprian backed by Fulgentius, in the Latetan council, in the revision of Charlemagne, the history of Victor, the Apostolos, the modern Greek confession of faith, &c. &c.*

Though I had by some pains and study qualified myself to pronounce the same sentence on Mr. Travis's book, I should have

---

* What these gentlemen say, in their concise manner, so well agrees with the observations scattered through the following letters, that, if I had met with their review sooner, I would have inserted it entire.

still kept my opinions to myself. My natural indolence, my engagement in other studies, my contempt of the work, hindered me from troubling the public with my thoughts. I read with a smile commendations* of Mr. Travis in print, and found no inclination to contradict opinions, which (with Vindex's leave) could only proceed from ignorance or bigotry. At last appeared, in the Gentleman's Magazine for August 1788, p. 700. a letter signed Eblanensis, challenging Mr. Gibbon to come forth in person and break a lance with that valiant knight of the holy brotherhood, Mr. Travis. So much ignorance of the question joined with an equal quantity of insolence, as well to Mr. Gibbon as to others, excited my indignation, and raised an hasty resolution of writing some remarks upon Mr. Travis's letters, and sending them to the same journal in which his own first letters, and this magnanimous challenge, had appeared. I meant at first rather to expose

---

* Gent. Mag. Aug. 1784, p. 565.—Aug. 1785, p. 584.—Sept. 1785, p. 686, 687.—March 1787, p. 211.

Mr. Travis's way of managing this controversy, than to enter into the controversy itself. But when I considered that it would be little more trouble to undertake the one than the other; that it would be a good deed to let the public know how far they might trust big words and bold promises; that, though many were fitter for this task than myself, some were averse to labour, and others perhaps afraid of consequences; when I considered all these things, I changed my plan, and determined, besides occasional animadversions on Mr. Travis, to give a general abstract of the main question. *Mea fuit semper hæc in hac re voluntas et sententia, quemvis ut hoc mallem de iis qui essent idonei, suscipere quam me; me ut mallem, quam neminem.* In consequence of this resolution, I inserted seven letters (which make the five first of this collection) in the Gentleman's Magazine for October and December 1788, February, April, May, June, August, 1789. A gentleman who called himself Vindex, in the same Magazine for January 1789, p. 12. after mentioning " Mr. Gibbon's contemptuous inattention to Mr. Travis's irrefragable* de-

PREFACE.

fence," added the following note: * " A *Cambridge* correspondent has not rendered it less so by his feeble strictures in your Magazine for October last, p. 876. *Dat veniam corvis.*" I gave Vindex a gentle rebuke in my next letter (II. p. 17.), but he was too headstrong to take advice, and replied in the Gentleman's Magazine for March, p. 225. I shall only transcribe a part of his letter.

Mr. Urban,

Your [4] zealous, knowing, and discreet correspondent, in p. 101—105 of your last Magazine, who is happily exempt from " [5] the weakness that fools call candour," is pleased to insinuate that [7] " bigotry" alone can support the authenticity of the famous text 1 John V. 7. This surely is " [9] the excess of Christian benevolence." Let this literary Goliath " [10] beware of measuring the integrity of other men by his own narrow conceptions." * * * * * * As to Mr. Travis, " [3] with whom I have not the pleasure of being acquainted," I flatter myself that he will " [1] never be weary of answering" those opponents who " are never weary of repeating the same baffled and exploded reasons." Contemptuous inattention will justly be construed as " 'a proof of conscious impotence." Let him therefore, " ' compliments being passed, begin upon business." To him it may be safely left. In the mean time, " 'will you, Mr. Urban, advise" his supercilious antagonist in a whisper," not to issue his dictates *quasi ex cathedra*, though he may have a sufficiency of learning to fill the chair. But does not his " ' good mother" know him too well to place him in the chair. *Fœnum habet in cornu*.

I quote this trash merely to shew how ready any person is to decide upon these points, though neither qualified by nature nor art for the discussion of them, and to think he benefits the world by publishing his opinion. As if truth in these cases always depended upon a majority of voices!

But being tired of this tedious method of publication, I quitted it, as soon as I had finished the subject of Greek MSS. with a promise to resume the dispute in another form. Some time afterwards, while these letters were in the press, Mr. Travis sent to the

PREFACE. xxi

Gentleman's Magazine for January 1790 such a defence of Stephens and Beza, as Martin himself would have blushed to father. He there repeated, almost word for word, what he had already said in his book, and I had confuted. He had not even knowledge enough to see, or candour enough to own, the most palpable errors of the press; but still assumed, without shame, a position in itself absurd, and shewn by me to be totally groundless, the perpetual infallibility of Stephens's margin. I replied in the next month minutely to every article of the defence; and, as Mr. Travis, in his zeal for Stephens's character, had forgotten his own, I reminded him of a few offences that he had committed against his favourite virtue, Truth. But he declined my proposal of retracting or defending his his assertions, by calling me Thersites, saying that he *despised my railings*, and making a sort of promise, that when my volume came out, he would take it into consideration. We shall therefore soon see what efforts his ingenuous temper will make to acknowledge or excuse his errors.

PREFACE.

I here perform my promise, which perhaps Mr. Travis and my readers would have forgiven me for breaking. Such as these letters are, I deliver them to the judgment of the public. I shall make no professions of diligence and fidelity, for two reasons; 1. because I conceive, that such a profession is always implied in the very circumstance of becoming an author; and, 2. because in the present case it would be dangerous as well as unnecessary. For all that are well acquainted with Mr. Travis's book would infallibly feel either their suspicions roused, or their laughter provoked, if I pretended, like him, that "Truth was the sole aim, object, and end," of the following letters. But before I take my leave, I would gladly prevent two or three objections, which I foresee;——That I have treated a grave subject with too much levity; and a dignitary of the church with too much freedom; and, what is a much more grievous crime, that I may be thought to defend heresy, and to attack the Catholic faith.

To the first and second objections I answer, that I could not treat the subject in any other manner.

PREFACE.

manner, if I treated it at all. To peruse such a mass of falsehood and sophistry; and to write remarks upon it, without sometimes giving way to laughter, and sometimes to indignation, was, to me at least, impossible. For the first, let Tertullian* plead my excuse. *Si et ridebitur alicubi, materiis ipsis satisfiet. Multa sunt sic digna revinci, ne gravitate adorentur. Vanitati proprie festivitas cedit. Congruit et veritati ridere, quia lætans; de æmulis suis ludere, quia secura est.* For the second, I am persuaded that every attentive reader, who believes me right in the statement of my facts, and the tenour of my argument, will allow, that even harsher expressions would in such a case be justified. Besides, I confess, I never much admired that mock politeness, which expresses a strong charge in a long-winded periphrasis of half a dozen lines, when the complete sense might be conveyed in as many words.

Je ne puis rien nommer, si ce n'est par son nom; J'appelle un chat un chat ＊＊＊＊＊＊＊＊＊＊＊＊＊＊

---

* Adversus Valentinianos, § 6.

Mr. Gibbon, after answering an accusation brought against him by Mr. Davis, thus proceeds: " I disdain to add a single reflection; nor shall I qualify the conduct of my adversary with any of those epithets, which might seem to be the expressions of resentment, though I should be constrained to make use of them as the only terms in the English language which could accurately represent my cool and unprejudiced sentiments." I desire to know whether Mr. Davis was at all obliged to Mr. Gibbon for this exertion of his good-nature? Or who sees not that such moderation proceeds from malice, and is only affected in order to possess the reader with a more lively resentment against the offender?

As a river tastes of the soil through which it last flowed, our style generally takes a tincture from the last book we read. This must be my excuse, if I have too much disregarded the laws of civility, that by reading Mr. Travis, I have been insensibly infected with his spirit. But whatever apology I owe to others on this score, I owe none to him. He thinks himself authorized to treat the most eminent men for learning and virtue with

with the utmost contempt and insolence. He is the last man that should be permitted to be angry with others for *railing*. *Idne alteri crimini dabis, quod eodem tempore, in eadem provincia tu ipse fecisti? audebisne ita accusare alterum, ut quo minus tute condemnere, recusare non possis?*

The truth of the third objection I deny. I maintain that my book is virtually a defence of orthodoxy. He, I apprehend, does the best service to truth, who hinders it from being supported by falsehood. To use a weak argument in behalf of a good cause, can only tend to infuse a suspicion of the cause itself into the minds of all who see the weakness of the argument. Such a procedure is scarcely a remove short of pious fraud. *Pro pietate nostra tam multa sunt vera, ut falsa tanquam ignavi milites atque inutiles oneri sint magis quam auxilio.* What good can we expect to work upon heretics or infidels by producing the heavenly witnesses? Will they submit to dispute with us, if we revive such stale and exploded reasons? Will they not believe, or affect to believe, that this text is the only, at least the chief pillar, of our faith, and that,

that, like Sir Martin Mar-all, we continue to fumble upon the lute, long after the mufic is over?

What candour or fairnefs in difpute, exclaims a Papift, can be expected from the Proteftant heretics, who ftill maintain the obfolete fcandal of Pope Joan, which has been fo frequently and fully confuted? What juftice, might a Mahometan exclaim, can we hope from the Chriftian dogs, who ftill propagate the ridiculous tale of the Prophet's pigeon?

If any expreffions occur, where I feem to fpeak flightingly of orthodoxy, let the reader confider, that in difputing againft a paffage generally fuppofed to favour the caufe of orthodoxy, my fubject fometimes compelled me to affume the perfon of an heretic. But when, for the fake of brevity, I ufe the word *orthodoxy* in a bad fenfe, I mean, not that refpectable orthodoxy, which defends the doctrine of the Trinity with fair argument and genuine fcripture; but that fpurious orthodoxy, which is the overflowing of zeal without knowledge—which is not contented with our profeffing the common faith, but would force

force us to defend it by all and singular the arguments, whether weak or strong, and all the texts, whether spurious or genuine, that have ever been employed in its defence;—which, whenever a rotten and ruinous outwork of religion is demolished, utters as hideous a shriek, as if the very foundations of the building were shaken, and the church of Christ nodded to her fall.

Yet why defend Mr. Gibbon, an enemy? I do not defend Mr. Gibbon, except by accident. I defend Erasmus, Sir I. Newton, La Croze, Mr. Griesbach, and other *Christians*. But where would have been the harm, if I had avowed myself the defender of Mr. Gibbon? Because he is an enemy? For that very reason I would defend him. And I wish that every writer who attacks the infidels, would weigh the accusations, and keep a strict watch over himself, lest his zeal should hurry him too far. For when an adversary can effectually overthrow one serious charge out of ten brought against him, the other nine, though they may be both true and important, will pass unheeded by the greater part of readers,

An

An impartial judge, I think, muſt allow, that Mr. Gibbon's Hiſtory is one of the ableſt performances of its kind that has ever appeared. His induſtry is indefatigable; his accuracy ſcrupulous; his reading, which indeed is ſometimes oſtentatiouſly diſplayed, immenſe; his attention always awake; his memory retentive; his ſtyle emphatic and expreſſive; his periods harmonious. His reflections are often juſt and profound; he pleads eloquently for the rights of mankind, and the duty of toleration; nor does his humanity ever ſlumber, unleſs when women* are raviſhed, or the Chriſtians † perſecuted.

Mr. Gibbon ſhews, it is true, ſo ſtrong a diſlike to Chriſtianity, as viſibly diſqualifies him for that ſociety, of which he has created Ammianus Marcellinus preſident. I confeſs that I ſee nothing wrong in Mr. Gibbon's attack on Chriſtianity. It proceeded, I doubt not, from the pureſt and moſt virtuous motive. We can only blame him for carrying on the attack in an inſidious manner, and

---

* Chàpter LVII. note 54.
† See the whole ſixteenth Chapter.

with

with improper weapons. He often makes, when he cannot readily find, an occasion to insult our religion; which he hates so cordially, that he might seem to revenge some personal injury. Such is his eagerness in the cause, that he stoops to the most despicable pun, or to the most aukward perversion of language, for the pleasure of turning* the Scripture into ribaldry, or of calling Jesus † an impostor.

Though his style is in general correct and elegant, he sometimes *draws out the thread of his verbosity finer than the staple of his argument.* ‡ In endeavouring to avoid vulgar terms, he too frequently dignifies trifles, and clothes common thoughts in a splendid dress, that would be rich enough for the noblest ideas. In short, we are too often reminded of *that great man, Mr. Prig, the auctioneer,* § *whose manner was so inimitably fine, that he had as much to say upon a ribbon as a Raphael.*

Sometimes in his anxiety to vary his phrase, he becomes obscure; and, instead of

---

* Chapter LIX. note 32.   † Chapter XI. note 63.
‡ Love's Labour Lost.   § Foote's Minor.

calling

calling his personages by their names, defines them by their birth, alliance, office, or other circumstances of their history. Thus an honest gentleman is often described by a circumlocution, lest the same word should be twice repeated in the same page. Sometimes epithets are added, which the tenour of the sentence renders unnecessary. Sometimes in his attempts at elegance, he loses sight of English*, and sometimes of sense.

A less pardonable fault is that rage for indecency which pervades the whole work, but especially the last volumes. And, to the honour of his consistency, this is the same man who is so prudish that he dares not call Belisarius a cuckold, because it is too bad a word for a *decent* historian to use. If the history were anonymous, I should guess that

---

* Chapter XLVII. near note 19. " Yet a *latent* and almost invisible spark still *lurked* among the embers of controversy." If it lurked, it was probably latent. Chapter L. near note 153. " The author of a mighty revolution appears to have been endowed with a pious and contemplative disposition." I might with equal want of precision say of Mr. Gibbon, " The author of a bulky history appears to be perfectly free from superstition."

these

these disgraceful obscenities were written by some debauchee, who having from age, or accident, or excess, survived the practice of lust, still indulged himself in the luxury of speculation; *and exposed the impotent imbecillity, after he had lost the vigour of the passions.**

But these few faults make no considerable abatement in my general esteem. Notwithstanding all its particular defects, I greatly admire the whole; as I should admire a beautiful face in the author, though it were tarnished with a few freckles; or as I should admire an elegant person and address, though they were blemished with a little affectation.

Yet, to say the truth, I have one censure in reserve. A candid acknowledgment of error does not seem to be Mr. Gibbon's shining virtue. He promised † (if I understand him rightly) that in a future edition he would expunge the words, *of Armenia*, or make an equivalent alteration. A new edition has appeared; but I have looked in vain to find

---

* Junius.
† Vindication, p. 75. Chapter XV. near note 178.

a correction of that passage. I am almost persuaded, that the misrepresentation of Gennadius was not wilful; but that Mr. Gibbon transcribing the Greek from the margin of Petavius, wrote by mistake αἰδοῦμαι for αἰδοῦνται. This error has now been so long published, that it is scarcely possible to suppose him ignorant of the charge. He has had an opportunity of confessing and correcting the mistake. Yet still it keeps its place in the octavo edition.

For my own part, having professed in the following letters to retract any mistake upon conviction, I here present the reader with a list of additions and corrections, which I have intermixed with the typographical faults.

If

ERRATA, ADDENDA, CORRIGENDA.

P. 7. l. 2. *for* p. *read* pp. N.B. p. 127, 375. means the corresponding pages of the two editions; pp. 9, 79. mean pages of the second edition; and all single references mean the second edition, when notice is not given to the contrary.
9, 19. *for* would *read* could.
21, 19. editions.
22, 18. "thirty-one".
24. ult. *for* 5 *read* 31.
25, 8. are, Et
ib. 20. ᾧ εἰσιν,

35, 15. the 9 excess
36, 15. The reader
37, 1. same with
42, 8. Aquinas.
44, 1. quotes
49, 13. that
51, 2. τρεῖς
ib. 9. εἷς
ib. 13. τρεῖς εἰς τὸ ἕν
52, 9. Martin, Verité, p. 171.
ib. 11. εἰς τὸ ἕν
ib. 14. 16. ἓν εἰσι
53, 7. ἅμα.
ib. 8. *efficiunt*

55, 7.

PREFACE. xxxiii

55, 7. p. 33)
58, 23, 24. clearer. In
ib. 25. Matthew
62, 14. addition
ib. 15. ἐν
ib. 17. εἰς
64. penult. MS.)
72, 16. *Le Long only says that he found* ELEVEN *MSS. which belonged to King Henry. For* ELEVEN *therefore read* EIGHT, *and blot out the next sentence.*
74, 8. refers, Emlyn,
75, 3. MSS.?
ib. 5. as it may,
ib. 8. sent them
78, 7. ἀγαθὸν ζητησάτω,
83, 20. *for* pp. *read* p.
84, 15. manuscript
ib. pen. ἀ. ιι.
91, 5. Gal. IV. 14.
ib. 15. 80. XXI.
ib. 23. IV. 31.
94, 9. where even
97, 18. it is
98, 4. ' In cælo,'
ib. 6, 7. Brugensis's editions,
99, 20. at last,
110, 8. p. 27. 43.
133, 22. ἐν τῷ
140, 17, 18, 19. adds *In Christo Jesu* in the eighth verse; which is added in the seventh by the author de Trinitate, published, together with the writer against Varimadus, by Chifflet.
147, 6. farther,
167, 17, 18. Mark IV. 9, &c. a great number of MSS. adds it in Matth. XIII. 23. XXV. 30. Luke
182, 6. *Add as a note:* Bengelius, who says on Apoc. XIII. 5. that Usean prints his additions in a different character, mistook the edition of 1698 for Usean's.
188, 16. *My memory has here grossly deceived me. For* meant to print *read* printed, and *blot out the note.*
190, 14. scripture?
218, 12. *add:* And Mr. Griesbach informs us, Symbol. Crit. p. 225. that the French King's MS. No. 60. reads, καὶ οἱ τρεῖς τὸ ἕν εἰσιν, the precise words quoted in the dialogue.

223, 6. *add this note:* From this place to l. 17. except the parenthesis, the Emperor Justin II. has stolen word for word in his epistle to all the Christians in the world; and towards the end of the epistle employs almost the very words of the parenthesis. *Evagrius* Hist. Eccles. V. 4. p. 422.
229. 5. in the epistle for
ib. 11. Instead of *spurious* I ought rather to have said *interpolated.* The words *licet carnaliter et visibiliter corporis et sanguinis Christi sacramentum dentibus premant* are rejected by all the MSS. (about twenty) that have been collated by the Louvain and the Paris editors. *Augustine*, Tract. in Joann. XXVI. near the end.
236. *Note* †. *Combefis*, Græc. Patr. Auctar. Noviss. Part II. p. 215.
272, 7. *On the word* Father * *add this note:* * How easily this might happen, will appear from the following passage of Epiphanius, Hær. LXVI. 69. p. 691... Οὐδεὶς γὰρ ἔνι ἕτερος θεός——ἀλλὰ εἷς πατὴρ ἐξ οὗ τὰ πάντα, καὶ εἷς Κύριος Ἰησοῦς Χριστός, δι' οὗ τὰ πάντα, καὶ ἓν πνεῦμα τὸ ἅγιον, ἐν ᾧ τὰ πάντα, ἀεὶ οὖσα ἡ τριὰς, μία ἡ θεότης.
275. *note* §. *Hæres.* XXX. 30. p. 156.
292, 19. *Read, for the sake of clearness,* happened to authors.
293, 7. *dele* a
301, 26. *Add this note on "* montesq; * *feros;" * I follow Markland's emendation, which Mr. Heyne has misrepresented. He imputes to Markland an absurd reading, *montesq; feras, silvasque,* and condemns the emendation for its aukward arrangement of the mourners, in putting the wild beasts between the mountains and woods. I mention this oversight, merely to strengthen an opinion, which I have long entertained, and shall always resolutely defend, THAT ALL MEN ARE LIABLE TO ERROR.
313, 5. would have been.   *
                                            316.

316. *antep.* or even
322, 11, 14. Priestley.
344 (or 345. *for I have no proof by me), after* Rom. VIII. 16. *add:* Compare also the nineteenth chapter of the first book. *And on the end of the paragraph add this note:* In *Sirmond's* works, Vol. I. p. 377 —400. is an anonymous treatise, entitled, *Breviarium Fidei adver-*

sus Arianos; the author of which borrows the substance of great part of the third book, with additions, transpositions, and alterations; but he too is silent upon the text of the three heavenly witnesses.
354, 17. fifth.
382, 15. or by chance.

If I discover any fresh mistakes, I shall be happy to have an early opportunity of correcting them. I should be extremely obliged to the candour or curiosity of the public, if they would give me this opportunity by calling for a second edition. On that joyful occasion, I engage to amend all the errors detected in this book, either by myself or others. Nor will I blot out the traces of these errors, as if I was ashamed of the common lot of authorship, but let them remain, and subjoin to each a correcting note. This will, I think, be the surest pledge of the innocence of my intentions, if any of my mistakes should chance to wear a suspicious appearance. With respect to a public confession of error, I should think it a duty, and not a merit, if I did not see how reluctantly and ungracefully most men submit to it. My example therefore may perhaps conduce to the instruction

of

of younger or more bashful authors, whom the dread of a recantation, natural in the outset of a literary career, might tempt to dangerous and dishonest concealments. I should rejoice to be able to add, that my example may conduce to the instruction of posterity, if I were not too well acquainted with the weakness both of my own and my adversaries abilities, to nourish so groundless an hope. Mr. Travis and I may address our letters to posterity; but *they will never be delivered according to the direction.*

CONTENTS.

LETTER I.

Of Mr. Travis's candour in correcting his mistakes. Instances in what he says of Erasmus, of the Dublin MS. and of Bede. Page 1—15

LETTER II.

Of Valla's Greek MSS. supposed to contain the disputed verse, 1 John V. 7. 16—40

LETTER III.

Of the Complutensian edition. 41—53

LETTER IV.

Of the MSS. used by R. Stephens and Beza.
                                54—100

LETTER V.

Of the MSS. supposed to be seen by the Louvain divines, of the Dublin and Berlin copies. An enumeration of all the Greek MSS. that omit the verse.   101—135

LETTER VI.

Of the Vulgate Latin version.   136—156

LETTER VII.

Of the Syriac and Coptic versions.   157—177

LETTER VIII.

Of the Arabic, Æthiopic, Armenian, and Slavonic versions. —— 178—208

CONTENTS.

LETTER IX.

Of the Greek writers that are quoted in favour of the verse. ——— 209—238

LETTER X.

Of the Latin writers before Jerome that are quoted in favour of the verse. 239—282

LETTER XI.

Of the later Latin writers that are quoted in favour of the verse. 283—362

LETTER XII.

Of the Greek and Latin writers, who, though they had sufficient occasion, have not quoted the verse. Recapitulation and conclusion.
363—406

TO

The Rev^d Mr. TRAVIS.

LETTER I.

SIR,

I AM of the same opinion with your friend Eblanensis * upon the passage quoted from Gennadius by Mr. Gibbon (which Mr. Davis † mentioned before you) and I think that Mr. Gibbon is bound in honour to retract and amend that sentence of his history. I also think that Mr. Travis's book is a composition *scarcely to be parallelled in any age,* but not for

---

* Gentleman's Magazine for August 1788, p. 701.
† Gentleman's Mag. 1782, p. 181. 1784. p. 419.

those qualities which Eblanensis supposes. For, in my judgment, the character which you give of Dr. Benson's dissertation (p. 98, 221) will much better suit your own book; that " for intrepidity of assertion, disingenuousness of quotation, and defectiveness of conclusion, it has no equal, stands aloof beyond all *parallel*, as far as my reading extends, either in ancient or modern times!"

Since this question, after having been long decided, is now revived, I mean to trouble you with some animadversions on your management of the controversy. But first let me pay a just tribute of praise to your candid and ingenuous temper. You had got a conceit into your head, that Erasmus did not publish Valla's Commentary before 1526; and, in consequence of this blunder, went on to charge Erasmus with a wilful suppression of the truth. Can a man, who writes of others at this rate, expect any tenderness for his own errors? When you found out, what you ought to have known long before, that Erasmus did publish Valla in 1505, you omitted the passages in your book which contradicted that fact, but without making the slightest flighteft apology for this fhameful treatment of Erafmus. On the contrary, you labour to bring frefh proof of that arch-heretic's roguery. For it is a maxim with you, Sir, that all Arians are wholly poffeffed by the devil, and that it is impoffible for them *to quote fairly, to argue candidly, and to fpeak truly*, (p. 127. 374.) While the orthodox may fay what they pleafe, and their bare word is taken without farther enquiry; nay, even Amelotte's teftimony was urged as an argument in the firft edition, but omitted in the fecond, at the defire perhaps of fome cautious friend, who feared it would be too barefaced an infult upon any tolerably well-informed reader. In the 17th page of your fecond edition you tell us, that you have omitted Amelotte's teftimony, but being loth to give him up entirely, you add, " the deductions from the whole of this accufation and defence, feem to be greatly in favour of Amelotte." You, Sir, blame Erafmus, p. 147. for *giving up the conteft in a moft unchearful and difingenuous manner.* If Erafmus were now alive, he might retort the accufation with tenfold force againft his accufer. But to return. In the fifth page of of the preface to your second edition, you confess your mistake about the time when Erasmus published Valla's collation; but, at the same time, you would fain make us believe that you knew of its being published in 1505, though not of its being published by Erasmus. You talk of *the only edition—in 1505, which is, perhaps, to be found in England (if not in Europe.)* What do you mean by *the only edition in* 1505? There never was but one edition in 1505. But if you mean *copy*, you might have spared your parenthesis, and corrected your mistakes by looking into Wetstein's Prolegomena, p. 55; who informs us, that he used a copy of that very edition. I intend, Sir, in due time, to produce other proofs that you have never read through Wetstein's Prolegomena (whether from idleness, or fear of being infected with the poison of Arianism, I leave to the consideration of others); at present I shall content myself with one instance, that will serve to shew the extent and accuracy of your reading. Your predecessor Martin in his defence of the spurious verse, 1 John, v. 7, had mistaken the date of Mark's Gospel for the date of the MS. itself,

itself, thus turning years in centuries (χρόνοι) and St. Mark into the transcriber, as Wetstein expresses it, Prol. p. 52. You copied this ridiculous blunder *(errorem valde ridiculum,* WETSTEIN) which Sosipater exposed in his remarks *. Now let the reader see with what grace a candid man retracts his error. Ed. 2. p. 158. " The words respecting the date of this MS. which were copied from it in the former edition of these letters, are here omitted; because they *may* † be applied to the time when St. Mark's Gospel itself was *originally written*." Diffident creature! you seem indeed still to retain your former opinion, but will not positively assert that the words admit no other construction. I sincerely congratulate you on this accession of knowledge, and consequently of modesty. I hope that in the next edition of your book you will be farther enlightened, so as to perceive that the words in question can possibly mean no-

* Commentaries and Essays, Vol. I. p. 525.

† Ay, upon proof *positive,* it *must:* but upon proof *presumptive,* it only *may*; that's a logical distinction, Madam. *Witwoud,* in CONGREVE's *Way of the World.*

thing but the time when the gospel was first written by the evangelist. I hope too, that you will then have acquired a little more charity than you possess at present; and that, from the recollection of your own blunders, you will find some softer names for the trifling slips of your adversaries, than *want of knowledge*, or *want of integrity* (p. 39, 79.)

"But why," you will say, "attack with such violence errors which the author himself has corrected in a subsequent edition? why reproach a man with his sins after he has repented of them?" Certainly, Sir, this would be unfair treatment, if you had really and sincerely repented of them. But repentance, I think, is never reckoned sufficient without reparation. And what reparation have you made? You publish letters to Mr. Gibbon, in which Erasmus, Dr. Benson, la Croze, Simon, Bowyer, and Mr. Gibbon himself, are frequently taxed, in the plainest terms, with ignorance or dishonesty. In a question that branches itself out into so many minute particulars, it is difficult for the most cautious or sagacious critic to steer clear of all mistakes. He might hope, however, in case of error, for a milder a milder alternative (or, if you please, *two milder alternatives*, p. 9, 79, 80, 143, 325, 326) than what you, Sir, have thought fit to grant those unhappy men. Did it never occur to you, while you were revising your own work, and correcting some of the most notorious errors, that it was possible for the offences, which you punish in others with such severity, to be the mere offspring of inadvertence and human infirmity? For haste you would hardly admit as a good excuse; at least you seem to have disclaimed this plea for yourself, p. 127, 375, though your friend Eblanensis is not ashamed to make this wretched apology for you. Would you be content to have these mistakes urged against you as arguments of your own *want of knowledge*, or *want of integrity*? And why should you think less favourably of others, unless plain proof appears to the contrary? As to your correcting your errors upon due notice and conviction, *I would applaud you to the very echo, that should applaud again*, but not without insisting on two conditions: 1. That you should fairly, without shuffling or prevaricating, recant; 2. That you should, in errors of any moment, give a separate set of additions and corrections for the use of the purchasers of the former edition. For whoever reads the former without the latter, which is likely enough to happen, will be as liable to believe and spread its errors, as if the latter had never been published. Till these conditions are fulfilled, I shall look upon myself as fully authorized to censure the faults of the first edition, whether they be corrected in the second or not. That one of these conditions has not been fulfilled, is plain to every body. That the other has not, I think will be plain, partly from what I have already said, and partly from what I am going to say.

You confidently affirm, in the preface to your second edition, that the *errors* there mentioned *do* NOT *at all affect the great question*. The opposers of the doubtful text had concluded that Bede knew nothing of it, because in his commentary upon the fifth chapter of the first Epistle of John, he is very diffuse upon the sixth and eighth verses, but makes no mention of the seventh. "No!" exclaim you boldly without understanding a syllable of the matter, "they might as well argue,

argue, that Bede knew nothing of John VIII. 53, 54. Acts II. 12—22. Rom. I. 20—22. becauſe he makes no mention of ſuch paſſages in his Commentary." This remark and theſe citations are ſuppreſſed in the ſecond edition: in the preface to which you ſay, if I take your meaning rightly, that this error aroſe from truſting implicitly to the information of others. Now I would fain know two things: 1. Upon whoſe information you made the aſſertion; 2. If you took it from Martin, as I ſuſpect (Diſſ. Part. 2. c. 5. p. 196.) how it came to paſs that you changed 1 *Pet.* to *Rom.* Martin quotes, for examples of Bede's omiſſions, 1 *Pet.* I. 20—22. *John* VIII. 53, 54. *Acts* II. *verſes* 12 *et les ſuivants juſq'au* 23.) Suppoſing this remark to be true, it might, perhaps, ſeem plauſible enough to ſay, that nothing would be preſumed againſt any particular verſe from Bede's ſilence, becauſe he has omitted many other paſſages; which yet all critics believe to be genuine. But if the premiſes be withdrawn, what becomes of the concluſion? Did you mean to prove any thing when you made this obſervation? If you meant it for a proof, ſurely your

your main argument must be weakened in proportion to the weight that such a proof would have had, if the facts, on which it is grounded, were admitted. Still I agree, that the *expulsion* of these errors *has not enfeebled or impaired your argument*. And, while I am in the generous humour of making concessions, I will farther allow, that the cause which you have espoused would have been in full as good a situation, if you had never written in its defence. When first I read your preface, I thought that, not having Bede's Works in your possession, you had enquired of some person at Oxford, (perhaps the same who gave you so exact an account of the *only edition* of Valla) and that this person had led you into the mistake. But being now convinced that you took your citations from Martin, I would gladly learn, why you expressed yourself in such vague terms as, " the other mistake arose in the same manner." Why did you not rather say, " the other mistake I copied from Martin." I think I can guess the reason of this management. Such a confession would have shewn you to be a servile copier, a blind follower of the blind, and

would

would have drawn upon you the same censure that you have passed upon Dr. Benson, p. 56, 119. If you demand, and certainly you have a right to demand, why I insinuate so injurious a suspicion, I shall at present refer you to pages 13 and 76 of your former edition. (See hereafter, Letter V.) If you are not satisfied with this answer, I promise to give you some additional reasons for my opinion, before I end my remarks upon you.

Another distinguishing quality of your extraordinary composition is what the base vulgar would call canting. For instance: " Theo-
" dore Beza, whose erudition and piety *

---

* His piety was so fervent, that an instance or two of it may not be amiss. He wrote a book to prove, that heretics may justly be punished with death. It is well known that Servetus was grievously afflicted with that pestilential disorder, heresy. Calvin prescribed roasting by a slow fire, as an effectual cure, which was accordingly tried, but the patient unluckily happened to die in the operation. Beza, speaking of this accident, in a note on 2 Pet. I. 4. facetiously adds, " and yet there are some who think the good man forsooth was very ill used." Emlyn indeed, Vol. II. p. 253, is pleased to complain of this as a cruel scoff, but he had no taste for raillery. I must own, to the disgrace of piety and orthodoxy, that Beza omitted this sentence in his latter editions.

" did

" did honour to the age, &c." p. 6. " The
" celebrated Durandus," p. 20. " This ce-
" lebrated commentator" (Walafrid Strabo)
p. 23. " The good Eucherius — " there
" was not a bishop more revered for learn-
" ing and piety." " The pious Jerome," p.
32. " This holy martyr" (Cyprian). p. 37.
" Jerome speaks in these glowing terms"
(glowing indeed!) " Qui sic non credit,
" alienus a Christo est," p. 108. But
enough of this drudgery. Neither shall I
take any notice of your confused manner of
stating the objections of the adversaries. One
thing ought to be recorded to the honour of
your diligence and learning, that at first you
either knew not or entirely neglected, Newton, De Missy and Griesbach, and very rarely consulted Emlyn, Bengelius, and Wetstein.
In your second edition, p. 17, you tell us,
that you are indebted for the knowledge of
De Missy to Maty's Review. I shall not expect
the reader to believe, but upon the testimony
of his own eyes, that in Mr. Gibbon's note
upon the very passage of his history, which
gave occasion to Mr. Travis to expose himself in print, there is an accurate reference

to

to De Missy; nor shall I expect him to believe, but upon the same testimony, that you, Sir, have favoured us with that selfsame note in p. 367. But you seem to have too high a spirit to receive instruction from an enemy. I shall leave you, for this time, with the following dilemma. If you have read through De Missy's Letters in the Journal Britannique, either your sense or your honesty is in imminent danger: your sense, that you have not seen cause to make more alterations in your book; your honesty, that having seen cause, you have suffered the obnoxious passages, to remain unaltered. But if you have not yet read through De Missy's Letters, I call upon you to justify your indolence to the public; an indolence, which in any writer, who aspires to the character of a patient and impartial investigator, (p. 375) amounts to a criminal inattention. *Sed hæc fuerit nobis, tanquam levis armaturæ, prima orationis excursio; nunc comminus agamus, experiamurque, si possimus cornua commovere disputationis tuæ.*

POSTSCRIPT.

POSTSCRIPT.

ΕΥΡΗΚΑ! What I despaired of finding, chance at last threw in my way. Many sleepless nights did I pass in endeavouring to discover why Mr. Travis, in copying Martin, should change 1 *Pet.* into *Rom.* But looking into the English translation of Martin's book, I saw the reason of the mistake. The translator, p. 168, instead of saying St. Peter's *first Epistle*, says, St. Paul's *first Epistle*. Mr. Travis solidly reasoned, that St. Paul's first Epistle was in our Testaments the Epistle to the Romans; set it down without farther enquiry, and fulfilled the old adage by robbing Peter to give to Paul. Are Bede's Works so very scarce or expensive, that they were inaccessible to Mr. Travis? Had he no correspondent at Cambridge or Oxford to examine them for him? Or could not " THE (where merit is preeminently conspicuous, *epithets* are needless) " PRELATE, to whom Mr. Travis's work is " humbly inscribed," p. 357, lend him a copy? Gentle reader, admire this *patient and impartial investigator*, who takes a quotation

tation at second-hand, and that he may enjoy every possible opportunity of blundering, consults even the copy of a copy. Thus in his first edition, p. 76. he quotes ἀντέλαβεν for ἀνέλαβεν, a mere typographical error in the English translation of Martin. To the same cause are owing the quotation and reference, both inaccurate, p. 74, 164.

N. B. See Vindex's remark upon the former part of this letter, in the preface, or in the Gentleman's Magazine for January, 1789, p. 12.

LETTER II.

SIR,

I HEREBY give notice, once for all, to you and my readers, that I pretend not to produce any new arguments upon so beaten a topic as I have chosen. It will be enough for me, if I can collect what is scattered through many works; dispose in a better order, or set in a clearer light, what others have written; so that those who want leisure or courage to wade through the whole controversy may form some general notion of the dispute, without the labour of collecting and comparing a multitude of polemical authors, or the danger of being misled by the hardy assertions of a partial and sophistical declaimer. Perhaps, after this confession, I shall be thought to stand in need of some excuse. I shall therefore shelter myself under the example of Mr. Travis, who has himself condescended to pick up the

blunted

blunted weapons that poor Martin wielded without succefs, and to brandish them against the Philistines. As the orthodox are never weary of repeating the same baffled and exploded reasons, we heretics must never be weary of answering them. For silence, as I learn from you, Sir, p. 369, is a proof of conscious impotence. I once thought that it might sometimes proceed from contempt*. But lest you should be wise in your own conceit, you shall be answered. I call myself an heretic, because I know that the disbelief of the authenticity of this text is the Shibboleth of the party; and that it would be equally absurd and fruitless, after the rash and unguarded opinion that I have advanced,

* Vindex also, with whom I have not the pleasure of being acquainted, in the Gent. Mag. 1789, p. 12, attributes Mr. Gibbon's inattention, with great justice, in my opinion, to contempt. In answer to Vindex's note, I would advise him in a whisper, to temper his zeal with a little knowledge and discretion. I must tell him at the same time, that the *strictures*, which he obligingly calls *feeble*, did not profess to enter into the merits of the cause; but only to convict Mr. Travis of ignorance and prevarication: in which, if I am not misinformed, they have had some success.

to make any proteftations of innocence. "It were to be wifhed," fays Martin, "that this ftrange opinion had never "quitted the Arians or Socinians; but we "have the grief to fee it pafs from them to "fome Chriftians, who though content to "retain the doctrine of the trinity, abandon "this fine paffage, where that holy doctrine "is fo clearly taught. *They have, however,* "*the misfortune to find themselves confounded* "*with the secret enemies of the doctrine.*" In vain may Simon, La Croze, Michaelis, and Griefbach, declare their belief of the doctrine; they muft defend it in the catholic manner, and with the catholic texts: nor is all this enough; but in defending the genuinefs of a particular text, they muft ufe every one of the fame arguments that have already been ufed, without rejecting any upon the idle pretence that they are falfe or trifling. I pity Bengelius. He had ⁵ the weaknefs (which fools call candour) to reject fome of the arguments that had been employed in defence of this celebrated verfe, and brought upon himfelf a fevere but juft rebuke from

an

an oppofer of De Miffy * (Journ. Brit. X.
133); where he is ranked with thofe, "wh
" under pretext of defending the three hea
" venly witneffes with moderation, defen
" them fo gently, that a fufpicious read
" might doubt whether they defended the
" in earneft; *though God forbid that we fhou*
" *wifh to infinuate any fufpicion of Mr. Beng*
" *lius's orthodoxy.*" You fee, Sir, what a mi
take I have made in taking my fide of tl
queftion. But there is no help; it is too la
to recant. *Fortem hoc animum tolerare jubet*
et quondam majora tuli. I wifh your frier
Eblanenfis had favoured us with the nam
of thofe eminent men who are convinced l
the extenfive learning and clofe reafoning f
which your work is fo remarkable. The
muft have been candid perfons, and extreme

---

* De Miffy's fate too has been fomewhat hard. I
was bold enough to attack Amelotte's veracity and Ma
tin's underftanding. This provoked a neft of horne
Four anonymous writers fell upon him; three with pe
fonal abufe; the fourth (who is here quoted) with m
lignity under the mafk of moderation.

open to conviction.* I will mention
many as I can recollect at prefent, who ha
publicly declared themfelves on your fide
Bifhops Horfley and Seabury, Bamptonia
Lecturers, Dr. Croft, and Mr. Hawkins †
and laftly, Sir, our good mother pays
due refpect to the merit of her fon. For
am credibly informed, that on the 30th
November 1788, at Great St. Mary's Churcl
Cambridge, the Rev. Mr. Coulthurft told

* The excellent Dr. Waterland being compliment
by Whifton and Emlyn (fee Emlyn, Vol. II. p. 236.) f
his impartiality in not infifting upon this text, thought pr
per in his "Importance of the Doctrine of the Trinity,
p. 271, to be convinced by Twells that it was genuine. [/
I mean to acknowledge a miftake or to fupply a defec
whenever I perceive it, I think it neceffary to obferve, th
the foregoing note contains the truth indeed, but not tl
whole truth. For I have fince learned that Dr. Wate
land had declared himfelf in favour of the fpurious ver
in the year 1723, but in a more guarded and doubtf
manner.]

† To thefe I ought perhaps to add the anonymous au
thor of "A Summary of the moft interefting Evidenc
on a moft important Tryal," who calls Mr. Travis
book, p. 9. a *mafterpiece of reafoning and compofition*. Bu
whether he be in jeft or earneft, depends upon a prev
ous queftion.

- brilliar

brilliant and crowded, as well as a learne[d] audience, that "the authenticity of 1 John V[.] 7, has been clearly and substantially establish[-] ed." When Eblanensis shall be pleased [to] increase this list with the names of his con[-] verts *of the first eminence*, they will all to[-] gether compose a very amiable set, and en[-] tirely free from [7] bigotry. And now, Sir, compliments being passed, I shall begin upo[n] business.

Mr. Gibbon affirmed in that sentenc[e] upon which Mr. Travis has written a lon[g] commentary, that the memorable text of th[e] three heavenly witnesses is condemned b[y] the silence of Greek MSS. of versions, and [of] fathers. In a note, he explains his senti[-] ments more openly with respect to the Gree[k] MSS. and the origin of the verse in our pre[-] sent edition. A writer in the Gentleman['s] Magazine (Nov. 1782, p. 521) to whom yo[u] yourself referred in your first edition, p. 3[,] sufficiently justified Mr. Gibbon upon th[e] subject of the offensive note. Since the e[x-] ternal authority of any text in scripture [is] founded on the concurrence of ancient MS[S.] of ancient versions, and citations of ancie[nt]

writers, it will readily be granted, that wher[e]
ever any of thefe three pillars of evidence
withdrawn or weakened, the fuperftructu[re]
which they were intended to fupport, mu[ft]
totter of courfe; and that if all three be u[n]
found, it muft be in great danger of fa[l]
ling.

Let us then enquire into the Greek MS[S.]
fuppofed to contain the difputed verfe. Yo[u,]
Sir, reckon up feven belonging to Vall[a,]
one to Erafmus, fome (you are fo mode[ft]
you will not fay, p. 280, how many) to t[he]
Complutenfian editors, fixteen to Robe[rt]
Stephens, and fome that the Louvain d[i]
vines had feen. You afterwards make,
282—5, a very pretty calculation (for yo[u]
are an excellent arithmetician) and find tha[t]
thirty-one [MSS.] out of *eighty-one*, or (mo[re]
than) *three* out of *eight*, or (nearly) ONE HAL[F]
of that WHOLE NUMBER —actually did e[x]
hibit, or do exhibit, the verfe 1 John, [V.]
7!" Inquifitive people will fay, how ha[p]
pens it that none of thefe MSS. now r[e]
main, except the Dublin copy, which We[t]
ftein is fo cruel as to attribute to the fi[x]
teenth century; for concerning the Berli[n]
MS[S.]

MS. they will, I fear, rather chuse to believ[e]
La Croze and Griesbach than Martin and M[r.]
Travis. But the answer is easy. The[y]
are lost. Either they have been burned, [or]
have been eaten by the worms, or bee[n]
gnawed in pieces by the rats, or been rotte[d]
with the damps, or been destroyed by tho[se]
pestilent fellows the Arians; which w[as]
very feasible; for they had only to get in[to]
their power all the MSS. of the New Te[s]tament in the world, and to mutilate or d[e]stroy those which contained *un des plus bea[ux] passages dans l'Ecriture Sainte* *. Or, if a[ll]
these possibilities should fail, the devil ma[y]
play his part in the drama to great advan[n]tage. For it is a fact of which Beza *po[si]tively* assures us, that the devil has been tam[pering] with the text, 1 Tim. III. 16; an[d] that Erasmus lent him an helping han[d.] Beza indeed, being a man brimful of can[n]dour, subjoins, that he believes Erasmus a[s]sisted Satan unwittingly †. This perhap[s]
ma[y]

---

* Martin.

† A diabolo depravatum: cui sane hac in parte (dica[m] enim libere quod res est) suam operam imprudens quide[m]

may be some excuse for Erasmus. But what hopes of salvation are left for your Wetsteins, your Griesbachs, your Sosipaters, who have the front to persist in their damnable errors; the two first in spite of 350 pages of Berriman, the other in spite of 400 of Mr. Travis. After all, I rather prefer the supposition that the Arians destroyed the said MSS. because it shews the orthodox in so superior a light; who have not, to my knowledge at least, destroyed a single MS. that omitted their darling text, while the Arians, in less than a century and half, suppressed thirty that contained it. Yet let us hear what may be said in their favour; not out of tenderness to them (they deserve no mercy) but merely for our own justification.

The earliest collator of Greek MSS. of the New Testament was Laurentius Valla, who had seven, according to you, Sir, p. 18. For this, p. 144, you quote his note on John VII. 29, where it seems, Valla " positively af-

---

(sic enim arbitror) sed suam operam tamen Erasmus commodavit. In Beza's first edition it is, SIC ENIM MALO ARBITRARI. *Lenior et melior fis accedente senecta!* See above, Letter I. p. 5, note.

firms"

firms" it. I can see no *positiveness* in Valla's expression; however, it is a word of exceeding good command, and is of great use elsewhere, as in pp. 178, 247, 280, 296. But I see a great deal of *positiveness* in the assertion, that *this passage was found in all Valla's MSS. and is commented upon by him*, p. 1 Valla's words are, [*Et hi tres unum su Græce est*, ET HI TRES IN UNUM SUNT, εις τὸ εισι. Now, Sir, point out, if you can, a sing Greek MS. in which the seventh verse thus read. (I except the Complutensian i visibles.) Explain why R. Stephens's sixte MSS. should, according to your own hypothesis, all agree in the other reading, whi is now adopted for text by common conse One very notable circumstance in the cop is, that they are such gregarious anima All Valla's MSS. agree in having *in und εις το εν εισειν*, in the seventh verse; and the Complutensian agree with them in t variation, and with one another, as well with the Dublin copy, in omitting the fi clause of the eighth verse. Seven of Stephens's MSS. omit the words εν τωι ουρα and the other nine, if we may believe N

Trav

Travis, for Martin is not quite so sanguin[e]
correspond with the received reading. A[ll]
the rest of the Greek MSS. which, if I hav[e]
counted right, amount to ninety-seven
ancient and modern, oriental and occidenta[l]
good, bad, and indifferent, do with one co[n]
sent, wholly omit the seventh verse, and th[e]
words ἐν τῇ γῇ of the eighth. You have sa[id]
I know, p. 339, that the words ἐν τῇ γῇ see[m]
to have been omitted in a few copies onl[y].
But this is a little pious fraud, which is ve[ry]
excusable, when it tends to promote the cau[se]
of truth and the glory of God. If you thin[k]
this charge of fraud too severe, I shall [be]
very happy to seize the slightest probabiliti[es]
that may acquit you of so odious an imput[a]
tion, and shall acquiesce in the milder accu[
sation of shameful and enormous ignoranc[e].
But be this assertion of yours owing to frau[d]
or to ignorance, I defy you to specify a sing[le]
Greek MS. that omits the seventh verse, an[d]
retains these words. Simon indeed mentio[ns]
No. 2247, as having the words, ἐν τῇ γῇ; b[ut]

---

* This must be understood only of Mr. Griesbach[']
list. See a more exact computation at the end of Le[t]
ter V.

it seems to be a mistake committed in th[e] hurry of copying, and to have proceeded fro[m] the idea of the vulgar reading, which w[as] then present to his mind: 1. Because F. I. Long (Emlyn Vol. II. p. 277.) testifies, th[at] having looked over all the MSS. quoted b[y] Simon, he could find ἐν τῇ γῇ in none [of] them: 2. Because Mr. Griesbach, who ha[s] re-examined the same MSS. with a particular view to this passage, sets down No. 224, as in perfect harmony with the rest, without taking notice of any variation. It is no[w] high time to awake you, Sir, from your na[p,] and to inform you, that Valla's note is wri[t]ten upon the eighth and not the seventh vers[e.] This is acknowledged by Martin, who though a simple man, and totally destitu[te] of taste and criticism, had yet more learnin[g] and honesty than his humble imitator. Marti[n] only argues that Valla had the seventh ver[se] in his Greek copies, because Valla is qui[te] silent. This argument, as every body know[s] that knows any thing of collations, is ve[ry] deceitful; for in half the collations that ev[er] were made, and more especially the near[er] we mount to the revival of letters, the edito[rs]

an[d]

and critics confulted their MSS. only upon difficult places, or where they themfelves felt any curiofity. And to conclude that Valla or any critic of that age, had any particular text in his MSS. becaufe he does not exprefsly fay that they omitted it, is to pufh a negative argument much farther than it will go by its own ftrength. But I fhall fpeak more fully on this head, when I come to treat of R. Stephens's edition. Meffieurs Martin and Co. feem at other times to decry all negative arguments; but that is only when the inference bears hard upon their favourite; when the admiffion of fuch an argument fuits their purpofe, they are as vigilant in feizing it, and as adroit in managing it as heart could wifh. You will fay, pp. 288, 313, (for you have a fine bold way of talking) "that the *invariable tenor* * of the eighth verfe in the Latin Vulgate is, with fo few exceptions as not to merit notice, *in unum funt*;" and confequently that Valla, who quotes fimply, *unum funt*, without the prepofition,

---

* Mr. Travis had the affurance to affert this without any limitation, Ed. i. p. 100.

from

from the Latin, muſt mean the ſeventh, and not the eighth verſe. I muſt deſire you to produce a competent number of authorities for this *invariable tenor*. I have ſeen, I believe, as many MSS. of the Latin Vulgate as you. I have compared moſt of the editions printed in the fifteenth century, and many ſubſequent to that æra; particularly ſuch as have various readings; I have examined the early French, Italian, and Engliſh verſions (which were all made from copies of the Vulgate) and I ſolemnly declare, that I have not been able to find, even in a ſingle copy, even as a variation, that reading which Mr. Travis affirms to be the *invariable tenor* of the eighth verſe. *Will he prove it to us? He does not attempt it. He truſts to find readers as full of zeal as himſelf; and then—no proof will be required**.

The

---

* This decent language is applied to Dr. Benſon, p. 83, 182. I ſhall here propoſe a conjecture, how Mr. Travis fell into this ſtrange miſtake. He knew nothing of the Latin copies: he ſcorned to ſoil his hands with muſty MSS. and editions; but Mr. Bowyer had ſaid (falſely indeed) that Cyprian has quoted *tres* IN *unum ſunt*; and

after-

The whole question is reduced to one point. Valla says nothing of this verse in his collation. Is his silence a good proof that the verse was in his Greek copies? By no means. That exactness of collation which is now justly thought necessary, was, unhappily, never attempted by the critics of the fifteenth and sixteenth centuries. The method in which Valla performed his task was, probably, to chuse the MS. that he judged to be the best, to read it diligently; and wherever he was stopped by a difficulty, or was desirous to know how the same passage was read in other Latin or in the Greek MSS. to have recourse

afterwards had supposed that Cyprian referred to the eighth verse. Mr. Travis seems to have joined these propositions together, and thence to have concluded that the reading of the Vulgate was IN *unum sunt*; in which opinion he might perhaps be confirmed by finding it thus quoted in the treatise *de Baptismo*, annexed to Cyprian's works. Part of this treatise Mr. Travis has printed in his appendix, which part contains the only Latin authority that I know for the preposition. Mr. Bowyer has led Mr. Travis into another mistake, and persuaded him pp. 91, [310], 311, to give Bishop Pearson the notes on Cyprian, which are the property of Bishop Fell. *I do not love thee, Doctor Fell!*

to them. So Erasmus, when he published his New Testament, gave the printer a MS. corrected in the margin from other copies; and this is the way in which first editions are printed, whose text is settled from different MSS. The editors select one, which they intend generally to follow, and sometimes correct it by the aid of the others. But as the faithful discharge of this office depends on the skill and industry of the corrector, no wonder that the good readings pass often unobserved or neglected, and that the bad are preserved or preferred. If, therefore, L. Valla found the seventh verse in the Latin copy or copies then before him, he might be so well satisfied of its authenticity, as not to think of consulting his Grecian oracles. If upon coming to the eighth verse, he found the Latin MSS. vary, some omitting *hi*, others the whole final clause, he might just cast his eye upon the Greek MSS. and having caught the words that he wanted, set them down for future use, without returning to the former verse, which he had already dismissed from his mind, and concerning which he had no scruples. Again: supposing that Valla perceived

ceived this omission of the seventh verse in his Greek MSS. is it certain that he would have mentioned it? He might know that the verse had been frequently quoted by the Latin writers of the later ages, as a strong proof of the trinity. Might he not therefore be apprehensive of the clamours of the orthodox, if he should disclose so unwelcome a truth, as the absence of this text from the originals? I dare not make the defence for Valla that Lee makes, who says that Valla did right, if the text were not in his MSS. to be silent, because to act otherwise would be *to furnish the heretics with horns to butt against the faith.* I can however easily imagine that in such a case Valla might have a prudent regard to consequences, and preserve himself by a discreet silence from the attacks, which an honest avowal of the fact would infallibly have provoked. Nor is this barely a surmise, but founded on reason and analogy. In the year 1698, Zacagni, an Italian, published among other things a collation of a Greek MS. containing the Catholic Epistles. This MS. agrees with all the others in omitting that much injured text of the three heavenly witnesses.

witnesses. Zacagni mentions this circumstance; and at the same time being sensible that it was necessary to seem to produce some authority in behalf of the common interpolation, he boldly says, that the seventh verse is extant in our Alexandrian. Who sees not that this assertion of a palpable falsehood was made only to stop the mouths of the bigots, and not meant to impose but upon voluntary dupes? *

But what if Valla's Latin MSS. omitted this verse? Certainly it is much more likely to suppose Latin MSS. that want the verse than Greek that have it. For the former, almost thirty in number, are real, visible, tangible, legible manuscripts, and not like those coy, bashful Grecian beauties, that withdraw themselves not only from the touch but from the sight

Quæ nec mortales dignantur visere cœtus,
Nec se contingi patiuntur lumine claro.

I argue therefore that this text might be absent both from Valla's Greek and Latin MSS. (which seems to be Mr. Griesbach's opinion)

* See a full and entertaining account of this whole farce, in De Missy's fourth letter, Journ. Brit. IX. p. 295—310.

and that his saying nothing about it does not prove that he read it. But that his Greek MSS. wanted it, is clear and certain, and fairly admitted by Bengelius. Here follows a list of propositions which you must demonstrate (at least the greater part) before Valla's collations will stand you in any stead.

1. That Valla intended to give a perfect and exact collation of all his MSS.
2. That he never mistook, or *omitted any thing through haste, inattention, &c. but collated them all and singular with the utmost accuracy.
3. That from his mentioning seven Greek MSS. upon John's Gospel, it follows that he had the same number throughout the whole New Testament; though in another place he speaks only of seven *Latin* copies; in a third says, *Tres codices Latinos habeo et totidem Græcos, cum hæc compono, et subinde alios consulo.* Besides it is well known that Greek MSS. of the Epistles, and especially of the Catholick Epistles, are much scarcer than of the Gospels.
4. That he had the perpetual use of these MSS. and did not only consult them

upon occasion, as the last quoted words seem to hint.

5. That Valla's Latin MSS. all agreed in retaining the seventh verse, together with the words *in terra* and the final clause of the eighth.

6. That if he had perceived the want of the seventh verse in his Greek MSS. he would have had courage enough to declare it.

After a blundering note, p. 143, which would lead us to think that Erasmus knew of Cassiodorus's testimony in favour of the verse, two hundred years before it was published, you proceed, Sir, in the excess of Christian benevolence, p. 147, to inform us, that Erasmus at last gave up the contest, being fearful of the argument deducible from Valla's MSS. You qualify indeed your accusation with an *as it seems.* But you play that trick too often. I find you generally most peremptory when you assume this air of moderation*. I shall therefore

---

* Not to tire the reader's patience, I shall trouble him only with a single instance, P. 8. *It* SEEMS *impossible to account for the behaviour of Erasmus—but upon one of these*

therefore in future omit such expletives, and by contracting the sentence restore it to its genuine meaning. Concerning this liberal insinuation, be it noted, that Erasmus, in his fourth and fifth editions says (what he had long before hinted in his answer to Lee) *Quid Laurentius legerit, non satis liquet*; plainly meaning that it was not clear whether Valla had this text in his MSS. or not. Martin affirms that this is not the true sense of the words; that Erasmus allows the verse to have stood in Valla's MSS. but that he was in doubt whether they had any slighter variations; (such for instance, as the omission of the words ἐν τῷ οὐρανῷ, &c.) the reader will hardly expect me to answer such absurdity. I give it merely for a scantling of that good man's reasoning, who, as De Missy says of him, *étoit fait pour déraisonner avec toute la confiance d'un vieillard à qui ses cheveux blancs, une réputation populaire et des complimens déplacés avoient faire accroire qu'il étoit fort capable.* I shall leave the subject of the Codex Britannicus

---

these *suppositions*, &c. p. 9. *A proceeding which* MUST *fall under one of these* INEVITABLE *alternatives,* &c. Compare ed. 1. p. 10. l. 21. ed. 2. p. 13. l. 17.

(which

which is the same with the Dublin MS. (whatever Mr. Travis may say) to another letter; at present it remains to vindicate Erasmus from another charitable innuendo. "You affect to doubt, p. 8, 9, and p. 66, 142, whether Erasmus could produce the five MSS. in which he alledged the verse to be omitted." I wish you, Sir, could defend all your allegations as well as I can this of Erasmus; for of the five Greek MSS. that Erasmus saw (if Erasmus affirms that he himself *saw* five, which I forget at present, not having the book at hand) four are still actually extant; the Vatican is extant, to which Erasmus appeals on the credit of an extract made by his friend Bombasius; a Latin copy, which Erasmus quotes as omitting this verse in the text, is now in the Berlin library. 10 Beware, Sir, of measuring the integrity of other men by your own narrow conceptions. I have dwelt the longer upon this article, because I have sometimes regretted that the opposers of the verse in question seldom explain their own arguments so copiously as might be expected, but study brevity too much, and do not sufficiently consult the apprehension of common readers.

D 3

ers. Thus sense is in danger of being overpowered by words, and reasoning by declamation. Besides, I should be happy to imprint some few elementary ideas of criticism upon the *rasa tabula* of Mr. Travis's mind. For I can assure him that at present he possesses not even the rudiments of that useful science.

N. B. See Vindex's answer in the preface or in the Gentleman's Magazine for March, 1789, p. 225. The passages which Vindex amused himself with quoting, are marked with corresponding numbers in his answer, and in the foregoing letter.

Postscript.

If I were writing for the learned, the inquisitive or the impartial, I should think that I had already trespassed too much upon their patience. But that the unlearned and less-attentive reader may be enabled, and the partial compelled to see how much credit is due to Valla's silence; I shall add a short observation or two to prove what I have asserted concerning the defects of his collation. 1. In 1 John,

1 John, v. 9, the Vulgate reads, *Quoniam hoc est testimonium Dei, quod majus est.* The clause *quod majus est*, is peculiar to the Latin translation. But Valla, who just now was so minute as to inform us that the Greek added two small words (εἰς τὸ) here says nothing of three (ἢ μείζων ἐστί) apparently more important. 2. Though the first epistle of Peter is not quite so long as the first of John, Valla has bestowed upon it almost twice as many annotations. If therefore it were probable that no various readings of consequence escaped him in the latter, much greater would be the chance that none escaped him in the former. At the end of the third chapter after *Dei* in the Latin copies we read *deglutiens mortem, ut vitæ æternæ hæredes efficeremur.* No Greek MS. has the slightest traces of this impertinent addition. But Valla, in spite of his dislike to the Vulgate, in spite of his readiness at once to display his own acuteness and to gratify his resentment, by confronting the version with the original, was either too negligent to detect this blemish or too merciful to expose it.

I am aware of an alternative that may be urged against this argument, which alternative I shall

all fairly state, and let it produce its utmost ect upon the mind of the reader. Either alla's Greek MSS. might be more bountiful an others, and contain this sentence; κταπιῶν τὸν θάνατον, ἵνα τῆς ζωῆς τῆς αἰωνίου κληρονόμοι γενοίμεθα) or his Latin MSS. might be more aring than others, and preserve the genuine ɛ, undebased by impure alloy. Which of e two suppositions be farther distant from e boundaries of reason, must be left a question, till a certain critic shall have made his tion in favour of one or the other.

LETTER III.

'Tis fit it should be shewn what an arguer he is, and how well he deserves for his performance to be dubbed by himself IRREFRAGABLE.* LOCKE.

> In school-divinity as able
> As he that hight IRREFRAGABLE*;
> A second *Thomas*, or at once,
> To name them all, another *Duns*.
>   HUDIBRAS.

SIR,

WE are now arrived at the Complutensian edition, in which the *honest bigotry* of the

---

* See Vindex on the use of epithets, Gent. Mag. for Jan. 1789, p. 12. I perceive, from the same Magazine for March 1789, p. 225, that he has not profited by the wholesome advice which I gave him. And how ungenerous it is, as well as cowardly, after swaggering and blustering, to sneak away from the combat, and leave Mr. Travis alone *to bear the burthen and heat of the day!* In the mean time I earnestly intreat Mr. Travis's admirers to refrain from boasting of their proselytes and repeating their defiances. Such quackery is unworthy any person who pretends to learning.

editors

editors has inserted the doubtful text. By *honest bigotry* Mr. Gibbon probably means, that the editors thought the verse genuine indeed, but inserted it contrary to their Greek MSS. If they thought it genuine upon such slight grounds as the authority of the Vulgate, of Pseudo-Jerome, and of Thomas Aquinus, they were *bigots*. But if they really thought it genuine, their *bigotry* was so so far *honest*. The same sort of bigotry predominated in your mind, when you quoted p. 286, the barbarous Greek of the Lateran council, and finding a chasm, supplied it by a still more barbarous translation of your own from the Latin. Thus would the Complutensian editors reason: " This verse is genuine, though it is not in the Greek copies. We will translate it therefore from the LATIN VERITY, and restore it to the context." But you, Sir, take for granted without proving (a vice very frequent in you, though you reprove others for it, p. 182.) that this verse was in all their MSS.; you hint Mr. Gibbon's wishes to be, that the editors had omitted it in opposition to all their authorities; and you profess an unwillingness (i. e. a willingness) nefs) to believe that Mr. Gibbon himself would in such a case have betrayed his trust. *Aerugo mera!* Mr. Gibbon justifies the intention of the Complutensian editors, and only blames their prejudice. And who can deny their prejudice in favour of the Vulgate to have been excessive and absurd, after reading the following sentence from their preface to the Old Testament? *Mediam Latinam beati Hieronymi translationem, velut inter synagogam et orientalem ecclesiam posuimus, tanquam duos hinc inde latrones, medium autem Jesum h. e. Romanam sive Latinam ecclesiam collocantes.* Or who can wonder that men, so blindly devoted to a version, should sometimes presume to correct the originals from that version, especially in a passage, * *in quo maxime et fides catholica roboratur, et Patris et Filii et Spiritus Sancti una divinitatis substantia comprobatur?* But in fact we have all the evidence necessary to prove that they actually paid this extravagant compliment to the Vulgate. For Stunica, who would have been extremely glad to have had the power of appealing to

* Pseudo-Hieronym. Prolog. in Epist. Canon.

the Greek MSS. against Erasmus, qotes none in favour of this unfortunate verse, but rests the whole merits of the cause upon the Latin copies, and the impostor who usurps the name of Jerome. You, Sir, to do you justice, think there is some force in this objection; and in a momentary fit of imprudence or modesty, p. 280, *own yourself unable satisfactorily to account for it.* But these are the last struggles of expiring shame. For though you saw the unavoidable consequence of this concession, you add, that you have proved the Complutensian Greek not to be a translation from the Latin. Your tacit inference then is, I suppose, that it could only come from the Greek MSS. But this inference is a little too hasty. The Complutensian Greek may be a translation from the Latin, though not an exact translation. Let us suppose that Mr. Travis, while he was disputing against Mr. Gibbon, had the use of a MS. which contained the suspected verse; would he neglect to produce its testimony in defence of this very verse and against a man whom he hated? If he believes this possible, or professes to believe it possible, I shall believe him

either

either mad, *aut illud quod dicere nolo*. I afk therefore what could induce Stunica, who is at other times fcarcely lefs virulent againft Erafmus than Mr. Travis himfelf is, what could induce him to be fo mild and tame in this particular inftance? What but the confcioufnefs that he knew of no Greek MS. which contained the paffage in queftion? Twells indeed has bethought himfelf of a falvo, and a precious falvo it is (Exam. P. II. p. 142.) that the labour of collating the Catholic Epiftles did not fall to Stunica's fhare. In the year when Stunica wrote his remarks on Erafmus, all his fellow-labourers were on the fpot, able and willing, I hope, to inform him of the manufcript readings of this or of any other paffage. For furely they had fome difcourfe together upon the difficult places, and did not perform each man his tafk in filence and folitude, without any confultation or communication. If Stunica had faid nothing upon this Epiftle of John, we might not perhaps be able to extract any certain conclufion from his filence. But Stunica quotes his Rhodian MS. frequently in oppofition to Erafmus, once upon the 16th verfe of the third

third chapter of this Epistle, once upon the 20th verse of this very fifth chapter, and both times in defence of the Complutensian reading. Yet upon the 7th verse, where there was a pressing necessity, if ever necessity existed, of supporting his opinion by the authority of the Greek MSS. Stunica appeals to none. "Where," cries Erasmus, "sleeps this Rhodian MS.?" But the Codex Rhodiensis was as deaf to the reproaches of Erasmus, as Baal to the sarcasms of Elijah. No man in his senses would ever omit to urge evidence that was so much wanted and that would have so much weight. Poor Stunica most piteously cries out, *Sciendum est Græcorum codices esse corruptos; nostros vero ipsam veritatem continere.* Now if this be not a full and clear confession, that he knew of no MS. containing the disputed verse, I cannot tell what is. If the Codex Rhodiensis had been orthodox, he would have written to this effect: *Quidam sane codices Græcorum hæc verba omittunt; Rhodiensis vero ipsam veritatem continet:* I need not observe, that since this MS. leans very much to the Vulgate and particularly adds, τοῦ Θεοῦ in the former of the two places above quoted,

words

words found in no other Greek MS. nor version whatsoever, its omission of the seventh verse of the fifth chapter will form a strong argument against the genuineness of the passage. Allowing then that the Codex Rhodiensis omitted, as it certainly did omit, this *excellent* passage, why did not Stunica consult others? Either he had no more to consult, or the other editors, and not Stunica, had collated them. If he had only the Codex Rhodiensis, why is he not ingenuous enough to confess it? If he or his brother editors had more, why did he not inform himself of their reading in this place, either from his own inspection or from those who had consulted them? They would naturally be anxious to confirm their own credit and veracity; they would be eager to tell him, if they could tell him with truth, that their MSS. gave the very reading which they had followed in their edition. When that edition was published, Erasmus's challenge had been made some time. While they were giving us a marginal note from *Beatus Thomas*, to account for their eighth verse, we should have esteemed it a favour if they had added a little postscript or preface,

face, to inform us of the state of their MSS. in the foregoing part of the sentence. Nay, they ought to have done it; and as you say, Sir, p. 223, *Where it is a duty to speak, to be silent is to be criminal.* To which I add, that where we should be sure to gain our cause by speaking, to be silent is to be foolish. "But if the Complutensian editors took not this verse from Greek MSS. whence did they take it?" I answer, as others have answered, from the modern copies of the Vulgate, from the spurious Jerome and the Angelic Doctor. "This would be to charge those *illustrious* editors with FORGERY." I should be loth to call it by so harsh a name; *honest bigotry* better suits the purpose; but such is the everlasting sophistry which you and Martin employ. You aggravate the faults or negligences of the Complutensian editors, of Stephens and Beza, into crimes; and then, from the enormity of the offence argue against the probability of its being committed. Your reasoning may thus be reduced to the form of a syllogism.

Stunica, Stephens, Beza, &c. did not insert this verse in their editions contrary to the authority of their Greek MSS. unless they were

impious

impious hypocrites, abandoned cheats, notorious impostors, &c.

But they were not impious hypocrites, abandoned cheats, notorious impostors, &c. *Ergo*, they inserted this verse from the authority of their Greek MSS.——

Q. E. D.

As I flatter myself that every unbiassed reader will see through and despise this paltry artifice, I shall give myself no farther trouble about it, but proceed to consider the objections that may be made to my position. You tell us, Sir, and truly too! That the Latin Copies differ from the Complutensian. They do differ; but only in the seventh verse by reading *(hi tres unum sunt)* οὗτοι οἱ τρεῖς ἓν instead of οἱ τρεῖς εἰς τὸ ἓν; which seems at first sight a considerable difference. You of course exult upon it, and civilly ask, p. 184, "Can any man be so much a *Bœotian*, as to imagine, that if these editors had meant to forge a *Greek* text, *to follow the reading of the* Latin *copies*, they would not have forged one which would have followed those copies exactly?" I confess, most *learned Theban*, that till I was enlightened by you, I was so much of a *Bœotian* as to imagine, that if the intention of the Complutensian editors was fraudulent, they might have wit or caution enough to make their tranflation vary from the Latin copies, the better to impofe upon the world by the apparent difference. They would difguife the child they had ftolen, in order to conceal the theft. But I, who poffefs more charity than perhaps any other perfon in the world (always excepting you, Sir, and your humble admirers, Vindex, Eblanenfis and Kufter*) will try to give a more candid reprefentation of this matter. The Complutenfian editors believed 1 John V. 7, to be genuine and determined to infert it in their text. They alfo believed to be fpurious and determined to expunge the final claufe of the eighth verfe.†

* Gen. Mag. March 1787, p. 211.

† This claufe is omitted in many of the Latin MSS. Mr. Travis, with his ufual modefty, afferts, p. 288, that *the* Latin *copies have univerfally the concluding claufe of the eighth verfe.* A direct falfehood! *Ufque adeo lectores fuos pro ftupidis et bardis habet, quibus quidvis imponere fibi licere fecure confidit.* I appeal to the reader, whether a man who is capable of making fuch round affertions wilfully or ignorantly, be not utterly difqualified to manage a controverfy, or to accufe others of mifreprefentation.

Thus

Thus then I suppose them to have translated the Latin into Greek; Ὅτι τρεῖς εἰσὶν οἱ μαρτυροῦντες ἐν τῶι οὐρανῶι, ὁ πατὴρ καὶ ὁ λόγος καὶ τὸ ἅγιον πνεῦμα, καὶ οὗτοι οἱ τρεῖς ἕν εἰσι, καὶ τρεῖς εἰσὶν οἱ μαρτυροῦντες ἐπὶ τῆς γῆς, τὸ πνεῦμα καὶ τὸ ὕδωρ καὶ τὸ αἷμα. In their Greek Manuscript or Manuscripts, they found, Ὅτι τρεῖς εἰσὶν οἱ μαρτυροῦντες, τὸ πνεῦμα καὶ τὸ ὕδωρ καὶ τὸ αἷμα καὶ οἱ τρεῖς εἰς τὸ ἕν εἰσι. What was now to be done? They were not willing entirely to abandon their originals; they accordingly patched up a motley text, and dexterously transplanted the clause καὶ οἱ τρεῖς τὸ ἕν εἰσι, to the end of the seventh verse. So that as far as they could without damage to the orthodox faith, they followed the reading of the Greek manuscript. They thought this clause of too great size and importance to be turned out of doors without ceremony; they therefore suffered it to stay, though they provided it with rather an indifferent lodging. If Mr. Gibbon observed this, he had a fresh reason for attributing their conduct to HONEST BIGOTRY. And it is no more than justice to allow that they at least did their work like workmen. They made good Greek of their Latin; a task to which the translator of the Lateran Decrees and the writer of the Dublin MS. were unequal. In my next I intend to travel through Stephens's, and the other manuscripts that have been said to contain this *excellent* verse.

I shall not quit this article without taking notice of an objection, which you, p. 185, and Martin seem rather to insinuate darkly, than to propose in form: " that the Complutensian reading of the seventh verse, εἰς τὸ ἕν εἰσι, weakens the evidence for the doctrine of the Trinity that might otherwise be drawn from this passage." Or that the words εἰς τὸ ἕν εἰσι may be understood of an unity of will and testimony; whereas the simple expression ἕν εἰσι must be understood of the unity of essence. Now, Sir, if I have rightly divined your meaning, be so good as to tell us whether we are to think the former reading genuine or not? If we accept it for genuine, and maintain, even from your own concessions, that the text is nothing to the purpose of the orthodox, all suspicion of fraud on the part of the heretics will be at an end, and you will be compelled to acquit the Arians of a
 scandalous

scandalous accusation, which at present you have neither courage enough to avow, nor generosity enough to abandon, (p. 339—341.) But to me, I confess, the Complutensian εἰς τὸ ἓν appears full as orthodox as the more common ἓν alone; and may be thus paraphrased; οἱ ΤΡΕΙΣ τό ΕΝ ΘΕΙΟΝ ἅμα συνlεκᾶσιν. *hi* TRES *conjuncti* UNUM *efficient* DEUM; in the same manner as ἔσονται οἱ ΔΥΟ εἰς σάρκα ΜΙΑΝ is exactly synonymous with οὐκέτι εἰσι ΔΥΟ, ἀλλὰ σὰρξ ΜΙΑ, Matth. XIX. 5, 6. To shew my uncommon civility, I advertise my reader, that I shall impartially transcribe every argument in your favour that has come to my knowledge; but I shall sometimes be content with transcribing them; for many are such as Patience herself would disdain to refute,

LETTER IV.

What! will the line stretch out to the crack of doom?

SIR,

How formidable an host you are now leading to battle! Sixteen MSS. of Robert Stephens, all containing the heavenly witnesses! We may however spare our alarms; for all these MSS. upon a nearer inspection will prove *Phantoms bodiless and vain, empty visions of the brain*. I shall first lay down the real state of the case, and then confute your cavils. Mr. Gibbon gives his readers the option between fraud and error. I am always unwilling to attribute to fraud what I can with any reasonable pretence attribute to error. But if any person be more suspicious than I am, he needs not be frightened from his opinion by your declamation. For when

he

he considers how Erasmus was worried for speaking his mind too freely, and with what jealousy R. Stephens was watched by the Paris divines, it cannot appear incredible that Stephens might make this seeming mistake on purpose; so far, like Zacagni (see Letter II. p. 13) honest in his fraud, that he furnishes every inquisitive reader with the means of detection. But as I am content with the other supposition, I say, 1. That Henry Stephens, and not Robert, collated the MSS. 2. That the collation was probably inaccurate and imperfect. 3. That it certainly was not published entire. 4. That Stephens's margin is full of mistakes in the numbers and readings of the MSS. 5. That the marks in the text are often misplaced or omitted. 6. That some of the very MSS. used by Stephens having been again collated, are found to agree in this critical passage with all the rest that have been hitherto examined. And, 7. That therefore the semicircle, which now comes after the words ἐν τῷ οὐρανῷ in the seventh verse, ought to be placed after the words ἐν τῇ γῇ in the eighth.

You, Sir, answer in the first place, that H.
Stephens

Stephens was not the sole collator of the MSS. "because there is no pretence *for* the assertion, and because reason, propriety, and probability, are all uniformly *against* it," p. 297. Now this is so fully proved in Wetstein's Prolegomena, p. 143—144, that I should even be tempted to hope that if you had read them before you wrote your letters, you would have spared yourself a considerable quantity of disgrace and repentance. I shall repeat Wetstein's last quotation. *Pater meus—cum N. T. Græcum cum multis vetustis exemplaribus* OPERA MEA COLLATUM, *primo quidem minutioribus typis—mox autem grandibus characteribus,* &c. To which add Beza's testimony to the same purpose. *Ad hæc omnia accessit exemplar ex Stephani nostri bibliotheca cum viginti quinque plus minus manuscriptis codicibus et omnibus pene impressis diligentissime collatum.* Thus Beza in his first edition of 1556. But in his second edition, when R. Stephens was dead, these important words follow after *impressis*; AB HENRICO STEPHANO EJUS FILIO ET PATERNÆ SEDULITATIS HÆREDE *quam diligentissime collatum.* Observe in all this proceeding the craft of a printer and editor. Robert

bert was aware that, by telling his readers who was the collator, he might infuse a suspicion into their minds, that the work was negligently performed: he therefore carefully avoided * mentioning that circumstance. Another instance of this management may be seen in the preface to his first edition, where he says, that he has not suffered a letter to be printed but what the greater part of the better MSS. like so many witnesses unanimously approved. This boast is indeed

---

* With the same caution, speaking of his No. 2, (now our Cambridge MS.) he calls it, *exemplar vetustissimum in Italia* AB'AMICIS *collatum*, ἀτιβληθέν. Without fairly confessing or openly violating the truth, that it was collated by his son Henry, he disguises the fact in a general expression. I have not forgotten Mr. Travis's masterly construction of the sentence, p. 284; "It was the *exemplar*, the *book itself*, then, (and not the *lections* out of it) which was *collected* or (rather) *procured for R. Stephens*, by his friends in *Italy*." I have heard of a learned Doctor in our university, who confounded the *collection* with the *collation* of MSS. but I never till now heard of a single copy being *collected*. That the reader may not suspect me of inventing nonsense for the pleasure of fathering it upon Mr. Travis (a supposition which at first sight may seem not improbable) I assure him that I have honestly copied the very words, and can only beg of him to verify my citation by the evidence of his own senses.

utterly

utterly false, as all critics agree, who have taken any pains in comparing Stephens's editions. They know that Stephens has not observed this rule constantly, because his editions often vary from one another, and his third edition often from all his MSS. even by his own confession. But because Mr. Griesbach took this point for granted; not foreseeing that a man would be found so hardy or ignorant as to deny it, you insult him, p. 298, and call his assertion *groundless, improbable, uncandid, and injurious.* These are the magic words that have charmed your converts *of the first eminence.* Editors and printers are such conscientious people, that we may be sure they will never practise any tricks of their profession, or give their own publications undeserved praise. And whoever offers to think that they may sometimes bestow extravagant commendations on their own labour, diligence, or fidelity, is totally void of *literary candour and Christian charity,* (p. 59, 125.) But an example will make this position clearer in the eleventh verse of the second chapter of Mathew, all the MSS. the Complutensian edition, nay the very MS. from which

Erasmus

Erasmus published his edition, have εἶδον instead of εὗρον, but Erasmus upon the single authority of a faulty copy of Theophylact, altered it to εὗρον; Stephens in his third edition followed Erasmus, and εὗρον infects our printed Testaments to this day. I can only excuse Stephens by the universal custom of dealers who think it an innocent deceit to cry up the value of their wares. Stephens inserted nothing in his text (mistakes excepted) which he did not find in the Complutensian edition, or in Erasmus, or in his MSS. But he frequently quits all his MSS. to follow his printed guides, and frequently follows Erasmus without attending to the rest, of which partiality I have already given a specimen. Let us be no more pestered with the stale common-places of honour, honesty, veracity, judgment, diligence, erudition, &c. If R. Stephens's MSS. all omitted the controverted passage, he would still retain it in his edition; because he has the same vicious complaisance for many other passages, without having equal seeming authority. Here he had the consent of both editions for his warrant; in other places he follows Erasmus alone. You, Sir, prove, with admirable conciseness,

ciseness, in something less than six pages, (p. 78--81, 172--177) that Stephens did NOT take this verse from the Complutensian edition. Granted. He did not take it *wholly* from the Complutensian. He took it partly from the Complutensian and partly from Erasmus. He differs from Erasmus in adding the article thrice, and in transposing the word ἅγιον; and in these four differences he followed the Complutensian edition and the genius of the language.

Mr. Griesbach asserts, as quoted by you, Sir, p. 297, that there are in R. Stephens's MSS. many good readings, which are not inserted in his margin. You answer him by a flat denial. This is indeed a compendious and convenient method of answering; but I would counsel you not to make it too cheap by frequent use. Mr. Griesbach thought, that this and some other of his assertions were so generally allowed, that it would be waste of time and paper to prove them in form. At last up starts a grave and reverend gentleman, and tells us with a serious face, that it is not day at noon. And this trash we are expected to refute, or the *Mumpsimus* regiment

regiment will boaſt hereafter that we have not accepted their leader's challenge. Let us however undertake the tireſome taſk of flaying the ſlain. Firſt then I affirm, that Stephens has omitted to mark in his margin at leaſt one half of the Complutenſian various readings. Have you a mind to diſpute this, Sir? Will you give Mill the lie as you have Sandius (p. 199) and others? Now, if the collator was ſo negligent in noting the various readings of an edition, *which was printed from moſt ancient copies, and had a wonderful agreement with Stephens's own MSS.* (STEPH. Præf. ad N. T.) is it not extremely probable, nay, morally certain, that he was equally inattentive to his MSS.? I ſhall therefore aſſume, what ſems to me ſufficiently proved; that Stephens's collation was imperfectly publiſhed; which if you chuſe to deny, you muſt confute Wetſtein alſo, who ſays that Beza produces from Stephens's MSS. above an hundred various readings not noticed in Stephens's margin. When Emlyn argued from Mill's authority, Prol. 1226, p. 126, that Stephens's collation was imperfect, and preſſed Martin with this objection, that good old man told him,

him, for want of a better anſwer, that Stephens had only neglected the trifling variations of the Complutenſian edition, and ſelected the important. Not to infiſt, that by this method an editor claims the right of judging for the reader, what is trifling and what important; the fact is notoriouſly falſe: for whoever will look into Stephens or Mr. Travis, p. 79, 172, will find, that of *four* differences from the Complutenſian upon this very place, Stephens mentions not fewer than—*one*. He mentions only his omiſſion of εἰς τὸ in the ſeventh verſe, and is altogether ſilent upon the adition of οὗτοι; upon the change of ἐπὶ τῆς γῆς into ἐν τῇ γῇ in the eighth verſe, and upon the addition of the whole clauſe, καὶ οἱ τρεῖς εἰς τὸ ἕν εἰσιν. After this flagrant inſtance of Stephens's inaccuracy, I expect to hear no more of his diligence and fidelity.

R. Stephens had fifteen MSS. ſeven of which—*Fifteen!* cries Martin in a rage; he had *ſixteen*. You, Sir, *qui cum* Martino *errare malis, quam cum aliis recte ſentire,* ſing to the ſame tune, p, 55, 116, and to prove it, quote from the preface to Stephens's third edition, *cum ſedecim ſcriptis exemplaribus.* You bright
wits

wits foar far above the reach of common sense, or else you might have compared these words with the following: *Iis namque placuit, primo, secundo, ad sextum decimum usque nomina imponere, ut primo Complutensem editionem intelligas, quæ olim ad antiquissima exemplaria fuit excusa.* This sentence to an ordinary reader would be very intelligible, but Mr. Travis is no ordinary reader. Can any thing be plainer than that Stephens calls the Complutensian edition a MS. when he reckons his sixteen copies in the gross, because that edition had with him the weight and value of a MS. And if it was really printed, as Stephens believed, from *most ancient manuscripts*, he was reasonable and moderate enough in treating it as a separate MS. But if besides No. 1, which signifies this edition, Stephens had sixteen MSS. his sixteenth MS. would then be marked No. 17. Unluckily no such number appears in any part of the margin. However, as I love to be generous, I will help you to an argument, that will not only prove what you want, but something more: No. 19. (*ιθ*) is quoted in the margin, Matth. XXIV. 20, from which deducting one for

the

the Complutensian edition, there will remain *eighteen* MSS. belonging to Stephens, and a fortiori *sixteen*. I know that foolish people who are called critics will start an objection. They will affect to think it, with Mill, a misprint for 12; (θ. β.) but you, Sir, will wisely disregard what such fellows think. *Your soul never came into their secret, nor to their assembly has your honour been united.* But what am I doing? Teaching the rudiments of arithmetic to a couple of *Clotens, who can't take two from twenty for their hearts, and leave eighteen*! (Cymbeline.)

Whether Stephens had sixteen or only fifteen MSS. in all, is not of so much consequence as the next question, how many of these contained the Catholic Epistles. Martin (Verité, p. 171) part of whose reasoning you have adopted, (p. 80, 175) says, nine at least; and thus he argues: If Stephens had only seven MSS. in all, he would not have made a particular enumeration, but have said, π. or ἐν πᾶσιν in the margin. If he had only eight, he would have said, π. πλὴν (adding the number of the dissentient MS. such being his custom in other places.) I answer,

1. That

1. That Stephens could not, consistently with truth, as Martin himself owns, use the mark π. in this place, because the Complutensian edition, his No. 1. dissents; nor, 2. could he, consistently with himself, say, π. πλὴν—, because he never does say so in his second volume, the epistles and apocalypse. But you are not content with Martin's scanty allowance, your lively imagination hurries you beyond the bounds of sober reason; and in one of your happy inventive moments you set down the whole sixteen, p. 284, as containing *this disputed passage*. A jolly company! What luck old Robert had to light upon these MSS. and settle the true reading from them, before Satan and his Arians had laid their claws upon them! Did you ever hear, Sir, of any large collection of MSS. all containing the whole Greek Testament? Or, to deal liberally, let the apocalypse be excepted, did you ever hear of so many as fifteen all containing the remainder? Take the trouble of consulting fifteen at hazard, you will be very fortunate if seven of them contain the Catholic Epistles. Or do you piously believe, that an editor who has not

described his MSS. may have found only such as are complete, while scarce a sixth part of those MSS. which have been particularly described, contains the N. T. entire, even with the exception mentioned? You inform us, p. 275, (see also p. 295-6) " that it does not follow from R. Stephens's not citing all his MSS. to all parts of his Greek Testament, that all his MSS. did not contain all the Greek Testament." But I can tell you what does follow. If R. Stephens's MSS. all contain the whole N. T. either the MSS. so rarely cited had a miraculous agreement with his text, such as never has been since found in any one MS. or R. Stephens's collator was so infamously negligent, that his silence and his testimony are equally undeserving of regard. A ray of light however pierced through the Egyptian darkness of your mind, when you wrote the following sentence, p. 136 : " The MS. of R. Stephens marked 15, does not seem to have contained the Gospel of St. John at all ; FOR there is no reference to this MS. in the margin. But to what purpose do we prolong this childish play ? Newton, Wetstein, and Mr. Griesbach knew well enough

enough that Stephens's No. 2 was once quoted upon the Epistle to the Romans, No. 5, twice upon the apocalypse, No. 7, upon the Acts, &c. but they expected that an adversary, who had the least share of sense or candour, would not build any argument upon the infallibility of a printer or compositor. They knew too, that Stephens's margin was full of mistakes in the numbers of the MSS. and they judged it much more likely that β should be a mistake for some other letter, (perhaps for ẟ) than that the same MS. which in the Gospels and Acts was so prolific as to produce near four hundred various readings, should become so barren on a sudden as to yield only one in the epistles. Whoever can bring his mind to believe this, possesses a faith that disdains all intercourse with reason; a faith that not only can remove, but has actually removed mountains. Nor would it be difficult to rectify many of these mistakes from the internal evidence of the margin. For instance, No. 5, ought to be 15 in both places of the apocalypse; and, though it may seem strange, that the letters α and ζ should ever be confounded, I can with certainty pronounce this to have have happened in Acts XVII. 5. But let a single number be once quoted in Stephens's margin, you boldly set it down as *beyond all contradiction*, p. 295, containing that whole book of the N. T. where the marginal reference is found. In the first place, you take for granted that no MS. of Stephens was mutilated. Secondly, though Stephens has given us as vague and unlearned an account of his MSS. as if he intended to keep us in the dark, we are yet, with the few lights we have, often able to detect his mistakes. This argument therefore will do you no service, unless you can shew that it was impossible for Stephens to err in his marginal numbers. I know such an accident is impossible in your creed; yet I have been told that it sometimes happens in printing; and perhaps you may find, that in your own enumeration of Stephens's MSS. p. 295, (where, by the way, you have been able to reckon up only fifteen) by the author's or printer's fault *is* is left for *id*. I shall therefore, Sir, *request your permission* (p. 16) to believe that Stephens had only seven MSS. of the Catholic Epistles, and that if any of them

omitted

omitted 1 John, V. 7. they all omitted it. To which important discussion we now proceed.

Nearly two hundred and forty years are past since R. Stephens published his famous Greek edition of the N. T. with various readings. The marginal note upon the contested place would undoubtedly say, if there be no error, that his seven MSS. all have the seventh verse, except the words ἐν τῶι οὐρανῶι. But that seven Greek MSS. collected by the same person from different places; seven MSS. of different ages and merits, should all consent in a reading, that no critic or editor has been able, during the space of two centuries and an half, to find in any other MS. whatever, Greek or Latin, is such an excess of improbability, as the very men who maintain here, would be foremost to ridicule in any other dispute. For let us suppose, by way of argument, that some other Greek MSS. retain the text, still these retain at the same time the words ἐν τῶι οὐρανῶι. How comes it to pass, that none of these seven orthodox MSS. agrees with that noble pair the Dublin and Berlin in rejecting the final clause of the eighth verse?

verse? And what makes the wonder of the thing is, that the seven MSS. which omit the words ἐν τῶι οὐρανῶι should all fall into the same hands, perform the task imposed upon them, and then vanish for ever. All these difficulties you obviate by answering, that the MSS. are lost. If such MSS. ever existed, they are certainly lost; but how do you prove that they ever existed? Because R. Stephens and T. Beza say that they existed. What says the former? He puts a mark in his margin that implies such an assertion. Surely this is not the eighteenth century, the age of criticism and learning, when such arguments as these are heard with patience, and thought to need a serious refutation. Does an editor, when he marks various readings in the margin of his edition, intend solemnly to pledge his word, or to take an oath upon the truth of every assertion which those marginal notes virtually contain? If such be the conditions of publishing ancient authors, the publishers are of all men the most miserable; and no man in his senses will undertake so painful and thankless an office. A critic who expresses his various readings without abbreviations,

tions, has a much better chance of avoiding miſtakes; and yet miſtakes occur very frequently, notwithſtanding all precautions. Thus Grotius, in his note upon this paſſage *ſolemnly declares* and *poſitively affirms* that our Alexandrian MS. omits the final clauſe of the eighth verſe. What would you, Sir, ſay upon this, if you found it your intereſt to defend Grotius? Any thing rather than acquieſce in the true ſolution, that Grotius did not rightly underſtand or rightly copy the collation that was ſent him from England. " That Grotius was a man of ſo much ſenſe and veracity, that he could neither be deceived nor deceive; and that therefore the Alexandrian MS. wanted this clauſe: that to ſuppoſe the contrary would be to accuſe Grotius of telling a wilful lie; or that the MS. which he quotes upon this verſe was not the Alexandrian, &c." This, Sir, I take to be the ſubſtance of what you would ſay in Grotius's defence; which would make a very handſome figure when it was trimmed in your gorgeous eloquence, and ſpread through two pages in a mixture of declamation and invective, in which *it would be affected to teach us*, that *teaching* Mr. Travis *would be in vain*, (p. 125—126.)

But how could-seven MSS. be lost at Paris? Many MSS. used by editors of that age are still preserved. Beza's two, the Clermont and Cambridge, are still extant, and in good condition. Most of the MSS. which Erasmus used, are still extant, and in good condition. Were they in safer places or more likely to survive than Stephens's? What was Robert doing not to restore to the king's library the eight MSS. that he had borrowed? Le Long's testimony would indeed save Stephens's honesty; but alas! at the same time it would demolish a main support of the verse. For Le Long says, that *eleven* of the very MSS. that R. Stephens used (not *fifteen*, as you imagine, p. 128) are now in the king's library, four of which omit the disputed passage. We might hence conclude, that R. Stephens had restored all the eight that he had borrowed, and meant to give the library the rest of the fifteen that were his own. But you, Sir, are so offended with this testimony, that Le Long, Stephens, and the whole world, shall be liars, sooner than this

charming

charming text shall come to any harm. You therefore find a trifling error or two in Le Long's* account, make several more, and thence take occasion to set aside his whole evidence. But your chief argument is a tacit assumption, (which I have already considered) that Stephens could not commit a typographical error. This however is so important an axiom, that you ought beforehand to be very sure of its truth. Again, Le Long says, that the eleven MSS. in the king's library have the insignia of K. Henry II. upon the covers. Then, you exclaim, they are not the MSS. of Stephens; for his were borrowed of Francis, Henry's predecessor. The minor of this argument you have omitted, but the same *thinking minds*, that you have pressed into your opinion, p. 270, will be compelled, I doubt not, to acknowledge it for an eternal and self-evident truth, *viz.* that

---

* Le Long is mistaken, 1. In making Stephens's No. 15, contain only seven Epistles of Paul, which contains also the Catholic Epistles, and the Apocalypse; and, 2. In making No. 16. contain two of the Gospels, which contains only the Apocalypse. See Mr. Travis's Appendix, p. 47—48.

no king * ever sends his books to be new-bound. I told you, Sir, in my first letter, that you never read through Wetstein's Prolegomena. I now add, that you have not read through Wetstein's note upon the very passage that you defend. For there you would have found these words (to which also Le Long refers, (Emlyn, Vol. II. p. 274) quoted from R. Stephens's answer to the Paris divines: *Postulant afferri vetus exemplar—respondeo non posse fieri; quod non unum esset, sed quindecim relata in bibliothecam regiam, quæ mihi precario data fuerant.* You say, "that it does not concord with the known probity of R. Stephens, that he, who had only borrowed eight MSS. from the royal library should return *fifteen* thither, for no other purpose, as it should seem, than to abuse the confidence of those friends, who had lent to him the other MSS. and to deprive them of their property." Who told you they were lent ? *Quæ undique corrogare licuit.* Does *corrogare* signify so

---

* Stephani 11. Codex Reg. 2869. Compactus est iterum Henrico II. Galliarum Rege, WETSTEIN. Tom. II, p. 12.

strictly

strictly to *borrow*, that Stephens's friends could not have made him a present of these MSS. The word ηθροίσαμεν in the Greek preface intimates nothing about borrowing. But be that as may, R. Stephens affirms two things, 1. That he once had fifteen MSS. (not sixteen); 2. That he now had them no longer, but had them sent to the king's library. There is indeed a small inaccuracy in this account, but of no consequence. Stephens probably spoke from memory. The manuscripts had long been returned; and it concerned not his examiners, who required him to produce them, to know the exact history of every MS. its quondam possessor, &c. It was enough to tell them in general terms, that he was unable to comply with their demand, that the manuscripts were gone out of his hands; that they belonged to the royal library, and were now restored. Or he might perhaps forget the precise words of his answer to the examiners, and only retain the substance. However, if you chuse to take advantage of this slight mistake, and to give Stephens the lie, what will become of your pathetic declamation about

about *worth* and *probity* and *honour?* (p. 59, 125.) I cannot help observing how amiable this concern for Stephens's character is, and how well it fits upon a man, who, though he is shocked at the idea of that learned printer cheating his friends, feels no scruple in making him cheat the king, and carry off the royal manuscripts to Geneva, as his own private property. From this confession of Stephens in the year 1552, four years before Beza's first * edition, that he then had no Greek MSS. in his possession, it follows that Beza never had the use of any from Stephens, and that all your assertions and conjectures upon that subject fall to the ground.

But why, Sir, do you attempt to confute Le Long, and leave Wetstein untouched? Wetstein affirms, that he with his own eyes saw at Paris five of the seven MSS. that Stephens used in publishing the Catholic Epistles

---

* Beza first published his N. T. in 1556, though Mr. Travis erroneously, as his manner is, (p. 7. ed. 1 and 2) makes it 1551. In his second edition he twice contradicts himself, and says 1556, pp. 130, 275. With no less exactness he makes (p. 111, 337) Erasmus publish his Paraphrase in 1541, several years after his death.

(4, 5,

(4, 5, 7, 9, 10.) and that thefe all omit from the words ἐν τῶι οὐρανῶι to the words ἐν τῆι γῆι, inclufive. And I have fuch an opinion of Wetftein's fenfe and honefty (though he was an heretic) that I fhall venture to think him in the right, till you, Sir, talk fomething more to the purpofe. If you afk, how Wetftein came to know, that they were the fame manufcripts. I anfwer, by collating them, and finding them agree with Stephens's margin in other places. And left you fhould reply, that the readings of thefe MSS. as given by Wetftein fometimes differ from the readings of Stephens's margin, *cognofce ex me, quoniam hoc primum tempus difcendi nactus es,* that in thefe cafes a general and remarkable fimilarity is a ftronger argument for the affirmative, than a few variations for the negative. If we reject this canon, fuch a monftrous abfurdity as this will enfue; that if a collator makes here and there a miftake, whoever afterwards confults the fame manufcript, muft not infer the identity of the manufcript from the perfect agreement of the reft of the collation. Thus the manufcripts will be daily multiplied, in

the

the joint ratio of the number and neghgence of the collators.

Having before shewn that R. Stephens's work was in general inaccurate and imperfect, I proceed in the next place, to point out some particular faults. In 1 Pet. III. 11, the words ἀγαθὸν ζητσάτω, are omitted, contrary to all manuscripts, versions, and former editions. Was this the effect of fraud or mistake? If we dare to suspect any fraud, you will remind us that *it will become us to consider how we can justify ourselves either in literary candour or Christian charity*, &c. (p. 10, 13.) And we shall get very little by taking *the other* [part of the] *alternative*, that Stephens omitted these words by mistake. For, by the help of the *Travisian* logic, which is *of the sort that deduces* QUIDLIBET EX QUOLIBET, I will prove that Stephens omitted them upon the authority of manuscripts. *Now he omitted them* NOT BY MISTAKE; *because he would in that case have replaced in his subsequent edition of 1551, a passage which he had left out of this edition by mere oversight.* NOT BY MISTAKE; *because a man who had been so painfully accurate as to point out in his errata the misplacing of one comma,*

comma, and the omission of another, cannot be supposed to have suffered two such important words to have escaped his notice. NOT BY MISTAKE; because the words in question are omitted in the edition of *John Crispin* 1553, who was the friend and fellow-citizen of Robert Stephens, and must be concluded to have published with his assistance, for it is impossible to suppose, that Crispin would not, &c. NOT BY MISTAKE; because the Latin version in the edition of 1551, which is placed by the side of the Greek, contains these words, and must consequently force them upon the attention of Stephens, whose duty and interest would conspire to make him insert them in the original, unless he had (upon good grounds doubtless) determined to reject them. If such laboured nothings (which I have faithfully imitated from you, p. 57, 122, except that I have retrenched some of your redundancies) had any force, what would they prove ? That a reading is supported by authority, which, as far as I can learn, every man hitherto has believed to be a mere error of the press. Yet this error passed at least four editions * with-

* Stephens, fol. 1550. 8vo. 1553. Crisp. 8vo. 1551. Francf. fol. 1601.

out

out obfervation or correction. With refpect to the marginal numbers and the marks in the text, errors abound in Stephens's edition. To fet this matter in a clear light, I will give a collation of two pages of the Apocalypfe 176—177. In thefe two pages Stephens's margin omits eighteen various readings of the Complutenfian edition, and notes nineteen. Of thefe nineteen two are inaccurate and two palpably falfe. Three times the femicircle which ought to determine the quantity of text is omitted, and in a fourth paffage it is at leaft once mifplaced, for it is twice printed. Twenty-fix * faults in the compafs of two pages! In Apoc. XV. 2. καὶ is marked as wanting in two copies, whereas καὶ is extant in thofe copies and the four following words ἐκ τοῦ χαράγματος αὐτοῦ are wanting. If then Stephens could, as I have proved, place both his obelus and femicircle wrong, I am furely very moderate, when I only contend for half of this miftake in a cafe of neceffity. I am certain at leaft, that *the tremulous ball of orthodoxy muft be almoft invi-*

* Twenty-feven. See Poftfcript.

fible

sible, if it vibrates within the narrow limits * of this momentous semicircle. "But Stephens ought to have corrected this mistake, if it was a mistake, in his errata." Yes, to be sure he ought; so he ought to have corrected many others, some of which I have mentioned; but he has not done it, and therefore no particular reason obliged him to do it here. The transposition of a stop or a mistake in orthography, is easily rectified; but those errors, which are in truth of the greatest consequence, are at the same time most difficult to detect, a sophisticated text or a falsified margin. It was full as easy to misplace a semicircle as a comma, for they are nearly of the same size and shape, and are frequently confounded in Stephens's edition; but if the semicircle were misplaced, it might elude all discovery, unless the editor either carried all the various readings in his memory, or would undertake the pleasing task of performing the whole collation anew. In short, when we consider, that these seven manuscripts of Stephens, on the one supposition give a reading which has never been

* Gibbon, Vol. II. p. 253. 4to. III. 335. 8vo.

found

found in any manuscript, Greek or Latin; that they destroy the antithesis between *heaven* and *earth*, which the context, if the verse were genuine would plainly demand; that Stephens often misplaced his marks; that no manuscript can now be found in the library to which Stephens returned his manuscripts that exhibits this reading; while on the other hand, if we only suppose a single semicircle wrong placed, we shall have a text agreeing with all the other Greek manuscripts, or at least with more than one hundred; when we add to this, that Wetstein found at Paris five manuscripts, which agreed with five of Stephens's manuscripts in other places, but here contradicted his margin, none will hesitate to pronounce, that Stephens's copies followed the herd, and omitted the seventh verse, except only those, who by a diligent perusal of Tertullian have adopted his maxims of reasoning, and measure the merits of their assent by the absurdity * of the proposition to be believed.

* Crucifixus est Dei filius; non pudet, quia pudendum est: et mortuus est Dei filius: prorsus credibile est, quia ineptum est; et sepultus resurrexit; certum est, quia impossibile est. TERTULLIAN *de Carne Christi.* 5.

I have already quoted the passage from Beza's preface or dedication, which proves that he had not the ocular inspection of Stephens's MSS. I have likewise proved that Stephens, by his own confession, had them no longer in his power in the year 1552. I might therefore safely dismiss the subject; but it may possibly divert the reader to see Mr. Travis's alacrity in blundering. You say, that Beza detects mistakes in R. Stephens's collation, whence you argue that Beza had the use of the same MSS. A most exquisite reason! Stephens, in printing the collation made by his son Henry, sometimes committed a mistake; Beza, by the help of Henry's autograph, corrected the mistake.* Is this so hard to conceive? It is also pleasant to observe, that Emlyn tries to prove a truth by a falsehood, and that you gravely follow him, pp. 124, 275. For Beza detects no mistake in the passage to which

---

* Distinguendum inter collationem accuratam et editionem collationis accuratam: Cl. de Mastricht accurate quidem contulit codicem Cæsareum; sed collationem non accurate edidit; quin plurima suppressit. WETSTEIN. Proleg. p. 160.

Emlyn refers, but perfectly agrees with Stephens's margin *. But that the reader may see what stuff has imposed upon some persons for *irrefragable reasoning*, I will transcribe a part of your note, p. 124. " It would have been well worth Mr. Emlyn's pains to have apprized us how Beza could possibly have detected a mistake of this kind, in Stephens's book of collations, unless by resorting to the manuscripts themselves." If this note did not proceed from the profoundest ignorance ***** State it in English, and it will answer itself. How could Beza detect a mistake in Stephens's printed collations, but by resorting to the manuscripts from which Stephens printed those collations? *Pudet quidem talibus immorari; sed quid facias? Ut adversarii sunt, ita morem geras, et infra te nonnunquam descendas necesse est.* Again, " Beza says in other places, *ego in omnibus nostris inveni. Sic legitur in omnibus, quæ quidem mihi inspicere licuit,*" &c. The former of these notes

---

* Neque extant in Complutensi editione neque in alio quodam vetusto codice ex nostris. BEZA ad Apoc. I. 11. Emlyn understood it as if it were *quæquam*. ↔ H. STEPH. marg.

Beza

Beza had afterwards the modesty to withdraw. As for the other, and any expressions of the same sort, we must either soften them by a gentle interpretation, or be obliged to fix an imputation upon Beza, which would ill suit his *erudition*, and still worse his *piety*. Beza too is sometimes very lax in his assertions. Matth. I. 11. he at first published from an interpolated manuscript of Stephens. In his later editions he restored the common reading; but that he might seem to have adopted the other upon better grounds and authority than he really had, he goes on, *Robertus Stephanus ex vetustis codicibus excudit*, &c. Now R. Stephens did never so print it in his text, but only puts it in his margin as the reading of one single manuscript. Such was Theodore Beza's good faith and exactness in sacred literature! Besides, any impartial reader will be convinced by the conduct of Beza himself with regard to this verse, that he had not the immediate use of Stephens's manuscripts. For having written in his first and second editions, *legimus et nos in nonnullis*, he afterwards changed his tone, and in the succeeding impressions only says, *extat in nonnullis*.

nullis. How meek and modeſt! Such a ſweet tempered man as Beza, armed with the authority of ſo many manuſcripts, would not have thundered his anathemas againſt the *ſeſquiheretic* * Eraſmus for wreſting the capital texts out of the hands of the faithful. Inſtead of charging the oppoſers of this verſe with aſſiſting the devil, he is ſo faint-hearted in his later editions, as to hint a doubt whether the ſeventh verſe ought not to be expunged. If we may believe you, Sir, pp. 130, 275, R. Stephens himſelf *expreſsly declares* that he had lent Beza the manuſcripts, which he (Stephens) formerly uſed. I wiſh you would pay a little attention to the truth of your facts, and not quote books without conſulting them. Stephens is ſo far from affirming what you put into his mouth, that upon an attentive peruſal, he would appear to affirm the direct contrary. His words are, *Quod ad exemplaria attinet—ſunt autem cum alia tum ea omnia quæ in regis Gallorum bibliotheca extant, &c.* If they were then in the French

---

* Attuli Novum Teſtamentum ab *Eraſmo* verſum. Ab *Eraſmo?* Aiunt illum eſſe *ſeſqui*-hæreticum. ERASMUS Colloq. Adoleſcentis et Scorti.

King's

King's library, how could Beza have them at Laufanne? If Stephens had kept them and lent them to Beza, he would have expreffed himfelf in this manner:—*Quæ ex regis G. b. utenda habui*—*Quæ ex regis G. b. mihi precario data funt.* Having at laft difcuffed the fubject of Stephens and Beza's orthodox manufcripts, I am compelled to decide (with forrow I pronounce it!) that they have difappeared; perhaps they were too good for this world, and therefore are no longer vifible on earth. However, I advife the true believers not to be dejected; for fince all things loft from earth are treafured up in the lunar fphere, they may reft affured, that thefe valuable relics are fafely depofited in a fnug corner of the moon, fit company for Conftantine's donation, Orlando's wits, and Mr. Travis's learning.

POSTSCRIPT.

Though I am almoft afhamed to have wafted fo many words upon fo plain and eafy a fubject as Stephens's manufcripts, I cannot forbear offering fome farther obfervations.

The beauty of Stephens's edition is such, that it dazzles the eyes of the ignorant beholder, and this circumstance, joined to the vulgar but erroneous perfuasion that Stephens's editions are free from typographical errors, naturally creates a strong prejudice in favour of its correctness. But all the learned are agreed, that scarcely any critical benefit can be derived from it. For instead of giving an accurate and particular description of his manuscripts; what parts of the N. T. every one contained; where it was mutilated or defective; what was its probable age, &c. he leaves us to gather information where we can find it. However, if he had scrupulously noted all the various readings in his margin, and attributed each to its proper parent, we might by a careful comparison of the external authority since produced, and the intrinsic goodness or badness of the readings, form a tolerable judgment upon the antiquity and merits of his manuscripts. But instead of doing this, he has favoured us with only a part of the various readings, (probably less than half) and has frequently set down a reading as from one manuscript which belonged

longed to another. Of thirteen hundred various readings of the Complutensian edition, he has omitted seven hundred; of four upon the most curious place of the whole N. T. he has omitted three. Since therefore he has been so negligent of a printed book, it is utterly unlikely that he should take more pains with his manuscripts, the majority of which were less easy to read. Again: in his folio edition, Stephens was so servilely addicted to Erasmus (see Mill, Prol. p. 126) that though he follows his manuscripts only in thirty two places, and the Complutensian in thirty one, he follows Erasmus's fifth edition in ninety-nine! Surely then an edition to which he pays much more deference than to any other single authority, might deserve a place in his margin, when he deserts it. To what motive shall we ascribe Stephens's obstinate silence? I am inclined to think, he was afraid of acknowledging himself indebted to an heretic for any assistance in sacred criticism. Thus much may serve for omissions. To the examples of error that I have produced in the body of my letter, I shall now add a few more. John XVI. 14. If Stephens's margin be correct

rect, seven of his copies read λαμβάνει for λήψεται. Let Mr. Travis believe so if he likes; but every body else will quickly see that the marginal note belongs to λήψεται in the next verse. Act IX. 31. a reading which manifestly belongs to one and the same manuscript is split into two, and the parts given to different copies. Two of the proofs that Martin and Mr. Travis bring against Le Long carry internal evidence against themselves from the very order of the numbers. Act. XXV. 14. α. ια. η. XIII. 15. ιδ. ια. Upon the first I have nothing to propose; the second ought, I believe, to be, δ. ιι. ια. for these three manuscripts agree together in the same chapter once against all Stephens's other authorities, and once against all but the Complutensian. The same number is twice repeated in the margin of Apoc. XII. 2. α. ιε. ιε. (read α. ιε. ιϛ.) Nor is this edition free (however that silly fancy has gained credit) from the most glaring typographical errors. Thus pages 212 and 213 are numbered 213 and 214, and in the running titles of pages 85 and 212, ΜΑΤΘ. is printed for ΜΑΡΚ. and ΕΥΑΓΓ. for ΠΡΑΞΕΙΣ. Acts IX. 24. τὰ πύλας in the text; 1 Cor. XVI.

14. ἀ, γαπη is violently rent asunder, as I have here represented it. I have counted above forty places where the semicircle is omitted; sometimes neither the obelus nor the semicircle appear; Rom. XVI. 24. Gal. 14. Sometimes neither figure of reference nor semicircle; John XI. 30. Acts V. 33. VII. 57. Sometimes the text directs us to the margin for a various reading, where the margin is silent; Mark XIII. 19. Apoc. XVI. 1. Sometimes the semicircle is twice printed; 1 Cor. VII. 33. Apoc. II. 7. Sometimes the figure of reference is misplaced; Rom. XIII. 3. Apoc. II. 20. (correct my former collation, p. 29.) XXI. 6. XXII. 11. sometimes the semicircle; Matth. V. 48. XI. 23. Act. VII. 21.* &c. sometimes both the figure and semicircle: Act. I. 26. Yet none of these mistakes are rectified in the errata, where Stephens has been *so painfully accurate*, according to Mr. Travis, p. 58, 123, as to set commas and points exactly right. If then these plain and

* Gal. IV. 3 v. the semicircle is placed after the word ἐλευθέρας, which ought to follow και in the next verse V. 1. The same mistake for which we contend in 1 John V. 7.

palpable

palpable faults, most of which are such as the smallest share of knowledge or attention would be sufficient to detect, if these could escape Stephens or his corrector, how much more easily might they miss the error of this reference, for the discovery of which a good memory, a strong judgment, or a painful attention was necessary?

But supposing that R. Stephens, or any other editor, had affirmed in express terms, that he possessed seven manuscripts of the Catholic Epistles, in which was read the verse, 1 John, V. 7, except the words ἐν τῶι οὐρανῶι, who would be bound to believe him? This ground is so smooth, easy and pleasant, that the defenders of the said verse are perpetually pacing it over. After judiciously improving a marginal abbreviation into a solemn and formal asseveration, which must irrevocably decide the character of R. Stephens for honesty and veracity, they deafen us by bawling in our ears old scraps of sermons against the crying sin of uncharitableness. For my own part, I declare, that let any editor affirm, as positively as he will, that he has seven manuscripts of an ancient author, consenting in a certain reading; if an hundred manuscripts of the same author being afterwards collated are found all to agree in another reading, and to contradict the supposed seven manuscripts; whatever may be such an editor's general reputation for veracity, I shall certainly reject his testimony in this particular, either as a mistake, or (if his indiscreet friends will suffer no compromise) as a wilful and deliberate untruth. Ψευδοίμην ἀΐοντος ἅ́ κεν πεπίθοιεν ἀκουήν. In Horace, A. P. 65, *palus* has its second syllable made short, contrary to a known canon, and the constant usage of all good Latin poets. And to render the case quite desperate, Servius and Priscian expressly cite the verse for an example of this extraordinary licence. What says Theodore Marcilius to all this? He *produces,* if we may take his word for it, *the true reading from ancient parchments of Horace and Priscian.* Upon which Bentley observes, *strenue frontem perfricare Theodorum Marcilium,* in plain English, *that he is an impudent liar.* And to Bentley's sentence of condemnation, every person will subscribe, except Mr. Travis and his proselytes, whose *literary candour and Christian charity* will suffer them

them to think evil of none but heretics. *Ego huic testi, etiamsi jurato, qui tam manifesto fumos vendit, me non crediturum esse confirmo.* (Mosheim in Horsley's Tracts, pp. 159, 355, 489.) But I have no objection to put the debate upon a shorter issue. I will acknowledge the probability of Stephens's margin being right in this place, if another passage in the whole N. T. can be found, wherever three of his manuscripts agree with each other, and differ from every copy since examined.

Twelve years before the appearance of Stephens's first edition, his father-in-law, Simon Colinæus, published the Greek Testament. Both Mill and Wetstein allow that he faithfully followed his manuscripts, and Wetstein candidly vindicates him from Mill's harsh censure of rashness and presumption, rightly observing, that Colinæus had few guides to follow, and that his poverty, not his will, was to blame. These manuscripts, however, whether good or bad, many or few, omitted 1 John, V. 7; and consequently Colinæus leaves it out of his edition. If Colinæus borrowed his manuscripts from the royal library, they must have been some of those that were

after-

afterwards used by his son-in-law. If they were his own or lent him by his friends, still it is most probable that Stephens knew of them, and endeavoured to procure them for the service of his own edition. But if any manuscript of Colinæus containing the Catholic Epistles was afterwards used by Stephens, since that manuscript certainly was destitute of the three heavenly witnesses, it will furnish a new proof, if proof be wanted, of the wrong position of the semicircle, in this memorable sentence of Stephens's edition.

The freedom with which I have treated *that great work* (as Mr. Travis calls it, p. 129) may perhaps displease some of Stephens's idolaters; but the invidious praises that have been heaped upon it by ignorant or interested persons, have extorted these unpalatable truths. The early editions * of the N. T. considered as the publications of critics, are for the most part worse executed than editions of profane authors, and owe their chief value either to their scarcity or splendour. But when I pass

* See Mr. Griesbach's preface to the second volume of his N. T. p. 13—29.

this

this cenfure, I find fault not with the men, but with the times. They did not then poffefs, nor if they had poffeffed, would they have known how to employ, the materials that have fince been difcovered.

Of Beza's edition it is needlefs to fay more. As a critical work it has very little merit. Ignorant of the true ufe of various readings, he feldom mentions them but to fupport his own hypothefes; to which godly purpofe he warps both text and interpretation. He makes his commentary (as indeed he partly boafts himfelf) a vehicle for abufe upon Origen, Erafmus, and Caftalio; efpecially the latter; againft whom he indulges, * *without reftraint, the exquifite rancour of theological hatred.*

I have faid that the words *in cœlo* are omitted in no Latin manufcript, though Martin, I know, tells us (Verité, p. 170.) that thofe words are marked in Hentenius's edition 1547, as wanting in five manufcripts. It feems to be the fate of this † *marvellous text*, to lead

* Gibbon, Vol. II. p. 284. 4to. III. 377. 8vo.
† Martin.

both

both friends and foes aftray. For Simon himfelf, fpeaking of the edition of 1547, fays, that it commits the fame error as Stephens's Greek, and marks only the words *in cœlo* as wanting in five manufcripts, inftead of marking the whole verfe. Whether Martin was mifled by Simon or coined the error out of his own brain, I know not; but I know, that unlefs there are different copies of Hentenius's edition, which I hardly believe, Simon's affertion is totally falfe. For in the copy that I have feen, the whole feventh verfe is comprehended between the obelus and the femicircle. Nor could it be otherwife. Hentenius's lift of manufcripts includes the very Latin copies that Stephens had collated. Since, then, four of Stephens's manufcripts did certainly omit the whole feventh verfe, it was no lefs certain that, whatever Hentenius's margin may feem to fay, Hentenius himfelf meant to extend his marginal reference to the fame quantity of text. Perhaps Simon confounded a republication of the book with the original edition. For the Antwerp edition of 1570, omits both obelus and femicircle;

the Lyons edition 1573, places this mark], which anfwers to the femicircle in other editions, after the words *in cœlo:* the Antwerp edition 1572, thus reprefents the text, '*in cœlo,*' and in the margin has this note '5. But thefe miftakes are fet right in Lucas Burgenfis's edition, Antw. 1574, 1583. Martin fomewhere fays, if I recollect, that Herrtenius's edition 1565, omits the words *in cœlo,* but I believe him miftaken. From thefe facts it feems to me a certain conclufion, that Robert Stephens might eafily mifplace his femicircle upon this verfe, when we fee in two other editions the felf fame error committed in the very fame words. Still, if Mr. Travis wifhes to catch at a twig that may fave him from finking, I will be charitable enough to direct him to R. Stephens's Latin edition of 1545, but I expect his thanks for the information. In that edition Robert has printed two verfions, which he calls the Old and the New; the Old is the received Vulgate, the New is a tranflation from the Greek, made by Robert, or by fome learned man under his infpection. The Old, as might be expected,

expected, retains 1 John, V. 7; the New dismisses it from the text with ignominy, but puts a star after *testimonium dant* *, and adds in the margin, " * Pater verbum et spiritus sanctus et hi tres unum sunt. Et tres sunt qui testimonium dant in terra spiritus, &c. sic legunt quædam exemplaria Græca." Bengelius referring to this edition says; " Latina Stephani biblia lunulam suo loco exhibent, et disertam in margine habent annotationem: *Sic legunt* (scil. *in cœlo Pater, reliqua*) *quædam exemplaria Græca Britannicus NEMPE codex et Complutensis juxta Hieronymi lectionem* *. Nullum alium habuit quem citaret." But De Missy (Journ. Brit. IX. p. 63) taking Bengelius's explanation for Stephens's own words, bewildered himself in hunting for an edition that never existed. Now, if we put this marginal note to the torture, it will speak at least, and confess that some of its master's Greek manuscripts omitted the words *in cœlo*; for, upon adding the text and the margin together, they will exactly make up two verses, bating those two

* N. B. Bengelius's words are printed in the Italic character as I have here represented them.

words. If Mr. Travis be so cruel as to turn against me the point of the weapon with which I now present him, I must shield myself with Stephens's formal preference of the Greek copies that rejected the verse to those which retained it.

LETTER V.

SIR,

I ASSURE you that I lay a grievous tax upon my patience, when I condescend to throw away a few lines upon the Greek manuscripts, supposed to belong to the Louvain divines. In your first edition you were pleased, p. 13, to quote their words in this manner: " The reading of this text is supported by very many *Latin* copies, and also by *two Greek* copies produced by *Erasmus*, one in *England*, the other in *Spain*. *We have, ourselves, seen several others like these.* This verse is also found," &c. For this quotation you refer to Simon, Hist. des Vers. c. II. But in your second edition, p. 323, a short sentence is added; " The King's Bible agrees with the *Spanish* manuscript in this passage, as well as in every other. *We have ourselves,*" &c. Martin had omitted the same sentence, you implicitly copy him. To say the truth, notwithstanding all my candour, of which I have told you so often, that it is impossible for you either to doubt or forget it, this place made me almost suspect that worthy old gentleman's sincerity. For he argues from the close connection of the two sentences, that the Louvain divines can only mean manuscripts, by the words " several others." *Ces docteurs parloient des manuscrits—dire donc ladessus et* TOUT D'UNE SUITE, " *nous en avons vû plusieurs autres semblables,*" *n'est ce pas dire, qu'ils avoient vû plusieurs autres manuscrits Grecs?* Martin rightly refers to Simon, c. 11. but you, Sir, in evil hour took the Arabic for Roman numerals, and referred to c. II. What a quantity of belief some men have! Can the Roman Catholics shew such a faith as Mr. Travis's, who believes the infallibility of every individual, author, translator, transcriber, or printer, that is not tainted with heresy. But let us look at the Latin of the Louvain divines (or rather of Lucas Brugensis.) *Latinorum librorum plurimi suffragantur, quibus consentientes duos Græcos codices, unum Britannicum, alterum Hispanicum, Erasmus profert; Hispanico ut ubique et hic conformis est Regius*; *multos alios his consonantes vidimus.* Since editions as well as manuscripts are here called by the general name of *codices* (for *Hispanicus codex*, which you have transubstantiated into a Spanish manuscript, is the Complutensian edition, and *Regius* Montanus's edition, which in this passage exactly agrees with the Complutensian) none but such quicksighted critics as you and Martin could have made the next words, *multos alios*, signify manuscripts. The proper construction of the sentence is this: Most Latin manuscripts agree in this reading, together with Erasmus's British Greek manuscript, the Complutensian and Montanus's editions, and many others that we have seen. If a shadow of doubt can still remain, it will vanish when we learn that Lucas Brugensis published his annotations in 1580, 4to, separately, and afterwards in folio, subjoined to the edition of 1583. The note upon 1 John, V. 7, in both these editions is nearly the same in substance with the note already quoted, but varies considerably in the words. He there expresses himself in so plain a manner, that I should be amazed how Martin,

H 4   bigot

bigot as he was, could refift fuch evidence when it was laid before him by Emlyn, unlefs I knew what wonders obftinacy and prejudice can perform. *Quod pro textus lectione facit, cui Græca Complutenfis* EDITIO *et* QUÆ *ex ea funt, cum aliis* QUAS *vidimus non paucis confonant*. Take another fpecimen of obftinacy. Martin ftoutly denies that the Louvain divines meant to infinuate any doubt concerning Stephens's femicircle by the words, *inter omnes Stephani codices, ne unus eft qui diffideat, nifi quod feptem duntaxat τὸ* in cœlo *confodiunt*, SI TAMEN SEMICIRCULUS LECTIONIS DESIGNANS TERMINUM SUO LOCO SIT COLLOCATUS. And you, Sir, feem to be of the fame opinion with your principal, by breaking off your tranflation at the word *confodiunt*. The Louvain divines therefore have *affirmed* * nothing about Greek manufcripts, and there is no need of *difproving* what was never *affirmed*.

Make room there for the Irifh evidence! His teftimony, like your Victor's, p. 53, 112,

* The Louvain divines affirm, that this verfe exifted in feveral ancient Greek manufcripts of their times: and their affirmation has never been difproved. *Travis,* p. 105, 323.

is

is POSITIVE, *clear and pointed.* The Alexandrian and Vatican witnesses are grown old, and their memory is so decayed with length of years, that they cannot recollect a syllable of the disputed verse. But this deponent is in the full vigour of his intellect, of sound mind and memory. And this deponent maketh oath, and saith, *that there are three that bear record in heaven,* &c. All that is needful, you know, Sir, to give this witness a decent degree of credibility, is to shew that he is come to years of discretion; for the malicious pleaders on the other side maintain that he is too young to be admitted to take oath. But you and your brother-counsellor Martin prove the age of your principal evidence by two arguments. The first is, that he carries a certificate of his birth about him. This certificate, upon being examined, turns out to be a certificate of the birth of one of his ancestors, who lived fifteen hundred years before him. Or, to drop this inimitable allegory, the manuscript says in a postscript, that the Gospel of Mark was written ten χρόνοι after the ascension. That is to say, according

to

to Martin's glofs, this manufcript was written in the eleventh century. I fhall never like that ugly word χρόνοι again. Why did the tranfcriber write χρόνοι and not ἔτη? His view is too plain; to expofe a brace of painful divines to the fcoffs of heretics and infidels. Emlyn, Vol. II. p. 271. Wetftein, Prol. p. 52, and De Mifly, Journ. Brit. IX. p. 61, had ridiculed this grofs error of Martin; but alas! Sir, you had read through none of thefe when you publifhed your firft edition. I fhould not have mentioned this circumftance a fecond time, if you had not retracted your miftake in fo ungracious a manner, that the recantation ferves only to aggravate the offence. For * *a reluctant and imperfect retraction is more unfeemly than the firft error, be it ever fo enormous.* However, the other reafon ftill fubfifts in full force to prove the antiquity of the Dublin manufcript. " It

* Dr. HORSLEY's Xth letter to Dr. Prieftly, Tracts, p. 186. *But you allow it with fo ill a grace, with fo much reluctance and fhuffling about it, as takes off all the credit of a liberal and ingenuous conceffion.* MIDDLETON to Pearce, Vol. III. p. 171. 8vo.

has

has double points," say you, " over the ɩ and ϒ, and Montfaucon (a proper judge in such a case) informs us that such was the fashion a thousand years ago." But this argument is not quite decisive, unless you can prove these points never to have been in fashion since. Now I have seen many manuscripts of the fourteenth and fifteenth centuries with plenty of double points over the vowels. I have also seen two imitations of the spurious verse as it is written in this very manuscript, and though they are not so exact as I wish, I see that the Dublin manuscript is certainly not earlier than the fifteenth, and possibly as late as the sixteenth century. I see too, that this is the *codex Britannicus* of Erasmus. But this conclusion is controverted, because the Dublin manuscript has ἅγιον in the seventh, and οἱ before μαρτυροῦντες in the eighth verse, both which are omitted in Erasmus's transcript of the *codex Britannicus*. Therefore say Martin and you very wittily,

Martin,

Martin, Verité, p. 301. (174. Engl.)	*Travis*, p. 69, 149.
It is impoffible that one and the fame manufcript fhould actually have and not have the fame words, the fame fyllables.	It is impoffible that the fame manufcript fhould differ from itfelf; or, in other words, be *the fame*, and yet not *the fame* manufcript.

To this *mafterpiece of reafoning and compofition*, I anfwer, 1. That the place where the manufcript has been found, countenances my fuppofition. What more likely than that a manufcript which was found in England, about the year 1520, fhould be carried into Ireland, and there remain in quiet till the revival of the controverfy concerning this celebrated verfe drew it from obfcurity? 2. Erafmus was a very rapid writer, and his hand was often not over-legible. We know that he was in a great hurry when he compofed his apology againft Stunica, and therefore might himfelf omit a word, or his printers might overlook it. 3. Erafmus, when he firft added the feventh verfe in his third edition, inferted ἅγιον in his text, though he left it out of his notes. He had not then feen the Complutenfian edition. It is not probable

able that he added it of his own mere motion from the Vulgate. It is therefore probable that his original extract contained the epithet, but that Erasmus in copying it hastily, made the omission. 4. The omission of the article οἱ is so trifling in itself, so easy for a modern transcriber to make, that to lay any stress upon such an argument, proves a deplorable scarcity of better. You, Sir, especially, have the less cause to insist upon it, who in quoting the eighth verse from the Complutensian edition, p. 79. ed. 1. pp. 172, 287. ed. 2, omit the article τὸ before αἷμα. 5. Erasmus has elsewhere committed similar or greater mistakes in copying. He quotes a sentence from Theophylact (Wetstein. Prol. p. 124,) which, by leaving out πᾶσιν and writing τοῦ ἀνοήτου for τοῖς ἀνοήτοις τοῦ, he has turned either into nonsense or impiety. And this error passed through all his five editions. But you may prove by the help of your *nostrum*, that the manuscript of Theophylact, quoted by Wetstein, is not the manuscript which Erasmus used. 6. A general and remarkable conformity, as I have before observed, is in these cases a stronger argument for the affirmative, than a few disagreements for the negative. The omission

of

of the article six times, and of the whole final clause of the eighth verse, is a sufficient proof that the Dublin MS. is the *codex Britannicus* of Erasmus, a proof not at all weakened by the additional omissions of Erasmus's transcript. But I dare say that you will be better pleased with an illustration taken *(ex fumo lucem)* from your own appendix, p. 37, 43, which contains, among other curious things, the preface of the Complutensian editors, and their note upon the famous verse. In transcribing the preface you have written *et* for *quod*, *quod* for *quam*, *epistolas* for *epistolam*, *cuique** in your first, and *quicquid* in your second edition for *quicquam*, *quod* for *quia*, *aliquo* for *aliquando*, *collocato* in your first and *collocare* in your second edition for *collocate* (i. e. *collocatæ*) you have also omitted *ex* before *apostolica*. In the note, though not very long, you have omitted *et* after *ibidem*, and s. (i. e. *scilicet*) after *terra*. I shall excuse your *lectori* for *lectorem*, and

* *Cuique* and *collocato* are altered to *quicquid* and *collocare* in the larger list of errata to the first edition. I love a wary and judicious critic, who exchanges one blunder for another, and calls it correcting. *You are a wise man, Mr.* Foresight; *if you do wrong, it is with a great deal of consideration and discretion and caution.*

nobis

nobis—tam for *non—sed*, because they are amended in the second edition. Might we not argue from these variations, that Mr. Travis did not copy that part of his appendix from the Complutensian edition, or that he used a copy of that edition differing from all the others? But not to trifle any longer, experience teaches us, that such deviations from originals happen every day in copying, and either haste or ignorance will sufficiently account for them. I shall therefore equally divide the reasons between Erasmus and you. Erasmus himself confesses *haste*; and your humility, Sir, is such, that I know you will plead guilty to the charge of *ignorance*, to which I shall subjoin a civil question; what business has a man to prate about manuscripts and points of criticism, who cannot construe a Latin sentence, or read a printed book?

Erasmus said, in his answer to Lee, that if he had found a single Greek manuscript containing the three heavenly witnesses, he would have inserted them in his text. You, Sir, p. 8, think this conduct of Erasmus mean. Till the duties of an editor are exactly ascertained and defined, this charge may well be spared.

spared. But whether mean or not, the words of Erasmus might seem a kind of advertisement requesting any person who knew of such a manuscript, to give him notice of it. His industrious friends in England immediately began a strict search, and were so fortunate, in the interval between the second and third editions, as to discover a copy after their own heart. How seasonable was this assistance in so critical a juncture! Scarcely was Lord Peter more successful, when, after vainly hunting a long time in his father's will for a precept or permission to wear flame-coloured sattin, he called to mind a codicil written by a dog-keeper of his grandfather's, that, as good luck would have it, talked a great deal about that same flame-coloured sattin. I have said, that Erasmus never saw the Codex Britannicus, but had only an extract from it. It could not be expected that two such sturdy antagonists would let this pass without dispute. First Simon's *acknowledgment*, as you call it, p. 64, 138, is quoted to prove that Erasmus actually *saw* the manuscript. You ought to know, Sir, that no man is free from slight errors of this kind, which

which are never to be taken for deliberate opinions or assertions in which the writer stakes his veracity. Simon indeed says, that Erasmus inserted the disputed verse in his third edition from a manuscript that he had *seen* in England. But Simon (who is sometimes a little hasty and negligent) had no other means of information than Erasmus's own words. Where then does Erasmus say that he saw the manuscript? In two places, you answer, p. 139, ed. 2, which you thus quote, *In codice, unde* CONTULI *in Anglia fuisse scriptum,* &c. *Collationis negotium* PEREGERAM *in Anglia,* &c. "These are his words," you say, "when discoursing on this British copy." You will grant, I suppose, that Erasmus collated this manuscript, if he collated it at all, between the years 1519 and 1522, the dates of his second and third editions. But the biographers agree that he was not in England after the year 1518. He could not therefore collate the manuscript in England, and consequently in this passage he cannot mean the manuscript, which upon 1 John, V. 7, he calls the Codex Britannicus. The same answer will serve for the other sentence.

tence. If he performed the business of collation in England, he performed it in or before 1518, before he knew any thing of this manuscript. Thus it appears even from your own account, that your proofs turn against yourself, or at least do you no service. The fact is, that Erasmus carried over his manuscripts from Germany to England, and there prepared part of his edition. He says, therefore, *Collationis negotium peregeram in Anglia* ET IN BRABANTIA. The three last words you have suppressed, I doubt not, for the sake of brevity. *Collatio* is the general work of collation, not the collation of a single manuscript. Do you think that Erasmus collated his British manuscript partly in England and partly in Brabant? If the reader has not Erasmus's works at hand, let him consult Wetstein, Prol. p. 125, where both the passages above mentioned are quoted at length, and he will see that they have not the smallest reference to the *Codex Britannicus*. But when Erasmus speaks for certain of this manuscript, what are then his words? Surely not weaker than, *Repperi, vidi, inspexi codicem apud Anglos*; or *monstratus est mihi, missus est codex ab Anglis,*

Anglis, &c. Nothing less. *Repertus est codex apud Anglos.* Could he have used such uncertain, and indefinite language, if he had spoken from ocular inspection? Or would he have been contented with hinting his suspicion that the manuscript was corrected from the Latin version, if he had examined it himself? He would then have been enabled from a comparison of other places, to decide whether it were so corrected or not. Now, if the Dublin MS. has the Latin division of chapters, (which is Wetstein's opinion, Prol. p. 52) Erasmus's suspicion was very just. But you, Sir, in your next edition will clear up this circumstance. For as I hear that you have lately visited Ireland, I take for granted that you have diligently examined a monument so respectable, that, as Martin *positively* assures us, *divine Providence has visibly watched for its preservation**. In the mean time, to shew that the Codex Britannicus did not bor-

---

* La Providence divine, qui veille visiblement pour maintenir dans l'Eglise la vérité d'un Texte si respectable par la doctrine qu'il contient, m'a fait venir entre les mains l'Extrait d'un ancient Manuscrit Grec, &c. Vérité, p. 271.

row 1 John, V. 7, from the Latin Version, you again produce your favourite proof, the omission of the word ἅγιον. But if Erasmus himself omitted ἅγιον through oversight, what becomes of this Achillean argument. If it was really absent from the Codex Britannicus, might not an interpolator omit it? You seem to think that nothing less than absolute uniformity will prove one writer to have copied another. If such be your opinion, long may you live to enjoy it, for upon the commonly received principles of reasoning, you will be confuted in a moment; but if we grant you only the truth of a few impossibilities, you will undertake, like Belial or Socrates, * *to make the worse appear the better reason.* Though I should admit, what I now deny, that the Codex Britannicus was different from the Dublin MS. the omission of ἅγιον would not prove your point, unless all the manuscripts of the Vulgate agreed in retaining *sanctus.* But I myself have seen two Latin manuscripts in which that epithet is omitted; and Mr. Travis might have remembered that

* Milton, P. L. II. 113. Plato, Apol. Socr. p. 19. ed. Serran.

the

the same word is omitted in four of his own examples from the Latin writers, p. 28—31. The conclusions which I draw from these facts are, 1. That the *Codex Britannicus* is the MS. now called Dublinensis or Montfortius. 2. That it contains the controverted passage translated in a bungling manner from the modern copies of the Vulgate. For the omission of the final clause of the eighth verse is peculiar to them. 3. That it was probably written about the year 1520, and interpolated in this place for the purpose of deceiving Erasmus. This hypothesis will explain how it so suddenly appeared when it was wanted, and how it disappeared as suddenly after having atchieved the glorious exploit for which it was destined. It might have been hazardous to expose its tender and infantine form to barbarous critics. They would perhaps have thrown brutal aspersions upon its character, from which it might never have recovered. The freshness of the ink and materials might then have led to a detection of the imposture; but time would gradually render such an event less probable in itself, and less hurtful in its consequences.

I shall

I shall pass over in silence the shameful attacks on Erasmus, pp. 145—147, 348; where instead of accounting for his conduct from his natural timidity, and the violent clamours of his enemies, you make it spring from sheer Arianism, villainy and hypocrisy. Whoever fairly considers the temper of the times, and the peculiar situation of Erasmus, will find much greater reason to applaud his sincerity than to censure his *prudence*.

La Croze, a professed Trinitarian (though, I fear,* *(the leaven of Arianism fermented within his mind)* affirmed that the Berlin manuscript was copied from the Complutensian edition. *Mais* [M. Travis] *semble faire peu de cas du jugement de M.* La Croze. *Cela ne sied pas mal à quiconque fait grand cas de celui de M.* Martin †. In consequence of this persuasion, you retail Martin's reasons of straw; the first of which is, that the Elector purchased the manuscript for 200 crowns. This, it must be owned, proves the antiquity

---

* Compare p. 146 with p. 162.
† De Missy, Journal Brit. IX. p. 78.

of the manuscript not less clearly than the expences of Cardinal Ximenes prove the learning, diligence, and fidelity of his *illustrious congregated divines*; (pp. 179, 183) not less clearly than the immense price that the Duke of Lauderdale paid for Captain Thornton's bible*, proves the genuineness of that bible. 2. Hendreichius, Saubertus, Tollius, Jablonski, Spanheim, believed it ancient. Did these five men, or any of them, give their opinion after a careful examination? Did they persist in their opinion after doubts to the prejudice of the manuscript had been hinted? When a critic detects a forgery that has for some time imposed upon the world, his discovery casts no imputation upon those learned men who have been hitherto deceived. Besides, if La Croze convinced Spanheim and Hendreichius that the manuscript was a forgery, their conversion is more than equivalent to the hasty opinions of fifty others. 3. La Croze affirmed that he had made the matter plain to Martin himself, whereas Martin denied that La Croze ever had made it plain to him; and La Croze

* Lewis's History of English Translations, p. 47—49. ed. 8vo.

never replied; but left that venerable Senior master of the field. I see no great disagreement in these assertions. I take La Croze to mean, that he had given sufficient reasons for his opinion, and that Martin knew of those reasons. I believe therefore that La Croze was not mistaken in the nature and force of his proofs, but in the nature and force of his patient, whose case would have baffled the united powers of reason and hellebore. But why did not La Croze reply? If his excuse be unsatisfactory, as given by Wetstein, Prol. p. 59, and by you, p. 165, take his own words from the Journal Britannique, XI. p. 90. *Le bon homme M. Martin, n'avoit aucun goût ni aucun merite critique. Le respect que j'ai cru devoir à son âge et à son caractère m'a empêché de lui repondre. Il auroit mieux fait de se mêler de prêcher.* 4. Thus far you have only been skirmishing. Now you prepare for a decisive action. "The Berlin manuscript is not a transcript from the Complutensian edition, because it differs in many places." Martin had occupied the same ground, and to maintain it, had intrenched himself in twenty-three choice examples, twelve of which you borrowed in your first edition,

edition, without consulting the Complutensian. In your second edition, either by the suggestion of a friend or your own collation, you detected two mistakes adopted from Martin, and the list of examples dwindles to ten. However, Mr. Travis's arguments are like the Sibyl's books; they contain information of equal truth, and they increase in value by the diminution of quantity. One of the examples is so important that I cannot help quoting it. " In [Matth.] VI. 13, the Complutensian edition has the doxology complete—of which the Berlin manuscript has not a single word." Thus you had faithfully transcribed from Martin in your first edition, p. 76. Now the Complutensian edition (as you have since learned) omits the doxology in the text, and gives the reasons for this omission in the margin. Would not a writer, who had any regard for the public or for his own character, upon the discovery of such a mistake, blot out the whole sentence? You, Sir, in your second edition, p. 167, repeat the falshood with unblushing forehead, set down the same assertion, and qualify it with this elegant note: " This doxology stands in the margin of the Complutensian Testament." The argument then

then is, by your own confession, either false or trifling, and proves nothing but the ignorance or prevarication of its owner. But some writers seem to be incapable of distinguishing text from margin, originals from translations, or manuscripts from editions. Let the reader attend to the next observation; for the words of the wife, says John Dennis, are precious. " In *eight* of these examples this manuscript agrees with one or more of the manuscripts of *Robert Stephens*; in *one* example with a manuscript of *Casaubon*; in *two* with the *Codex Montfortius*; in *one* with the manuscripts of Saubertus; in *three* with the celebrated manuscript of *Cambridge*; and in the last example with the still more celebrated manuscript of *Alexandria*." From all which you most logically infer, p. 169, " THAT IT IS IMPOSSIBLE FOR THE BERLIN MANUSCRIPT TO BE A TRANSCRIPT FROM THE COMPLUTENSIAN EDITION." How perverse must those men be, that can withstand such a proof! But to strip the unbelievers of all defence, Mr. Zoellner is at hand in the appendix, p. 56, with six fresh examples. And yet loth as I am to dissent from Mr. Travis,

Travis, I am here compelled to it by the reafons which La Croze and Mr. Griefbach (Symbol. Crit. p. CLXXXI—CXCII.) have given for the contrary opinion. I fhall only mention feven or eight.

1. The Berlin manufcript has all the marks of novelty, fuch as frefh chalk, parchment, (ink not pale from its antiquity, but its natural weaknefs, adds La Croze,) &c. Mr. Zoellner, who, to fay the truth, fpeaks more like an advocate than like a judge*, confeffes that thefe appearances are fufpicious, and makes a very feeble anfwer, the amount of which is, that in his opinion a manufcript of Suetonius, written in 1472, looks rather younger than even the Berlin manufcript.

2. The characters refemble no manufcript whatever that has yet been feen, but are very like the types of the Complutenfian edition.

---

* Dixerit forfan codicis Raviani fautor—Nec tamen hic elabendi rima codicis Raviani defenforibus deeft, p. 54, 59.

3. It

3. It is written without accents and spirits. It ought, therefore, to be above a thousand years old. But as I suppose you will scarcely believe it to be quite so old (though I am far from wishing to stint you in your faith) I shall conclude that it is a copy of the Complutensian edition, which is also destitute of accents and spirits.

4. Though La Croze calls it a transcript, even to the faults of the impression, yet critics, as De Missy observes, never expect such a conformity as there is between *ten* and *twice five*; because it is next to impossible to transcribe a book so large as the New Testament without making many deviations. But you and Martin take it for a first principle, that no book can be copied from another, unless both agree exactly in every word, syllable, letter, and comma.

5. A general and remarkable likeness is allowed; and that, as I have more than once observed, is in these cases reckoned sufficient. Since La Croze supposes

supposes the imposture to be the joint product of fraud and folly, it is no wonder that differences from the original are occasionally found, some the offspring of knavery and some of ignorance.

6. These differences are strewed more plentifully through the Gospel of Matthew than any other part of the book. Who perceives not the drift of this contrivance? That if any morose critic should chance to collate the manuscript with the Complutensian edition, he might be deceived by the apparent variation before he had examined too far. *Nempe callide sibi prospexit impostor, ut in quovis N. T. libro— in promtu esset locus unus et item alter a Complutensi editione manifeste discrepans, quo commodum uti posset adversus eos, quibus fraus suboleret. Atque ob eandem hanc causam procul dubio plures Matthæo adspersæ sunt lectiones, &c.* *

---

* GRIESBACH, Symb. Crit. p. cxc.

7. The

7. The disputed verse in this manuscript exactly represents the reading of the Complutensian edition; and,

8. Lastly, every one of the sixteen different readings produced by you and Mr. Zoellner may be found in the margin of R. Stephens's edition. In short, every circumstance favours La Croze's determination, that the Berlin manuscript was copied by an ignorant transcriber from the Complutensian edition, with corrections here and there interspersed by his knavish employer from Stephens's margin. If instead of the eloquent paragraph which I have quoted above, you had been content with this short and simple expression, " In every one of these examples, the Berlin manuscript agrees with Stephens's margin," your argument would have recoiled upon yourself, the forgery would have stared us in the face, and the indignant reader would have exclaimed with Mr. Griesbach, *Itaque jam*

jam tenetur falsarius, manifesto furto prehensus!

The calculation at which I hinted in my second letter, p. 22, is (if that be possible) falser and fuller of mistake than the rest of the work. You assert, p. 282, that Wetstein's No. 49, contains only the Gospel of Mark, when Wetstein himself tells us, that it has also scholia upon the catholic epistles. Perhaps you think that the reading of the text can never be ascertained from scholia. If such be your notions, why do you not explain them? You would then believe an absurdity; now you assert a falsehood. "No. 56 is no more than a collection of some various readings noted in the margin of a printed book." Is it therefore to be set aside? On the contrary, it is at least a good single authority. A learned man had collated the catholic epistles with four manuscripts in the Medicean library, and had marked the various readings in a copy of Raphelengius's edition. Since therefore that edition contains the disputed verse, if the collator had been silent, it would not indeed have been certain that any of his manuscripts agreed with the

printed

printed text; (though Martin and you would have improved this silence into a demonstration;) but since Wetstein sets down No. 56, as agreeing with the other manuscripts, he could not act thus but upon the actual information of the margin.

In the following sentence, Sir, I must desire you to chuse between *deliberate falsehood* and *strange misapprehension.* " Of these sixty-five Greek manuscripts Wetstein admits that those marked 34, 44, 48, 51, 57, and 58, do exhibit this disputed passage. Six assertions and five of them false! Wetstein only admits, that No. 34, (the Dublin MS.) exhibits the disputed passage. No. 44 signifies Valla's manuscripts; and Wetstein is so far from admitting what you affirm, that he endeavours to prove (as I have done more at large) exactly the reverse. Numbers 48, 51, and 57, he sets down in the list of manuscripts that omit the three heavenly witnesses; and you rightly observe (from Mr. Griesbach) in the fifth line preceding this sentence, that No. 58 is a duplicate of No. 22. If then Wetstein admitted that No. 58 retained the three heavenly witnesses, he would admit that

that No. 22 retained them. But he has set down No. 22 in the omitting list. Either therefore you possess a copy of Wetstein's edition different from all other copies, and in it these important confessions exist; or, in five of your six assertions, *Truth and you will be found in two stories; and which are we to believe?* I own that politeness alone would induce me to prefer the lady, even without the magnificent character that you give her, p. 127, 374, " That she is all fair and artless, uniform and consistent, simple and sincere." Who shall hereafter doubt of Mr. Travis's *Christian charity*, when we find him thus honestly doing justice to his inveterate enemy? You charge Mr. Gibbon, p. 126, 371, in express terms with *forging* the authority of Gennadius. If Mr. Gibbon be guilty of *one* forgery, Mr. Travis is guilty of *five*: If a defender of Mr. Travis should argue, that it is incredible that Mr. Travis should wilfully attribute to an author opinions, which that author not only never maintained, but which he directly opposed; in the same manner, with equal right, may a defender of Mr. Gibbon argue. " But Mr. Gibbon has wilfully misrepresented reprefented Gennadius, becaufe his reference is exact." Truly I am fo dull as not to perceive the connection between the two propofitions. Would not the fufpicion be more reafonable, if the reference were general and inaccurate? You, Sir, p. 71, 157, make Montfaucon fay what Montfaucon never meant; and in the fecond edition the reference is exact. From your own principles, therefore, I might conclude, that you have " *wilfully* (for the reference is too exact to allow you fhelter under any fuppofed *inadvertence*) *mifreprefented*" Montfaucon. But I fhall fhew you more indulgence. I believe that you caught a detached fentence without confulting the fequel. Only remember, that a man who quotes in this negligent manner fhould be the laft to accufe others of forgery.

You end your calculation by telling us, that thirty-one manufcripts have the verfe to fifty that omit it. What only fifty? Making all poffible deductions from Wetftein's lift, I cannot allow fewer than eighty-fix that omit the verfe. But perhaps you have a new fyftem of arithmetic as well as a new fyftem of criticifm. Why did you not rather take Mr. Griefbach's

Griesbach's computation? Becaufe it increafes the number of heretical manufcripts, and *that way madnefs lies!* I muft try, therefore, my-felf to fubftitute a more exact account of all the Greek manufcripts that have been collated upon this chapter. I deduct No. 64, one lectionary, and two of Stephens's manufcripts that have difappeared. There will then remain ninety-feven in Mr. Griefbach's lift; for I myfelf have examined No. 63, and teftify that it omits the paffage. To which add, two of the oldeft manufcripts in the Efcurial, infpected by Edward Clarke*, a manufcript once belonging to Bentley (which I have feen in Trinity College library, Cambridge) another in Cafley's Catalogue, p. 3, another in the library at Vienna, lately collated by Profeffor F. C. Alter, and ten at Mofcow (one written in capitals) examined by Mr. Matthæi; the whole number of manufcripts now extant, omitting this *marvellous text*, amounts to one hundred and twelve. I fhall therefore not hefitate to conclude with

---

* Letters concerning Spain, 4to. 1763, p. 133.

Chandler (Pref. to Cassiodorus), Bengelius, Wetstein, Mr. Griesbach and many others, that this celebrated verse exists in no genuine Greek manuscript whatsoever; and partly with Mr. Gibbon, that it owes its place in our editions to the prudence of Erasmus; the honest bigotry of the Complutensian editors; the typographical error of Robert Stephens; and the strange misapprehension of Theodore Beza.

Postscript.

1. I have still a scruple remaining with respect to an incidental question. Simon quotes the note of Lucas Brugensis, which Mr. Travis has so grossly mistaken, as from the edition of 1574. Martin says, that it is in the preface. I have seen several copies of the Antwerp edition of 1574. All these were in octavo; none of them have notes, nor mention this text in the preface. Lucas Brugensis too speaks in such terms (Pref. to his notes dated 1579), as strongly imply that they were then published for the first time. Are there then different copies of the same notes,

notes, and did Simon use a copy containing such a note upon 1 John, V. 7, as he has represented? If that be the case, Lucas Brugensis seems to have been apprehensive that he had not expressed himself with sufficient clearness, and in consequence of that apprehension to have stopped the press, that he might alter his note so as to leave no ambiguity. But I shall be thankful to any learned reader, who can explain this difficulty, and either confirm or destroy my conjecture.

2. That I may shew my impartiality by correcting errors on either side, I shall observe that De Missy has fallen into a mistake by too much refinement. The word μαρ]υροῦντες in the Dublin MS. has its last syllable written in a contraction, and marked with double points, a circumstance not uncommon in modern Greek manuscripts. But upon this innocent circumstance he founded a false accusation against the manuscript, that it meant to proscribe the whole sentence from ἐν τοῖ οὐρανῶι to μαρ]υροῦντ῭ (inclusive), as doubtful or spurious. I have expended so many lines upon the identity of the Dublin manuscript, and of the *Codex Britannicus*, merely in obedience to the canon,

canon, that enjoins us not to enlarge the number of manuscripts without necessity. Else I would as readily admit as deny their diversity. For since they both are manifestly translated from the recent and corrupt Latin copies, the authority of an hundred such manuscripts is equal to the authority of one, and the authority of one is equal to nothing.

3. When I say, in the foregoing letter, that Mr. Travis prefers Wetstein's computation to Mr. Griesbach's, the expression is inaccurate. He misrepresents them both. He makes a shew of mentioning Mr. Griesbach's additions in these words, " to which Griesbach adds four others." Now besides the manuscripts which Wetstein constantly uses, he appeals, on 1 John, V. 7, to those which were collated by Simon, Burnet, Lami, Blanchini, &c. These make up thirty-one; to which Mr. Griesbach adds eight. These manuscripts, together with the fifty that Mr. Travis graciously allows us, would make eighty-nine. But Mr. Travis, either from hurry or from forgetfulness, or from whatever cause, has totally neglected these additional witnesses.

ses. Whatever was the cause, it certainly was no dishonest motive. For " to state authorities, and to urge arguments on *one side* of a question alone, is barely tolerable in an hired advocate," p. 125, 370.

Take notice, lords, he has a loyal breast,
For you have seen him open it.

LETTER VI.

SIR,

AFTER a long interval, which, I dare say, has been equally painful to us both, I wait upon you again according to my promise*. Having dispatched the Greek manuscripts, I proceed to the examination of those versions of the New Testament which contain the Catholic Epistles. You, who with an happy facility contrive to turn the balance in your favour, however the particulars may make against you, tell us, p. 205, 206, that, of the five ancient versions, the Italic, the Vulgate of Jerome, the Syriac, the Armenian, and the Coptic, three, the Italic, the Vulgate, and the Armenian, contain the

* Gent. Mag. Aug. 1789. p. 697.

disputed

disputed verse, 1 John, V. 7. Pray, Sir, where is this Italic Version to be found? Not in MSS. for you say, that there is not a single MS. of it now certainly known to exist in the world, p. 90. Why, then, must this version be pressed into the service? Because it is cited by the writers who lived before Jerome. This version, therefore, ultimately resolves itself into the authority of those writers; and the number of ancient versions shrinks into four, unless to fill up the vacancy, you will accept my gracious offer of the Sclavonian version, to which you ought to have no objection, considering that you have also inlisted that into the orthodox army, p. 92, 206. Leaving, therefore, the examination of your quotations from Tertullian, Cyprian, &c. to another letter, I shall endeavour at present to treat of the Vulgate version with all possible brevity. In order to pave the way to this subject, I desire the reader to ask himself the following questions:

1. Does the Vulgate always closely follow the Greek, particularly in scrupulously guarding against interpolations?

2. Do

2. Do all the MSS. of the Vulgate agree in retaining the three heavenly witnesses?

3. Do all that retain the seventh and eighth verses of 1 John V. represent them in the same manner, without any important alterations, omissions, or additions?

4. Have the orthodox MSS. the verse from the hand of the first writer, without rasures, interlineations, or marginal insertions?

5. Are they generally the oldest and best?

Unless these questions can be answered in the affirmative, the main prop and pillar of your cause will be in a very lame and tottering condition. For I need not tell you, Sir, because you must deny, nor need I tell the learned, because they cannot but know, that the chief support of this contested verse is the authority of the Vulgate. But whoever has enquired with the least share of diligence into the state of the Latin MSS. knows, that not one of these questions can be answered in the affirmative.

I allow you in advance, that a great majority

jority of the Latin MSS. are on your fide. Perhaps for one that omits the three heavenly witnesses, forty or fifty may be found that retain them. I fearched, I confefs, a long while without finding any others; and, that my readers may be as wife as myfelf, I will give them a collation of fifty MSS. or more, that I had the patience to confult.

1. Of this number thirty-two omit the final claufe of the eighth verfe; eighteen retain it, but one has it in the text underlined with red lead, two in the margin, one from the firft, the other from a fecond hand.
2. One omits the final claufe of the feventh verfe.
3. Two read *filius* inftead of *verbum*; with which two French MSS. fold by Meff. Leigh and Sotheby, May 29, 1789, agree. (*li fils.*)
4. Two omit the epithet *fanctus*.
5. Nine change the order of the verfes; but of thefe nine one begins the eighth verfe with *et* and the feventh with *quoniam*; on the other hand, one MS. that preferves the common order,

order, begins the seventh verse with *et* and the eighth with *quoniam*.

6. The MSS. that retain the clause of the eighth verse read invariably either *et tres unum sunt*, or *et hi tres unum sunt*.

7. One adds the heavenly witnesses in the margin from the same hand; another is so fond of them as to insert them in the text, both before and after the others.

8. *En terre* is wanting in one French MS. and *in terra* in a Latin MS. at Ulme, quoted by Mr. Griesbach, p. 229.

With most of these variations some MSS. or other, collated by editors and critics, agree. One MS. at Toledo, collated by Blanchini, adds *in Christo Jesu*; which is also the reading of the author de Trinitate and the writer against Varimadus, both published by Chifflet under the name of Vigilius Tapsensis. You seem, Sir, to acquiesce in Chifflet's judgment. But if you shall hereafter choose to make them two distinct witnesses, my candour is such, that I am determined to have no objection.

The

The same faithful and judicious writer*
against Varimadus quotes for the earthly
witnesses in the eighth verse, *aqua, sanguis,
et caro*; and so reads the margin of a Colbertine MS. quoted by Simon. If this reading
had become fashionable, it would have prevented an objection which the heretics have
made against the double mention of the
spirit.

The addition *in Christo Jesu* I take to have,
at first belonged to the eighth verse, and to
have been written by some pious person who
meant thus to explain the verse; that the
spirit, the water, and the blood, concur in
bearing witness to Christianity. But when
the seventh verse was framed upon the model
of the eighth, they whose copies had received
this addition, transposed it together with the
rest of the clause to the end of the seventh.
One of my reasons for this opinion is, that
some of the MSS. of Ambrose add these
words at the end of the eighth verse.

I shall take little notice of the trifling
omission of *in* before *unum*, because I think

---

* See the Postscript to this Letter.

that it neither affects the sense of the passage, nor the credit of the Vulgate. The Greek MSS. from which that version was made, without doubt omitted εἰς from the identity of the three preceding letters in τρεῖς. The preposition is omitted from the same cause in a passage of Cyril, and in the Greek MSS. of Euthymius Zigabenus*.

If all these various readings were presented in one view to any person endowed with common sense, moderately instructed in the principles of criticism, and uninfluenced in the present debate by interest or passion, he could not help concluding, that the number and importance of the various readings furnish reasonable ground for a suspicion of corruption. That a passage, which so often adds, omits, or alters particular words; which now precedes, now follows the unsuspected part of the text; which is sometimes seen in the body of the work, sometimes in the margin; sometimes by the same, sometimes by a dif-

---

* Panopl. Dogm. Tit. XII. near the end, fol. 112. col. 1. ed. Tergovist. See Mr. *Matthæi* on the Catholic Epistles, p. 141—143.

ferent

ferent hand; sometimes after a rasure; which, in short, changes shapes faster than Proteus or Empusa; that such a passage is exceedingly questionable, whatever shape it assumes; and that, though it were not absolutely omitted by any MS. an editor might yet hint his doubts, or even avow his disbelief, of its genuineness, without justly incurring the censure of *blasphemy or impiety**.

But, allowing that this verse had been extant in the Vulgate even from the end of the second century, and without any of these suspicious appearances, is the merit of this version so high as to ratify and render genuine every word and sentence in which its MSS. conspire? Was it in no place corrupted in the days of Tertullian and Cyprian? If we are certain of any reading having constantly kept its place in the Latin copies, we are certain that they never read otherwise than QUOD in 1 Tim. III. 16, instead of DEUS. You, Sir, will probably defend the latter reading; nor shall I dispute it. But if we take the liberty

---

* *Emlyn*'s Enquiry is called *blasphemous and impious* in the Layman's Address to Convocation, 1717, p, 18.

of rejecting the authority of the Vulgate, when it is so consistent with itself, and so well supported as it is upon 1 Tim. III. 16. why may we not with equal right reject it, when it is the principal, if not the sole, support of a contested verse? Was the addition of the clause in 1 Pet. III. 22, made by the first framers of the version from the warrant of Greek MSS.? Yet that has the general consent of the present Latin copies. Whoever undertakes the defence of such passages, may pretend that his aim is to establish the genuine text, but in fact he is exerting all his force to weaken and undermine its authority.

Thus I should argue, if all the MSS. consented in the received reading. I should think it an hazardous step to prefer any version to the unanimous consent of all the Greek MSS. now known to exist. Still less should I venture to rely upon such a version, which, by having been more frequently copied, has also been more frequently interpolated than any other. The subsidiary streams which the river has received in its course have neither made the water more clear, nor more wholesome.

But

But we are told, p. 42, that, by the command of Charlemagne, Alcuin was employed in a revision of the Vulgate; that in Alcuin's Correctorium " the testimony of the three heavenly witnesses is read without the smallest impeachment of its authenticity;" and that this very volume was extant at Vauxcelles in the life of Baronius. You then add a supposition (for of suppositions you have a plentiful stock), that Alcuin and his assistants, in order to settle the text, referred to the Greek MSS. and not only to the Greek MSS. but to the best and oldest Greek MSS. some *in all probability* as old as the Apostolical age. A lively fancy, Sir, is an indifferent accomplishment for a critic. You cannot prove that Alcuin ever saw a Greek MS. much less that he collated any for the use of his edition. The knowledge of Greek was so scarce a commodity in those days, that the contrary supposition, which is expressly affirmed by Vallarsius*, is much the more probable of the two. It was labour and honour enough for Alcuin to collate the copies of the Vulgate. Neither can you prove that the MS.

---

* In *Blanchini*'s Vindiciæ Veteris Vulgatæ, p. 328.

at Vauxcelles is the original of Alcuin. For it is so customary to transcribe titles from older MSS. that the name of the corrector is no proof of the MS. being written by the corrector, or in the same age. Besides, the ignorance shewn in orthography* (as Wetstein observes) would tempt us to believe that it was written by an unskilful transcriber of Alcuin rather than by Alcuin himself. You will be delighted, Sir, I doubt not, to hear, that this *treasure of inestimable value* is still in being. Blanchini has given a specimen of the character in his Evangeliarium Quadruplex, from which it appears, as far as I can judge, to be less ancient than he would make it. But in these matters most editors are naturally apt to be a little partial. When you say, that 1 John V. 7. is found in this famous MS. without *the smallest impeachment of its authenticity*, what do you mean by *the smallest impeachment?* Would you have

---

* Such, for instance, as *Canoniorum* for *Canonicarum*, &c. *Vitali* seems to speak of another MS. written by Alcuin, and representing 1 John V. 7. in the same manner; but what he says is very obscure, and therefore I shall not urge it.

the writer of the MS. inform his readers, by a marginal note, that he had inserted a spurious verse in his edition? An editor would hardly be mad enough to become such a *felo de se*.

But I shall advance one step further, and maintain, that this MS. upon which so much stress is laid, is at least as much against the verse as in its favour. For how is the verse read in this MS.? Not in the text, but in the margin are added these words:—Sicut *tres sunt qui testimonium dant in cœlo, pater, verbum, et spiritus sanctus, et tres unum sunt.* The text has only these words, *Quoniam tres sunt qui testimonium dant, spiritus, aqua, et sanguis, et tres unum sunt.* Between *sunt* and *qui* the same hand has interlined *in terra* *. Now, Sir, this is so far from being a *small impeachment* of your favourite verse, that it is a direct and violent attack upon it: for it plainly says, that the Latin MSS. varied; and it more than hints, that the older surviving MSS. were without the addition of the heavenly witnesses. If, then, this MS. was only a copy of Alcuin's

* *Vitali* in Blanchini's Evang. Quadr. Part I. p. 567.

autograph, Alcuin might be unacquainted with this verse, though without its aid he believed the doctrine which it is supposed to contain, as appears from his treatise on the Trinity.

I have purposely omitted, in my former account of the various readings, one of the most important, that I might introduce it here. The reader will easily guess that I mean the connection of the seventh verse with the eighth by the intervention of SICUT. In three MSS. that Bp. Burnet saw, the seventh verse follows the eighth; and they are *pinned* together, as the bishop well expresses it, by a SICUT. In a MS. at Ulme* the passage stands thus: *Quia tres sunt qui testimonium dant, spiritus, et aqua, et sanguis, et tres unum sunt,* SICUT *in cœlo tres sunt pater, verbum, et spiritus, et tres unum sunt.* This various reading not only gives fresh suspicion of interpolation, but shews us the means by which it gradually insinuated itself into the text. Whoever duly and attentively weighs this circumstance, will perhaps see less cause to think the idea of a marginal gloss so *affected and absurd* as

---

* *Griesbach*, tom. II. p. 229. SICUT is also read in a MS. of Card. Passionei.

you modestly pronounce it, p. 342. But they who believe things that are impossible, generally disbelieve other things both possible and probable. We know for certain that some of the most learned and renowned fathers interpreted the spirit, the water, and the blood of the Trinity. Could all the diligent Christians who perused Augustine, Eucherius, and Facundus, with the intention of extracting explanations of scripture, and noting them in the margin of their bibles—could they all miss this sagacious interpretation? Would no member of the churches over which these bishops presided, approve and endeavour to perpetuate his diocesan's sublime discovery? When once such a copy existed, with a marginal note of this sort upon 1 John V. 8, *Sicut tres sunt qui testimonium dant in cœlo, pater, verbum, et spiritus sanctus, et hi tres unum sunt;* the next transcriber, in a fit of politeness, might think that if this sentence was not text, it deserved to be, and might compliment it with a place in the middle of his page. Perhaps you think it *an affected and absurd idea* that a marginal note can ever creep into the text: yet I hope you are not so ignorant as not to know that this has actually happened, not merely in hundreds or thousands, but in millions of places. *Natura,* says Daillé*, *ita comparatum est, ut auctorum probatorum libros plerique omnes amplos quam breves malint; verentes scilicet, ne quid sibi desit, quod auctoris vel sit vel esse dicatur.* To the same purpose Bengelius †, *Non facile pro superfluo aliquid hodie habent complures docti viri* (he might have added, *omnesque indocti*) *eademque mente plerique quondam librarii fuere.* From this known propensity of transcribers to turn every thing into text which they found written in the margin of their MSS. or between the lines, so many interpolations have proceeded, that at present the surest canon of criticism is, *Præferatur lectio brevior.*

I have hitherto been arguing as if all the Latin MSS. had the disputed verse in some shape or other; which you know, Sir, is not the case. You say indeed, p. 210, that "there is a greater number beyond all comparison in which this text is found." I have already

---

* De Lib. supp. Dionys. et Ignat. II. 3. p. 238.
† In Apocalyps. I. 11.

allowed

allowed you the full benefit of your majority. Make the moſt of this conceſſion; for it would be unkind to deprive you of an advantage which you ſo ſeldom enjoy. But take care of this argument; for, if you puſh it too forcibly, it will pierce the heart of your own cauſe. If the majority of Latin copies be a good proof that this verſe was early in the Latin verſion, the majority of Greek MSS. is as good a proof that it never was in the original. However, I will make what I think a fair propoſal. Produce two actually exiſting Greek MSS. five hundred years old, containing this verſe, and I will acknowledge your opinion of its genuineneſs to be probable. If you are unable to do this, and I produce you above twenty Latin MSS. all greatly exceeding that age, you cannot, I think, in common decency, refuſe to be a convert to my opinion. Let us then come to the fact. There are now exiſting twenty-nine Latin MSS. in general the oldeſt, the faireſt, and the moſt correct. Wetſtein reckons twenty-five, to which Mr. Grieſbach adds the Harleian, 1772, and ſays, *plureſque poſt Wetſtenium inſpectos.* I know nothing about any of theſe *plures,* and therefore

fore I shall make no appeal to them. All these MSS. in 1 John V. instead of our present seventh and eighth verses, give no more than—*Quoniam tres sunt qui testimonium dant*, spiritus, aqua, et sanguis, et tres unum sunt.* In the Harleian catalogue, No. 7551 contains three copies of the first epistle of John. The first copy seems to be of the tenth century, the second of the ninth, and both omit the heavenly witnesses. In the first copy the line, as appears from the space, originally stood thus; *sp̄s, aqua, et sanguis, et tres unum sunt.* But another hand has erased the whole sentence, and written, *spiritus, sanguis, et aqua,* stretching out the letters to make them fill the line. In the margin is added, by the same hand, I suppose, that made the rasure, *in cœlo pater, verbum, et sp̄s, et tres unum sunt, et tres sunt qui testimonium dant in terra.* After *aqua*, a third hand (unless it were the second in a repenting mood) adds, *et hi tres unum sunt.* The second copy has the genuine words

---

* If any of these MSS. add *in terra*, as perhaps one or two may, I am content that they be struck off the list.

without any rasure, interlineation, or marginal note. Casley, in his catalogue, p. 15, gives an account of another Latin MS. agreeing with these as it was first written; but afterwards thus interpolated: *Quia tres sunt qui testimonium dant* in tra sps *aqua et sanguis, et* hi *tres unum sunt.* et tres sunt qui testimonium dant in cœlo, pater et filius, et sps sanctus, et hi tres unum sunt. The same hand has very liberally scattered corrections through the rest of the book, sometimes right, but oftener false and absurd. I hope, Sir, by these instances, you will begin to perceive that it is at least possible for an interpolation sometimes to gain footing in the text. I shall trouble you with the mention of only one Latin MS. more. Mabillon found at Lisieux, and published, a Gallic* Lectionary, which is reputed to be now about 1200 years old, and contains the entire epistle of John, except the three heavenly witnesses. But these it barbarously omits, and only has *Quoniam tres sunt qui testimonium dant, spiritus,*

---

* Twells and Bengelius, by a strange mistake, affirm that this Lectionary was not written in Latin, but in Gallo-Teutonic.

aqua,

aqua, et sanguis, et tres unum sunt. The authority of this MS. cannot but be thought of great weight, if we consider its age; to which I shall add another argument in its favour: it omits (see Mabillon, p. 475) that interpolation 1 Pet. III. 22. from which no other Latin copy, so far as I know, is exempt.

But, to close this long discussion, the question is, To which side shall we give credit, to age or to numbers? On one side the witnesses are grave, elderly persons, who lived nearer the time when the fact happened which they assert, and they are all consistent in their testimony; while the other party, though vastly superior in numbers, yet lived too late to be competently acquainted with the cause: many carry a brand of perjury on their front; and, after all their collusion and subornation, their testimonies frequently clash, and contradict one another. In short, the few Latin MSS. that reject the verse, are as much superior to the herd of incorrect and modern copies that retain it, as a small well-trained band of soldiers to a numerous rabble destitute of discipline and unanimity.

POSTSCRIPT.

Postscript.

Abbot Joachim compared the final clauses of the seventh and eighth verses, whence he inferred, that the same expression ought to be interpreted in the same manner. Since therefore, said he, nothing more than unity of testimony and consent can be meant by *tres unum sunt* in the eighth verse, nothing more than unity of testimony and consent is meant in the seventh. This opinion the Lateran council and Thomas Aquinas confuted by cutting out that clause in the eighth verse. Thomas tells us, that it was not extant in the *true copies*, but that it was *said* to be added by the Arian heretics to pervert the sound understanding of the foregoing authority. My blood boils whenever I think of those sacrilegious Arians, sometimes forging and sometimes erasing scripture. Thus Thomas Aquinas tells us, that they were *said* to have added this clause. Bugenhagius thinks they inserted the whole seventh verse. Yet some part of my indignation is involuntarily diverted to the holy fathers of the church, who

who seem to have been in a sleep approaching to a lethargy, while the enemy came and sowed the tares. In taking the method above-mentioned, the Lateran council, it is true, followed Dr. Ovid's advice, *immedicabile vulnus Enfe recidendum*, NE PARS SINCERA TRAHATUR. But if they had given their minds to good reading, they would have found in the treatise against Varimadus an easy way of curing the wound that Joachim had made in the common faith, without having recourse to the desperate process of amputation. For the author of that treatise, as if he had foreseen, and meant to confound, the stratagems of the Arians, thus quotes the passage from " the epistle to the Parthians;" *There are three that bear record on earth, the water, the blood, and* THE FLESH, *and the three are* IN US; *and there are three that bear record in heaven, the Father, the Word, and the Spirit, and they three are one.* What would then have become of Joachim's argument?

LETTER

SIR,

YOU will perhaps accuse me of a capital neglect, in not taking notice of your argument from the Prologue attributed to Jerome, the author of which boasts to have restored * this verse from Greek MSS. I confess that I was rather doubtful in what class of proofs I should place the Prologue; but at last I thought it more properly belonged to the head of quotations. I shall therefore treat of it in my review of the *pious* Jerome. In the mean time, the next versions upon our list are the Syriac and Coptic, which I intend to make the joint subjects of this letter.

---

* Mr. Travis quarrels with the word *restored*, p. 51, 105, " because," says he, " the verse was never lost." Surely an editor may be said to *restore* a passage, that was only in a part of the copies, and consequently in danger of being lost.

You

You and Martin find the testimony of these versions so unfavourable to your cause, that you are resolved, at all events, to demolish their authority. But the heat of a prejudiced accuser often hurts himself more than the party accused. Your eagerness to disable the credit of the Syriac and Coptic versions has so utterly deprived you of judgment and reflection, that I am not without some hopes of making an impression upon your own head or heart:

―――― *for so I shall,*
If they be made of penetrable stuff;
If damned custom have not braz'd them so,
That they be proof and bulwark against sense.

I shall not dispute with you about the precise age of the old Syriac version. I have several reasons for this forbearance; one of which is, that I know very little of the matter. I shall only observe, that your argument against its being older than Chrysostome, because it contains the doxology, is not valid, unless you allow that the doxology is spurious. If you allow this, you reject a reading, that has, upon a moderate computation, thirty times

times as many witnesses in its behalf, as your present client. It is found in all the Greek MSS. except eight; in two of the oldest Latin copies; in some MSS. of the Arabic and Persic; in the Syriac, the Armenian, the Gothic, and the Æthiopic. If you had a sixth part of this evidence for 1 John V. 7. how you would triumph over all that dared even to insinuate the smallest suspicion! But you despise the aid of external evidence. It is the nature of the texts and the doctrines supposed to be contained in them that permits or forbids omissions to be conclusive arguments. If I had a mind to argue in your way, I could say, that only a single version, the Coptic, is found, which uniformly omits the doxology; " that this version is faulty beyond belief, leaving out many whole verses; and that no argument can be drawn from *any* omission of *any* verse, by *any* transcriber, like this;" p. 90, 196.

I now come to your arguments against these obnoxious versions; which, as they are of the same kind, I beg leave to consolidate. " They are," you say, p. 87—90, 190—196, " faulty and incorrect, almost beyond belief.

They

They pass over not words or sentences only, but even whole verses, which are admitted by all to be genuine." The instances of this sort which you produce from the Syriac, are John XIV. 3. XVI. 14. Acts VIII. 37. XV. 34. XXVIII. 29. 1 Pet. IV. 14. You might have strengthened this argument by an observation which I have seen, that this version omits whole epistles, and therefore might easily omit a short sentence of a single epistle. If you think this objection of any weight, you are welcome to the use of it. Your instances of omission from the Coptic are Matth. V. 44. XVIII. 1. XX. 22, 23. XXVII. 35. Mark VII. 16. XI. 26. Acts VIII. 37. XXIV. 7. To save your readers the trouble of looking for the places, and the fear of being deceived by any misprint in the numbers of reference, you have courteously transcribed the entire passages. But, before I go farther in this subject, I request you, Sir, to answer the following queries.

 1. Are you sure, from your own inspection, that the Syriac and Coptic versions are chargeable with these omissions?

2. Do

2. Do all the MSS. of this or that version agree in rejecting the verses specified? For, if the MSS. vary, some retaining and some omitting a passage, it is absurd to blame that for a fault in the version itself, which may be corrected from better copies.

3. Do they omit the whole quantity of text that you have transcribed?

4. How do you know that these passages are admitted by all to be genuine? Have you had the patience to collect the opinions of all who have written upon these subjects? Or do you believe that every syllable of our common Greek Testament, as it was settled in the year 1624 by Elzevir and other inspired men, is the genuine text of the Evangelists and Apostles?

Leaving you to chew the cud upon these queries, I shall proceed to consider a few of these passages.

"Matth. V. 44. is entirely left out of the Coptic."—Let us then transcribe the context without this verse, and see what excellent sense it will make.

43. *Ye have heard that it hath been said, Thou shalt love thy neighbour, and hate thine enemy;*

45. *That ye may be the children of your Father which is in heaven; for he maketh his sun to rise on the evil and on the good,* &c.

Strange, that the reason of a precept should be given, and the precept itself not appear! Notwithstanding your " right to command our full assent when you only affirm a plain fact, which you are compleatly competent to ascertain," p. 59, 126; notwithstanding my own *literary candour and Christian charity*, I assure you, Sir, that sooner than believe such an absurdity of the Coptic, I should have the audacity to charge you with *strange misapprehension*.

Matth. XXVII. 35.—Is this whole verse, too, Sir, wanting in the Coptic? If it be, I will own such a version to be of very little value, and shall make no difficulty of delivering it up to your resentment. But when I consider that, if the verse be expunged, there will remain no direct mention of Christ's crucifixion, I cannot believe that either translator or transcriber could in his most careless mood overlook so important a sentence.

Throw

Throw out Matth. XVIII. 1. XX. 22, 23. John XVI. 14. the sense indeed will not be totally destroyed, but the construction will appear abrupt and unconnected. In Acts XXIV. 7. whoever will cast his eye on the Greek text will see that your account cannot be true, for the eighth verse begins with κελεύσας, which, if the seventh verse be omitted, will have no substantive to govern it.

Thus far I have thought fit to take the high *priori* road of reasoning; that if I have any attentive readers (besides your friend Kuster) they may learn to weigh the probabilities of an assertion before they agree to its truth, and to distrust all inconsistent relations, however solemnly vouched by the relater.—

——— Σώφρονος δ' ἀπιστίας
Οὐκ ἔςιν οὐδὲν χρησιμώτερον βροτοῖς.

I shall now, Sir, descend to the level of your understanding, to the plain fact. I assert then that the Syriac version omits only three whole verses of the six you have been pleased to quote: Acts VIII. 37. XV. 34. XXVIII. 29. Of your eight examples from the Coptic, you are right only in three; Mark VII. 16. XI. 26. Acts VIII. 37. However, I shall be merciful to you in your last instance, Acts XXIV. 7. because you are seldom guilty of asserting too little. For the Coptic version there omits not only the whole seventh verse, but parts also of the sixth and eighth.

John XIV. 3. XVI. 14. the later Syriac editions represent exactly as they are in the Greek. Widmanstad and Tremellius indeed omit the former part of one *(And if I go and prepare a place for you)*, and the latter part of the other *(And shall shew it unto you)*; but in Guido's edition both these clauses are replaced from a MS. 1 Pet. IV. 14. the Syriac only omits, *On their part he is evil spoken of, but upon your part he is glorified.*

Matth. V. 44. the Coptic thus shortens: *But I say unto you, love your enemies, and pray for them that persecute you.* XVIII. 1. the Coptic does not omit, nor any other version, nor any Greek MS. that I can find. Instead of XVIII. 1. you ought to have written XVIII. 11. which the Coptic does omit. XX. 22, 23. In each of these verses the Coptic only omits the words, *and be baptised with the baptism that I am baptised with.* XXVII. 35. the Coptic omits the application of of the prophecy, and only retains, *And they crucified him, and parted his garments, casting lots.*

Thus, Sir, in your fourteen examples you have made eight mistakes. Will you accept of my corrections? The list will not be much lessened in number, for there will then remain twelve examples; but several of them will be of less consequence. These twelve examples amount only to eleven passages; Acts VIII. 37. being twice quoted. Are then these eleven passages *admitted by all*, as you affirm, *to be genuine?* You must correct again, Sir. This general assertion of yours contains in effect eleven separate assertions, and in ten of them you are wrong. Eight times Mill approves the shorter reading; two of the other omissions are patronized, one by Erasmus, and one by Bengelius; nay, Whitby himself, who * *put in the front of his book that* SPLENDID FALSEHOOD THAT THE VULGAR READING MAY BE ALWAYS DEFENDED, agrees to expunge Matth.

---

* VALCKENÆR. Orat. de Critica in N. T. non adhibenda, p. 308.

XXVII. 35. Three of your *genuine* paſſages Mr. Griesbach has diſcarded from his text; Matth. XX. 22, 23. XXVII. 35. Acts VIII. 37. and upon ſix more he ſets a mark to render them doubtful; Matth. V. 44. XVIII. 11. Acts XV. 34. XXIV. 6—8. XXVIII. 29, 1 Pet. IV. 14.

Let us now enquire into the merits of ſome of theſe readings. In Matth. V. 44. the ſenſe is the ſame, whether we acquieſce in the received reading, or prefer the ſhorter reading which has the Coptic and other authorities on its ſide. It is a mere point of criticiſm to decide whether the ſentence was firſt abridged by the haſte of copiers, or lengthened by the admiſſion of the parallel paſſage, Luke VI. 27, 28. To me, I own, the latter opinion ſeems more plauſible.

Matth. XVIII. 11. is omitted not only in the Coptic verſion, but in ſix Greek MSS, one very ancient Latin copy, one MS. of the Syriac quoted by Profeſſor J. G. C. Adler*, nor is it mentioned by Origen, Jerome, &c.

* De Syriacis Verſionibus.

Many Greek MSS. the Æthiopic, Arabic, and latter Syriac verſions add $\zeta\eta\tau\tilde{\eta}\sigma\alpha\iota\ \varkappa\alpha\grave{\iota}$; a circumſtance which makes it more than probable that the whole verſe is interpolated from Luke XIX. 10. In like manner many copies of Matth. XXIV. 36. have a clauſe added from Mark XIII. 32.

In Mark VII. 16. though no more than four Greek MSS. agree with the Coptic, I cannot but ſubſcribe to Mill's judgment, who thinks it ſpurious. What confirms me the more in this opinion is, that the tranſcribers of the Greek MSS. have in other places been very prone to ſtuff out the text with the ſame ſentence. Not contented with its having quiet and acknowledged poſſeſſion in Matth. XI. 15. XIII. 9. Mark IV. 9. a great number of MSS. adds it in Luke XII. 21. XXI. 4. In Mark XI. 26. ſeveral of the Greek MSS. agree with the Coptic.

The reſt of the omiſſions which you lay to the charge of theſe verſions are ſupported by ſo many conſiderable authorities, that whoever ventures to decide poſitively againſt them, will incur the imputation of great raſhneſs.

rashness. And what is remarkable enough is, that they all have the concurrence of at least some Latin MSS. By this time I hope the intelligent reader will perceive, that, in fact, there is not, among all the instances you have brought to prove the Syriac and Coptic versions faulty, above one or two that can reasonably be pronounced corrupt; and, that in the rest they rather create a prejudice against the luxuriance of the common reading, than the common reading against their frugality.

But " though it was greatly your duty, it was no part of your design," p. 71, 157, to say what might be said in favour of these versions. The unlearned reader therefore is left to suppose that one or the other of these versions is so incorrect as in many important instances to stand single, and contradict the united authority of the Greek MSS. the other versions, and the citations of the fathers. It is curious, too, that of the passages you produce, you only note the agreement of the Syriac and Coptic in one omission, whereas they really agree in five. And I cannot but condemn your imprudence in mentioning

even

even that single instance of their agreement, Acts VIII. 37. It might awaken the suspicions of some inquisitive reader, who by this glimmering of light would perhaps be led to a farther examination of the subject, and consequently to a detection of Mr. Travis's errors. I shall only add, that wherever the Syriac and Coptic versions agree in any deviation from the common reading (be it alteration, addition, or omission), and that deviation is countenanced by a reasonable number of Greek MSS. it will require better critical abilities than yours to prove them in the wrong.

" These are examples," you add concerning the Syriac, " which have escaped even the critical eye of Theodore Beza." How lucky that they *escaped* not *the critical eye* of Mr. Travis! But if Beza was so purblind as not to see such manifest omissions, with a Latin translation from the Syriac before him, I assure you, Sir, without flattery, that your *eye* is at least as *critical* as his. When you have read a little more concerning this subject than you have already, that is, when you have read at all, you will find, that Beza does

actually

actually mention four of these six examples; John XIV. 3. Acts VIII. 37. XXVIII. 29. 1 Pet. IV. 14.

I feel myself here treading upon slippery ground. When I reflect upon the heinousness of the charge that I have brought against you, I am almost afraid of being myself suspected for a false accuser. There is one advantage in telling enormous rather than moderate falshoods. Mankind are in general so lazy and credulous, that when once they are prejudiced in favour of any person's veracity, they will regard another as a calumniator who endeavours to convince them that they have bestowed their approbation upon an unworthy object. They will argue, as I have already observed, from the enormity of an offence, and the easiness of detection, against the probability of its ever being committed.

But if I shall be fortunate enough to have one reader of learning and probity, I request him, I exhort him, to peruse this letter, and the other passages where I pawn my own word, with particular attention. He will then find that I have stated the facts simply as they are, and that however astonishing the instances of of Mr. Travis's aſſurance may ſeem, I have ſpoken of them without diſtortion or exaggeration.

I ſhould indeed have almoſt diſtruſted the evidence of my own ſenſes, when I ſaw you commit above twenty groſs and palpable errors in leſs than half a dozen pages, if I had not been acquainted with the ſource from which they flowed. Your French friend Martin* makes a few miſtakes, which you like a true Engliſhman have greatly improved. Martin ſays, Diſſ. p. 166. (91 Eng.) "This Syriac verſion is full of faults, and eſpecially of omiſſions. Beza has given abundance of inſtances—and we could add thereto a great many others——I ſhall give only a few, and thoſe in whole texts." He then ſpecifies the very ſame verſes which you have quoted (except that you have omitted one of his examples); but becauſe he was content

---

* Mr. Travis may perhaps alledge in his defence, that he refers to Martin in the bottom of his page 88, 192. This is true; but I would defy any reader to gueſs from ſo ſlight and naked a reference that he had borrowed the ſubſtance of five pages from Martin.

to mark the numbers without reciting the words, you set down the whole verses without enquiry. To the Coptic he makes the same objection, and gives for examples of omissions the same numbers with which you have obliged us. But by ill luck, instead of Matth. XVIII. 11. his printer, by overlooking a figure, made it XVIII. 1. Now if Martin had been less sparing of his ink and labour, he would have written the passages at full length, and saved his admirer the disgrace of this ridiculous plagiarism. How very rude too was it to express himself so ambiguously, " Beza has given abundance of instances—and we could add thereto a great many others." If you look at these words again, you may perceive, Sir, unless *some devil has cozened you at hoodman-blind*, that they do not necessarily imply all the instances there given to be such as had *escaped the critical eye of Theodore Beza.*

There is another little circumstance which you have not condescended to mention. Besides the copies of the ancient Syriac version, commonly called the *Versio simplex*, there came to England in this century a copy of Philoxenus's loxenus's verſion, reviſed by Thomas Heracleenſis, and collated in the margin with the old Syriac and ſeveral Greek MSS. The margin and text of this reviſion ſo often make additions, that if the collator had found the three heavenly witneſſes in any MS. Syriac or Greek, he would not have envied his readers the valuable diſcovery. Yet this villainous copy is obſtinately ſilent both in the text and in the margin. The ſame malignant demon* that has preſerved the Dublin MS. to mock at human credulity, ſeems to have brought to light this new Syriac verſion to abet the Arians in their impious oppoſition.

Accipe nunc Danaum inſidias. In the year 1599, Menezes, Archbiſhop of Goa, preſided at the Synod of Diamper, and made the Indian Chriſtians correct their Syriac copies by the Latin verſion. Among the paſſages thus judiciouſly corrected, 1 John V. 7.† could not fail to be included. This the Archbiſhop ordered to be reſtored, as *having been ſuppreſſed*

---

* Journ. Brit. tom. IX. p. 64.
† La Croze, Chriſtianiſme des Indes, III. p. 342.

by

by impiety. Tremellius, not finding this passage either in Widmanstad's edition or the Heidelberg MS. ventured not to insert it in his text, but translates it into Syriac in the margin, and says, *sic restitui possit.* At last Gutbier boldly thrusts it into the text, and tells us that the Arians expunged it. Schaaf could not help applauding so good an example. " This verse," says he, " is wanting in the former editions, but Gutbier and I have transcribed it from Tremellius's notes and inserted it in the text." Schaaf afterwards sent a copy of his edition to the Bishop of the Malabarian Christians of St. Thomas. The Bishop in return sent him a Syriac MS. of the N. T. This *treasure of inestimable value* is still preserved* in the Amsterdam library, and contains that precious jewel, the cause of so much strife and shedding of ink. With what face will the infidels now assert, that the Syriac version omits the three heavenly witnesses, when a Syriac MS. confirms their authenticity? Perhaps they will make two

---

* ADLER de Syriacis Versionibus, p. 31—33.

trifling

trifling objections; 1. That this MS. was written as late as the year 1700, and therefore is too modern to have any authority; especially as we know that the Syriac copies had been interpolated with this very text a century before. 2. That in this MS. the verse is written thus in the margin, *in cœlo pater et filius, et spiritus sanctus, et hi tres in uno sunt. Et sunt tres testes in terra.* But you, Sir, who are as well pleased with margin as with text, and with Dublin or Berlin MSS. as with Alexandrian or Vatican, will despise such arguments, and manfully defend the credit of your witness. I hope, however, that some who have formerly entertained sublime notions of the morality of the Complutensian and other editors, will upon reflection abate of their confidence, and acknowledge that when a man is (no matter how) convinced of the genuineness of any reading, he will not be so scrupulous as to throw it out of his text merely because his MSS. chance to be refractory. In particular, the zeal and eagerness that have been shewn for the establishment of this verse, sometimes upon very slender authority and sometimes upon none, may

may serve to check the wonder of those readers, who are apt to put implicit trust in the professions of editors.

I must not forget a gentle censure of La Croze's upon the Syriac version, that * " respectable as it is, by having been retouched several times, the copies have many variations, and that it does not deserve quite so much credit as it has commonly obtained." But this observation, however it may detract from the general authority of the version, rather strengthens than weakens its evidence in the present case. For since many Greek interpolations have been admitted from time to time into the Syriac, its constant omission of this verse in the successive collations of Greek MSS. proves that the verse was uniformly absent from the early Syriac version and the Greek copies upon which the later translation was formed.

To conclude, the MSS. of the Coptic version unanimously, the old Syriac version, and the later version made by Philoxenus and collated again with Greek MSS. and the for-

* Christianisme d'Ethiopie, I. p. 40.

mer

mer Syriac by Thomas Heracleenfis, are three strong and diſtinct evidences againſt the authenticity of 1 John V. 7. The Syriac MSS. proteſted againſt it till the end of the ſixteenth century, when the copies of ſuch owners as were obedient to the conſcientious Menezes began to be adulterated in compliance with his orders. With equal judgment and fidelity ſome of the Syriac editors have admitted this verſe into their text, without the ſlighteſt authority, but merely from a marginal note of Immanuel Tremellius.

But whatever weight theſe verſions may be thought to have in the deciſion of the preſent queſtion, every attentive reader muſt ſee and confeſs that Mr. Travis is a ſervile copier and an hardy aſſerter. I ſhall therefore diſmiſs him to the contempt of the learned, and the reproaches of his own conſcience.

LETTER VIII.

SIR,

THE remaining versions to which Dr. Benson appeals, are the Arabic, the Æthiopic, the Persic, the Armenian, the Russian, and the old French. By the old French version I suppose him to mean the Gallic Lectionary published by Mabillon, of which I gave an account in my sixth letter. I frankly consent to exclude this from the number of versions. I have only produced it as a copy of the Latin version, though for a single authority I lay great stress upon it. The Persic, which Martin seems generously to yield to his opposers, Dr. Benson accepts, and you acquiesce in his claim. If there really be in print such a Persic version containing the Catholic Epistles, I must take shame to myself, and confess my ignorance; comforting myself, however, that Mill, Wetstein, Mr. Griesbach,

Griesbach, and others, seem to be as ignorant as I am. To the Arabic and Æthiopic you object, because they are copied, according to Simon and Dupin, from the Syriac. But in the note, p. 193, you tell us, that Renaudot deduces the Æthiopic, and Michaelis some of the Arabic versions, from the Coptic. The solution of this question must be left to the curious in Oriental languages. Perhaps those learned men were hasty in their judgments, and founded their sentiments upon a partial conformity. Perhaps both these versions were made from Greek MSS. though the MSS. might have a general likeness to those which were used by the compilers of the Syriac and Coptic. At any rate, amidst these jarring opinions, it will be impossible to make a well-grounded choice, till more accurate editions are published from Arabic and Æthiopic MSS.

But not caring to talk learnedly without understanding the subject (though that is a very common fault, as you, Sir, no doubt, have observed), I shall not press this argument; nor assume a point in my own favour, merely because it cannot be proved against me.

me. I shall only use the concurrent testimony of these two versions as an argument for the consistency of their parents. If the disputed verse had been once in the Coptic or Syriac, and was afterwards lost out of the later copies, it might have been preserved in the Æthiopic or Arabic from early and uncorrupted MSS. But since these too omit it, the agreement of the Syriac and Coptic versions is strengthened by a fresh accession of evidence.

Having thus dispatched the Arabic and Æthiopic versions, we come to the Armenian, which La Croze* has dignified with the august title of *Queen of Versions.* But, alas!

————*Kings,* QUEENS, *and States,*
Maids, matrons, nay, the secrets of the grave,
This vip'rous Slander enters.

For a king and a bishop (Haitho and Uscan), who were intrusted with the education of this *queen,* have been accused of sullying the purity which they ought to have protected.

---

* *Beausobre* and *Lenfant's* Pref. to N. T. p. 211. *Whiston's* Pref. to Moses Chorenensis, p. 9.

This

This slander had gained ground upon the report of Simon, Sandius, and La Croze; and the world in general seemed disposed to believe it; when a champion entered the lists, and with more than a Quixote's gallantry threw down his gauntlet in behalf of injured innocence.

>*En quoi certes & sa bonté,*
>*Et son zéle & sa charité,*
>*Se firent d'autant plus paroître,*
>*Qu'il n'a l'honneur de la connoître;*
>*Semblable à ces preux Chevaliers,*
>*Ces Paladins avanturiers,*
>*Qui defendant des Inconnuës,*
>*Ont porté leur nom jusqu'aux nuës.*

You will perhaps, Sir, interrupt this raillery by asking me, whether I understand the Armenian language? Truly, Sir, no better than yourself. But that I know something more of the subject than you, I will endeavour to convince my readers. We are happily agreed that Uscan published this version, and that it contains 1 John V. 7. You add indeed, " without any mark of doubt or suspicion." You are very fond, I perceive, of these expletives. Has any other passage of Uscan's bible any mark of doubt or suspicion? If not, what confequence can be drawn from his filence on this place? For my own part, not having your heroic talent for affertion, I cannot pofitively affirm, but I fully believe that Ufcan has fpared himfelf all trouble of that kind. Your next arguments cannot have juftice done them, without being more largely tranfcribed.

" 1. Michaelis affirms, on the authority of Sandius, that Ufcan did not find the paffage 1 John V. 7. in his MS. although it ftands in Ufcan's editions.

" But the account fo given by Sandius, was evidently (to fay the leaft of it) a miftake. [*Anglicè*, was evidently a lie.] For M. Simon was acquainted at Paris with Ufcan, whilft he was employed in executing his important commiffion. And M. Simon (who was not only a very learned, but on the whole, a candid opponent of this verfe) exprefsly admits, that Ufcan's impreffion could not but be very accurate. *The bifhop* (fays he), *who was a judicious and difcreet perfon, brought with him* THE MOST CORRECT MSS. *which he carefully followed. And thefe particulars I learned* FROM THE BISHOP HIMSELF."

Here,

Here, Sir, your fidelity in copying Martin's tranflator has let you into a fmall error. You ought to have divided Simon's words into two quotations. But if a tranflator will omit *ailleurs*, who can help it?—This, however, you call the confeffion of an adverfary, overthrowing his own prepoffeffions. To make this a complete confeffion, and a counterpoife to the evidence of Sandius, Simon ought to have feen Ufcan's MS. or MSS. with his own eyes, and to have teftified that he there read the difputed verfe. But he only fays that the bifhop brought with him good MSS. which he faithfully followed. We cannot erect this into a teftimony, unlefs we know alfo, that Simon examined the MSS., compared them with Ufcan's edition, and found them to agree. But this we know he did not, becaufe he confeffes, in another place, that he learned thefe particulars from the bifhop's own mouth. Thus Simon's confeffion, that was to work fuch wonders in favour of the verfe, fhrinks into the folitary declaration of an editor. The bubble that we admired at a diftance, and purfued with eagernefs, vanifhes into air the inftant we touch

touch it. Bengelius would have said (what he has said in effect) of the Complutensian editors, that they had good MSS. and followed them faithfully. And I myself would say the same of other editors. But Bengelius allows that the Complutensian editors had not this verse in their MSS. And if any person should take advantage of my general expressions, that an edition was published from MSS. and argue that therefore it faithfully followed the MSS. in this or that particular passage, I should begin to be in pain for the state of his intellects. Still less credit is to be given to the interested professions of a publisher. But you suppose men who commend the goods which they expose to sale, to have as nice a conscience as if they were taking an oath in a court of justice. Thus Erasmus's encomium upon Jerome you gravely bring, p. 253—255, as a contradiction to his less flattering opinion. Erasmus was a great, and upon the whole an honest man, though, like other editors, he sometimes descended to practise the tricks of the trade. Nobody else believes half the praises

that

that he heaps upon Jerome, nor did he himself believe them all.

But supposing that Simon really made this confession which you have extorted from his words, how does his testimony disagree with Sandius's? Sandius says*, that an Armenian MS. 400 years old, which he saw in possession of the bishop of the Armenian church at Amsterdam, omitted 1 John V. 7. You, Sir, I suppose, will not only allow, but insist, that Uscan had more than one MS. of the Catholic epistles. If he had two, one containing, the other rejecting the verse, who can doubt that he would have placed it in his text, and thought himself obeying the laws of sound criticism? *Præferatur lectio plenior et magis orthodoxa* would be his canon, especially when the common editions of the Latin, the only version that he understood, would confirm him in his decision. If therefore the Armenian MSS. varied in this place, Sandius's testimony is not contradicted either by Simon's acknowledgement or by Uscan's professions.

* Append. Interpret. Paradox. p. 376.

But Simon, Sir, makes no such acknowledgement. In the very letter of his, which you have quoted without seeing, Simon observes that the three heavenly witnesses were indeed in Uscan's edition, but adds, that Uscan, knowing something of Latin, probably borrowed them from the Vulgate to enrich his edition. This conjecture of Simon's receives some colour from La Croze's information, that Uscan confesses in one of his prefaces, with seeming complacency, that he altered some things from the Vulgate. But this proves nothing in your opinion, " because Uscan makes no such confession respecting 1 John V. 7." I am not violently disposed to accuse Uscan* of the interpolation. I only mention this as a specimen of your masterly reasoning. Uscan says that he added some things from the Vulgate. He specifies none. Therefore he did not add this. I answer, that whatever passage be suspected, you will always have the same reason at your

* If Uscan be really guilty of this insertion, the passages in the acts of the council are probably corrupted by Galanus.

beck.

beck. For Uscan makes no confession respecting any passage. Therefore he has altered none, and of course tells a lie when he says that he has. Excellent logician! But I am ashamed of such trifling.

In the thirteenth century the Armenian church became intimate with the Roman. Haitho in particular was much devoted to it, and tolerably acquainted with the Latin language. In preparing a new edition of the bible, it was impossible for him to neglect the authority of a church with which he had contracted so close a friendship. A clear proof of his reverence for his spiritual ally, is, that he translated all the prefaces attributed to Jerome, and among them the Prologue to the Canonical Epistles. When therefore Haitho borrowed this Prologue, which complains of unfaithful translators, and pretends to restore the heavenly witnesses from Greek MSS., how could he resist the testimony of Jerome, and, as far as he knew, the uniform authority of the Latin church? If the Armenian version was before his time defective in this important passage, he was bound upon such weighty reasons to patch up up the flaw. You say, " that Haitho's translating Jerome's prefaces does not prove that this verse was not in the Armenian MSS. before he was born." True; it does not entirely prove it. But it proves, that if this verse was not in the Armenian MSS. of that age, he would have taken it from the Vulgate, and added it to his own edition. That this verse was not in the Armenian MSS. of that age, appears from the testimony of Sandius concerning the only MS. known to be of that age. The testimony of Sandius is, 1. not contradicted by Simon's confession, for Simon confesses nothing, but that Uscan told him that he had brought Armenian MSS. from which he meant * to print his edition; nor, 2. is it contradicted by Uscan's own practice, for though Uscan has really inserted this verse in his edition, he might do this upon the authority of one or some only of his MSS. and not of all; and yet he would then have acted up to his own ideas of fide-

---

* I have not Simon's Bibliotheque de Sainjore at hand; but, as far as I recollect, Uscan was at Paris long before he printed his edition.

lity,

lity, and agreeably to the custom of editors. Nor, 3. is this testimony of Sandius at all improbable in itself; for there is no difficulty in conceiving that an Armenian MS. should agree with all the Greek MSS. extant, with the Syriac, Coptic, Arabic, Æthiopic, *Slavonic* versions, with more than twenty of the oldest Latin MSS. &c.

You next produce a confession from Michaelis, that this verse is quoted thirty-seven years after Haitho's death by an Armenian council. This, Sir, I acknowledge; and you ought to acknowledge in your turn the generosity of the adversaries; for La Croze first discovered * these passages. It may likewise be added to the advantage of La Croze's candour, that having at first suspected Uscan himself of the interpolation, he confessed his mistake. He found Uscan's edition agreeing with the Vulgate in adding passages of which no traces were visible in an Armenian MS. at Berlin. And by comparing this circumstance with Uscan's confession, that he had altered

* So Le Long first told the public, that the verse was found in the Dublin MS.

some things from the Vulgate, he inferred, that Ufcan had inferted 1 John V. 7. folely in compliance with the Vulgate. But this opinion he retracted upon finding the foregoing quotations.

From thefe paffages you argue, that, if the verfe had been reftored by Haitho, the members of the council would *certainly* have given fome note to inform the reader that it had once been loft, and now was *reftored*; or have made fome acknowledgement to the memory of Haitho for its *reftoration*. How long, Sir, muft a new edition of the bible be publifhed, before it is lawful to quote it for fcripture: The members of the council bufied themfelves, no doubt, in fcrupuloufly marking the paffages in which the old verfion differed from Haitho's! In our Englifh bibles this very fentence was once marked as fufpicious. I forget the precife year in which it was made free of the text. Would not a common Chriftian, nay, perhaps the clergy in convocation, if they quoted this verfe the next year, probably quote it without troubling themfelves about the hiftory of its infertion? The greater part of mankind, even thofe those who call themselves literary men, scarcely ever examine critically the passages which they occasionally quote. They take them from the edition that first occurs, or sometimes from another writer, on whose good faith they repose. (Of the truth of this position you, Sir, are a woeful proof.) It was natural then that an edition of the bible published by a king and a saint should in thirty-seven years become authentic. The person who drew up the account of the proceedings in council, might not possess, might not even have seen, a copy of the former edition. And though he did know that the passage was otherwise read in the older MSS. his orthodoxy, his natural propensity to the ampler reading, his respect for the piety, erudition and dignity of the deceased editor, would induce him to adopt the emendation. But were the writers of those days so exceedingly addicted to criticism, that they admitted no scriptural quotation into their works, without a full enquiry into its claims to be read in this or that manner? Did the members of those assemblies nicely weigh the authorities, and verify the citations, produced

duced by each other? In the present age, which is infinitely more learned and critical than either the thirteenth or the fourteenth century, I question whether every reader or writer gives himself this trouble. Some persons of high rank, Sir, it is said, have given your book great praises; have approved your reasonings, and subscribed to your conclusion. Have they all diligently examined your facts and your quotations? It is with pain I pronounce, that this question cannot be answered in the affirmative. In short, your argument is built upon two assumptions: 1. The council ought to have mentioned the various reading, if there had been one: 2. The council acted exactly as it ought to have acted, and therefore would have mentioned the various reading, if there had been one. But I have been informed, that the latter rule is sometimes deceitful. Neither perhaps did the council know of the obligation that Mr. Travis has lately imposed on them.

All this while, the reader must needs suppose, from what you have said, that the council quotes this verse to prove the doctrine of of the Trinity, or some branch of it; or at least to apply the words in some manner or other. How will he be surprised to learn, that though indeed this verse is thrice transcribed in the Councils, p. 436, 461, 478, in none of the three places is the slightest use made of it, nor any kind of reference to it in the sequel. What need then had the compiler of the Acts of the Council to quit his subject for an impertinent digression? Suppose that an English divine, soon after our translation had received its last correction, writing on the nature of Antichrist, thus quoted the present Epistle II. 23. *Whosoever denieth the Son, the same hath not the Father; but he that acknowledgeth the Son, hath the Father also.* Would it be worth his while to stop and inform his readers, that the second part of this verse was once wanting in our translation, or to make an acknowledgement to the church for having *restored* it? It is of small consequence whether a writer quotes a doubtful part of scripture or not, if he takes care to argue only from what is genuine. Nobody therefore, unless he were very critically inclined, would waste his time in explaining why he

O   preferred

preferred one reading to another, of a passage which he barely quoted, without intending to employ it in his argument. But let us examine the passages. The last I shall quote at length, p. 478; *Etsi verum illud esse fateri debemus, quod licet duo ista in se corruptibilia sint, in dominicæ tamen dispensationis sacramento mystice sumpta purissima et ab omni sunt corruptelæ contagio remotissima, eandemque cum Spiritu sancto purificantem vim et operationem sibi vendicant, quocirca magnus Apostolus ille Joannes in quadam ex Catholicis suis epistolis ait.* (1 John V. 7, 8. exactly as in the Vulgate:) *Vide ut tria hæc unam eandemque vim retinent; nam licet diversa secundum se, virtute tamen et operatione unum quid sunt divinum et purificans: baptismum enim præ se ferunt; aqua quidem juxta illud,* Ego baptizo vos aqua; *sanguis vero secundum id;* Calicem quem ego bibo, bibetis, et baptismo, quo ego baptizor, baptizabimini; *sanguinem hic intelligens: Spiritus denique juxta illud,* Ipse vos baptizabit in Spiritu sancto et igni.— The other two are exactly to the same purpose, and prove, from the water and the blood in the eighth verse, that water ought to be mixed with the sacramental wine. In this

this case there are three possibilities: 1. the council might quote these words from Haitho's version; or, 2. the copiers of the Acts, or, 3. Galanus himself might insert them. Whoever thinks that Uscan added 1 John V. 7. without the warrant of any MS. may adopt the latter supposition. But though I should not accuse the copiers or Galanus of forgery, if I chose to defend the second or the third supposition, yet to shew my fairness, and to shorten the dispute, I will be content with the first. Nothing however can be concluded thence, but that this verse was already extant in the MSS. used by the council. They might not know when or by what means it gained its situation. Or if they knew, it would have been worse than useless to have broken the thread of their discourse for so foreign a topic. They sent for an old acquaintance, whose help they wanted. He came, and brought with him a genteel young stranger. They gave the stranger a polite invitation, which he as politely accepted. In all this there is nothing extraordinary. It is the daily practice of mankind.

O 2   But

But we have not yet done with this *Queen of Verſions*. For " one Nicon, an Armenian, publiſhed a treatiſe *de peſſima religione Armeniorum*, in which he accuſed his countrymen of having interpolated their bibles in Luke XXII. 43, 44. and diverſe other texts; but he brought no charge againſt them concerning the verſe now in debate; which is a proof that it anciently was, as it now is, found in that verſion."

I did intend to examine this propoſition as minutely as ſome of the former, but I find it neceſſary to abridge. The errors thicken ſo much, that I am afraid of writing a folio inſtead of an octavo. I ſhall therefore ſtate the facts as conciſely as I can. If I had read your ſentence with implicit belief, I ſhould have ſuppoſed, that Nicon wrote after the date of Uſcan's edition; that he produced a long catalogue of paſſages beſides Luke XXII. 43, 44. where it was interpolated, but was ſilent upon 1 John V. 7. But as I knew ſomething of Nicon, and ſomething too of Mr. Travis, I was ſure that all you told us could not be true.

This

This Nicon, according to Fabricius*, was a monk of the tenth century. La Croze † and Beaufobre ‡, who call him *a Greek impoſtor*, ſeem to think him a different perſon. However, Greek impoſtor or not, he lived long before the age of printing, and at leaſt earlier, I ſuppoſe, than the time of Haitho. His treatiſe *de peſſima Religione Armeniorum* is extant in Latin §, but imperfect. It has been ſince publiſhed complete by Cotelerius ‖ from two Greek MSS. In ſmall Greek print this important treatiſe takes up about——two thirds of a folio page. Neither does Nicon accuſe the Armenians of interpolating, but of eraſing. Neither does he accuſe them of corrupting " Luke XXII. 43, 44. and *diverſe* other paſſages," but only one beſides, John VIII. 1—11. If Nicon's copy had 1 John V. 7. and he knew that the Armenian MSS. omitted it, in ſo ſhort a treatiſe, where he is

---

* Biblioth. Gr. Vol. X. p. 283.
† Hiſt. du Chriſtianiſme d'Armenie, p. 333.
‡ Biblioth. Germanique, tom. XXXIX. p. 40.
§ Beveridge, Not. in Can. Concil. Trull. p. 158.
‖ Patr. Apoſtol. tom. I. p. 235.

content with two examples, he might not have thought it neceſſary to record a third. If his copy omitted and the Armenian MSS. retained it, he might be ſilent for the ſame reaſon; or he might not be equally ſevere upon additions; or he might think that they preſerved the genuine text, and that his own copy was corrupt. But if, as we maintain, neither Nicon nor his contemporary Armenians knew of this verſe, how could he reproach them either with omitting or interpolating a ſentence, that never exiſted in Greek or Armenian till the thirteenth century?

In all this, Sir, I am ready to acquit you of fraud, except ſo far as it is a fraud to profeſs knowledge where you are moſt ignorant. You copy Martin and his references from the Engliſh tranſlation. This appears from your ſaying DIVERSE *other paſſages* (PLUSIEURS) inſtead of ANOTHER. Having drawn out this article to an unconſcionable length, I ſhall ſum it up in a few words. The ancient Armenian MSS. omitted the three heavenly witneſſes. But in the thirteenth century the Romiſh and Armenian churches became intimate.

mate. Haitho, king of Armenia, underſtood Latin, and was a diligent reader of the Vulgate. Perhaps from this circumſtance he firſt formed the deſign of making a new edition of the ſcriptures in his own language. However, from the Vulgate he tranſlated all the prefaces attributed to Jerome, and inſerted them in his own edition. He could not be ſo inattentive to the advice of a (ſuppoſed) critic and ſaint, not to *reſtore*, as he would think it, this valuable verſe to its place. Thirty-ſeven years after Haitho's death, the council of Armenia (perhaps) quoted it, but in company with the eighth verſe. And it is the eighth verſe only that concerns their argument. They prove from the earthly witneſſes, that the wine of the Euchariſt ought to be diluted with water. Three hundred years after Haitho, Biſhop Uſcan inſerted the ſeventh verſe in his edition. But that it has been uniformly in the Armenian MSS. from the time of Chryſoſtome, becauſe it has been in them ſince the union of the Latin and Armenian churches, is as likely as that it has been uniformly in the Greek MSS. becauſe it has been quoted by ſome Greek writers since the Greek translation of the Lateran council.

I have already asserted, in this letter, that the Slavonic version omits 1 John V. 7. I find, upon reading a little farther in your book, that you have asserted the contrary. That I may know, whether I ought to defend or retract my opinion, I shall examine your reasons, which are two, I think, one *presumptive* *, and one *positive*. Your presumptive proof stands thus: " The Russians, at the close of the tenth century, were converted by the Greeks, from whom they received the scriptures. But it has been proved that the *ancient* Greek church acknowledged this verse to be genuine. Therefore the Russian or *modern* Greek church acknowledged it to be genuine." Your *positive* proof stands thus: " This verse possesses its place in all the Russian New Testaments, and in the Russian confession of faith, drawn up by Parthenius in 1643."

First, I observe, Sir, upon the former of

---

* See Letter I. p. 5.

your proofs, that *La Croze, almoſt as good a judge of theſe matters as yourſelf, attributes the Slavonic verſion to the ninth century, that is to ſay, not quite an hundred years after Alcuin's reviſion. " It cannot be ſuppoſed, that the authors of this verſion would collate modern MSS. No! *candour* (I mean Mr. Travis's candour) obliges us to admit, that their reſearches were extended much higher, in all probability to the ſecond or third century." But my *candour* is more eaſily ſatisfied. I am content to produce the authority of this verſion for no more than a tolerable proof what was the uſual reading in the ſixth (or if, when you find it turned againſt you, you ſhould be zealous to depreſs its value) in the ſeventh and eighth centuries.

Next, I obſerve, that your preſumptive proof may eaſily be gained to the other ſide. The Ruſſians tranſlated the ſcriptures from Greek MSS. in the ninth century. But all the Greek MSS. of all ages omit 1 John V. 7. Therefore the Slavonic verſion omits it.

* Hiſt. du Chriſtianiſme des Indes, p. 229 or 343, and Addenda, p. 13.

You cannot controvert this conclusion, unless you can prove either that all the present Greek MSS. or all at least that are of the ninth century and older, retain this verse, or that it is frequently quoted by Greek authors of that and the preceding ages. For, till you can prove an universal or very general consent of the Greek MSS. how do you know but the translators lighted upon some of the defective and erroneous copies, such as the Syriac and Coptic interpreters had?

Thirdly, I observe, that you are so candid as to add a note which totally overthrows what your *positive* proof advances. " The Slavonian bible of 1663 has this text printed in its margin only. All the Russian bibles have it in the body of the page." Now, Sir, since the modern Russian bibles have no authority whatsoever, but what they derive from the ancient Slavonic, even from your own state of the case it plainly appears that this verse is an interpolation. If the curators of the edition of 1663 had a single MS. containing the verse, at a time when their Patriarch had admitted it into their confessions of faith, it is impossible that they should

set

set so disgraceful a mark upon it, as to exclude it from the text and degrade it to the margin. In this manner words and sentences utterly unknown to the author first gain admittance into the margin, and then become part of the text. Since we see this happen so often in printed books, we need not wonder at it in MSS. Whoever remembers what I have said concerning the Syriac version, will want no farther inducement to believe that the disputed verse was never in the Slavonic. But when once such passages are in possession, it is blasphemy to enquire how they came thither; it is want of candour and charity to hint a suspicion that any editor could be so *unworthy a betrayer of his trust, so unfaithful a steward of the oracles of* GOD, &c. &c. (I omit several thousand epithets for the sake of brevity) as to increase his edition with a verse which was not extant in his MSS. But how is this verse printed in the edition of 1663? You, Sir, who at other times are luxuriant enough in your quotations, here grudge us a short sentence. The Slavonic edition then thus represents 1 John V. 8. in the text: **And there are three witnesses* *nessing on earth, the spirit, and the water, and the blood, and the three agree in one.* In the margin the seventh verse: * *For there are three,* &c. Here, says Martin, the abrupt transition to *And* instead of *For* shews that it was a mere variation in the Slavonic MSS. You, Sir, may strengthen this reasoning, if you like, by observing that the words *on earth* refer to their opposites *in heaven*, and cry loudly for the insertion of the seventh verse. Besides, continues Martin, this edition professes in the preface closely to follow an elder edition printed at Ostrow in 1581. That edition therefore represents the passage in the same manner, being printed, no doubt, from a MS. that had the heavenly witnesses in the margin, either from the same or from a different hand. Martin and you, Sir, I knew long since, look upon margin and text as one and the same thing. But I hope that others, whose ideas are a little more distinct, will see, that, even allowing Martin's account to be true, the verse may justly be suspected of interpolation. For myself, I own, I am not so quick of belief. Having had a little experience of pious fraud, I am apt to exclaim, on such occasions, Κάκις' ἀπολοίμην, εἴ τι τούτων πείθομαι. Perhaps the reader will hardly believe, that the Ostrow edition has only these words in the text, without any marginal note: *Quoniam tres sunt testantes, spiritus, aqua, et sanguis, et tres in unum sunt.* Perhaps he will find greater difficulty in believing, that Newton, whose arguments you pretend to confute in your second edition, had already declared himself an eye-witness of this reading in the Ostrow edition. And I can assure you, if you will allow such a testimony as mine, that in this declaration Newton tells no lie. Newton refers also to Camillus de Antichristo*, who had seen one *Illyric* or *Russian* MS. as he calls it, six hundred years old, and possessed another of great antiquity, both which read the passage in the same concise way. Perhaps you will make an objection to this Camillus, because he was a Socinian. I shall leave him to your mercy. For no heretic's word or oath ought to be believed, who writes against this verse. But

* P. 156. His real name was *Thomas Pisecius*. See *Sandius* Biblioth. Antitrinit. p. 107.

how

how shall we elude the evidence of a Slavonic MS. lately collated by Professor Alter*, which is guilty of the same Laconic rudeness. Perhaps the Professor too is a concealed heretic, and has made a false report.

Let us now contemplate the honesty of the Moscow editors. They dared not all at once interpolate the text with this verse. They therefore put it into the margin, hoping that it might at last arrive at the honour of being received for undoubted scripture. To accomplish this godly purpose, they first altered *For* to *And*, v. 8. then added *on earth*, and both contrary to the authority which they professed to follow, in order to persuade the ignorant and credulous, that it was a mere casual omission of the transcriber. Surely never was so much fraud and forgery employed as in support of this marvellous passage!

I may now, I think, venture to affirm, that the ancient Armenian and Slavonic versions both were ignorant of the heavenly

* Var. Lect. in N. T. ex MSS. Vindobon. tom. II. p. 1036.

witnesses; but I shall affirm without scruple, that you, Sir, have proved nothing to the contrary; and that, every step you take, your ignorance of the question, joined to an implicit faith in your blind guide Martin, plunges you into fresh difficulty and mistake.

Postscript.

1. J. L. Frey told Wetstein in discoursing upon 1 John V. 7. that it was wanting* in his copy of the Armenian version. This conversation passed in 1719, before the deadly quarrel broke out between Frey and Wetstein. I am not so sanguine as Mr. Travis; else I should produce this for a decisive testimony in my favour. For it is possible that Wetstein's memory might deceive him, or that in the eagerness of his zeal, partly against the verse, and partly against Frey, he might

---

* Regessit neque exstare apud Patres, ne apud Cyprianum quidem, si recte inspiciatur, neque in MS. Sancto-Gallensi, aliisque veteribus codicibus Latinis, neque *in Versione, quam haberet, Armena.* Wetstein Prolegom. p. 192.

enlarge a simple conjecture into a positive assertion. The fact, however, is probable enough in itself, that Frey had seen, or that he possessed, an Armenian MS. containing the Catholic epistles. If such a MS. be still preserved at Amsterdam, it would perhaps upon examination turn out to be the same that Sandius saw in Uscan's possession. I throw out this only as an hint to those who may hereafter have inclination and opportunity to reconsider the question.

2. I learn from Mr. Matthæi[*], that the first edition of the Slavonic version was printed at Prague in the year 1519. He does not mention its form, but observes that it is remarkably scarce, and rarely found entire. I have seen an old Slavonic edition, which I guess to be the same. It is a small thick octavo, but I have not been able to find any date of time and place. Nor is it necessary to make any particular enquiry after so perverse and disloyal a book, which scarcely furnishes half its complement of text on this dangerous and distressing occasion.

[*] Append. II. ad Apocalyps. p. 346.

LETTER IX.

SIR,

I ALMOST feel an inclination to pity you, when I enter upon your Greek authorities, they are so scanty, doubtful, and suspected. According to your own computation they are only four; the Synopsis Scripturæ and the Dialogue against the Arians (both published with the works of Athanasius), the Panoplia Dogmatica of Euthymius Zigabenus, and the Greek Lectionary called Apostolos or Praxapostolos. Of these I mean to treat in their order.

First, the argument of this Epistle, you say, p. 49, 102. is generally allowed to be the genuine work of Athanasius. As far as I can learn, it is generally allowed to be spurious. In some editions of the N. T. it is attributed to Euthalius. It may be found in Oecumenius without any author's name. In Mill's

Mill's edition it is called Sophronius's, though Mill himself, Prol. 994. thinks it may be the work of Athanasius, *not the great prelate,* (FOR THE LEARNED HAVE LONG SINCE DECIDED IT NOT TO BE HIS), *but another, perhaps him who advised Euthalius to undertake his edition.* Certainly it would much lessen the character of the great Athanasius, if he were the real author of such a confused and imperfect abridgement. However, genuine or spurious, " this author *seems* plainly to refer to the verse in question." How different are opinions! Mill, Bengelius, Wetstein, and Mr. Griesbach, affirm that it is not cited in the Synopsis. But let us attend to the proof. " The verse—is not directly quoted—but the author of it seems plainly to refer to this verse in his summary or breviate of the fifth chapter:" *The apostle,* " says he," *here teaches the unity of the Son with the Father :* " for this unity is not taught in any part of that chapter, save in the seventh verse." This you had written, probably without looking at the Synopsis itself, and therefore added those useful words, *in his summary or breviate of the fifth chapter,* which vanish in the second edition.

tion. A common reader might hence fancy, that the Synopsis was a correct abridgement of the whole Epistle, chapter by chapter, and almost verse by verse, with the exactness and regularity of a modern commentator. But though you omit these words, you still say, at the end of the sentence, *in any part of that chapter*, which supposes the very assertion you have omitted. To make the argument complete, you ought to have said, as Martin had boldly said, *in any part of the epistle*, instead of mending his expression by an implied falsehood. Whoever will take the trouble of reading this same Synopsis, will find it an incoherent jumble without method or consistency. I once intended to transcribe the whole, but to avoid the fatigue and disgust of such a task, I shall set down in their order the passages which the author cites from this epistle. I. 1. I. 5. I. 2. V. 20. III. 8. II. 12—14. III. 10—18. IV. 7—12. IV. 19. 18. III. 10. IV. 2, 3, 6. V. 16. III. 14. IV. 8. [II. 23.] 22. III. 13, 14. V. 20, 21.

I may now safely appeal to every man of common sense, whether the place of any doubtful text in the Synopsis can determine its corresponding situation in the epistle. But perhaps the expressions are so peculiar as clearly to point out the seventh verse of the fifth chapter. " He also shews the unity of the Son with the Father." What! so brief that he cannot allow us the full sense of the passage, but breaks off a part and conceals the rest? Could he not have said, " He also shews the unity of the Son and the Holy Ghost with the Father," or " the unity of the three persons in the Godhead," or some one of an hundred other expressions, which every mind will suggest to itself? How strange is it, that he should transplant from the other parts of the epistle, so many phrases visible to the naked eye, and here make so minute a reference as requires the most powerful orthodox microscopes! Martin and you cautiously avoid quoting the entire sentence. " He also shews the unity of the Son with the Father, and *that he who denies the Son, neither has the Father.*" The reference here is made solely to II. 23. as Emlyn, in his Reply, p. 265. observed; to whom Martin Verité, p. 234. made so lame and shuffling a rejoinder, that, I fear, he was convinced of his error, though he he had not the courage to confess it. If you object that the verse II. 23. does not teach the unity of the Son with the Father, you must prove, 1. that the author of the Synopsis means unity of essence, not of consent; 2. that no ancient writer would or could interpret it in that manner. But, I hope, every person who has had the patience to read thus far, will be convinced that no mention is made of our verse in this Synopsis, but that since the author was perfectly orthodox, his silence is a probable argument that it was utterly unknown to him.

Your second authority is a dialogue between an Athanasian and an Arian, where " the verse is thus EXPRESSLY QUOTED; *Is not that lively and saving baptism, whereby we receive remission of sins, administered in the name of the Father, the Son, and the Holy Ghost? And St. John says, And these three are one.*" You have here translated rather freely, paraphrasing some words and omitting others. You might have greatly edified your readers, if you had favoured them with all the arguments by which the Athanasian convinces the Arian that the Trinity in unity is to be worshipped.

worshipped. I shall therefore give an abridged but faithful translation. "Why do the Seraphim, that Isaiah heard cry, Holy, Holy, Holy, neither exceed this number, nor fall short of it? Certainly because it is not lawful for any besides the Trinity to be thus honoured. Why did Moses teach the people to bend their neck and their knees three times on the earth, but to denote the worship of the Trinity in one Godhead? The divine Elijah raises the dead at the third breathing, to shew that no man can be worthy of eternal life, who shall not first receive with reverential faith a coequal and consubstantial Trinity, which like fire consumes deadly sins—— Neither could Paul otherwise have ascended to the third heaven, unless he had possessed in his heart the indelible and consubstantial faith of the Trinity——Likewise is not the remission of sins procured by that quickening and sanctifying ablution, without which no man shall see the kingdom of heaven, an ablution given to the faithful in the thrice-blessed name. And besides all these, John says, *And the three are one.*" [or rather, " *are the one.*"]

Concerning

Concerning this dialogue you tell us, "that whether it belongs to Athanafius or not, has been a matter of great difpute among the learned." Who is the author, may perhaps admit of a difpute. But all the learned at prefent, as far as I know, confefs it to be fpurious. Cave thinks it to be the compofition of fome doating monk. In general however, I believe, it is attributed to Maximus, who lived in the feventh century, and refided five years in Africa and ten at Rome. You, I know, fettle its date by an acute critical remark (taken, as ufual, from Martin), that becaufe the dialogue mentions the joint reign of Conftantine and Conftantius, it was written before the expiration of that joint reign, A. C. 337. I always thought, Sir, that the internal notes of time, unlefs they be very recondite, were not decifive in feigned dialogues. The greateft dotard of a monk in the feventh, or even in the feventeenth century, might write a dialogue and mention fo obvious a fact. It would be a part of his plan to throw in a circumftance of this nature, if he meant to fuftain his affumed character with propriety. Works may be proved (with certain exceptions) to be spurious, if they violate historical truth, but they cannot be proved genuine, because they do not violate it.

To the foregoing censure of Cave, which I am sorry gave that *worthy man, Mr. Martin, great uneasiness,* no reader of the least taste, who has perused my extract, will refuse his assent. How easily might a monk who could fix such remote, abstruse, or rather absurd senses upon other passages of scripture, interpret 1 John V. 8. of the Trinity? The words seem to convey at least a more mystical meaning than most of the other quotations. If he thought that such arguments as the Israelites thrice bending the neck, Elijah's thrice breathing, Paul's being rapt into the third heaven, &c. had made an impression on his antagonist, he might with equal modesty expect, that he would be completely vanquished with this testimony. It cannot be said, that this interpretation was not current among the Greeks, when Simon found it in the margin of two MSS. and Mr. Matthæi in a third. The latter scholium is this: *Three in the masculine gender, in token of the Trinity:*

Trinity: the spirit, of the Godhead; the water, of the enlightening knowledge to mankind, by the spirit; the blood, of the incarnation. These MSS. are of the tenth and eleventh centuries. Now if this explanation could thus creep into the copies, and be recorded by the scribes as a valuable memorandum, I should be surprized to find that no author had met with it in the margin of his MSS. or in the works of the holy Doctors, or in conversation; or that, having met with it, he should impiously suffer it to rust in his possession, instead of employing it in the service of religion.

But, interrupts Martin, the words are not the exact words of the eighth verse. I answer, neither are they the exact words of the seventh. But they much more nearly resemble the eighth than the seventh. The word εἰς, as I said before, was absorbed by the three preceding letters, and lost out of the Greek MSS. from which the Latin version was made. The same omission has happened in the copies of Cyril, of Euthymius Zigabenús, I may add, of Dionysius Alexandrinus, whom Martin cites to his own confutation. But whether the copy itself that the author of the

dialogue

dialogue used, or the scribe who copied the dialogue, be in fault, the fault is so trifling and natural, that I wonder, 1. why it has not been more frequent; 2. why Mill should hence take occasion to object that the eighth verse is not quoted by Maximus. For, says he, all the MSS. read in the eighth verse, εἰς τὸ ἕν. But this argument is not valid, unless all the MSS. of all ancient writers who quote the eighth verse, retain the preposition, which we have just seen not to be the fact.

In treating of the Latin fathers, I shall have occasion to examine more fully the subject of this allegorical interpretation. In the mean time I pass to your next Greek witness (next in the order of time) Euthymius Zigabenus, who in his *Panoplia Dogmatica Orthodoxæ Fidei " thus refers to this verse of St. John. *The term* ONE *denotes things, the essence and nature of which are the same, and yet the persons are different, as in this instance,* AND THREE ARE ONE."

---

* Compare Ephes. VI. 11—17.

Here,

Here, Sir, I mean to furprize you with my liberal conceffions. I grant that this paffage relates to the Trinity. And if it be a quotation from fcripture, I will grant that it is the claufe of 1 John V. 7. But before we admit this fecond propofition, I cannot help complaining that you have been lefs civil than Martin, who produces the Greek original from a MS. in the French's king's library: τὸ ἓν ἐπὶ μὲν τῶν ὁμοουσίων λέγεται, ἔνθα ταυτότης μὲν φύσεως, ἑτερότης δὲ ὑποςάσεων, ὡς τὸ, ΚΑΙ ΤΑ ΤΡΙΑ ΕΝ. You might have made your Englifh look fomewhat better by rendering, *And* THE *three are one*. But you will forgive me if I doubt a little whether Euthymius really meant this for a quotation of our verfe, becaufe he fo greatly varies the expreffion. The verb fubftantive, and pronoun, are omitted, and the mafculines turned into neuters. Thefe orthodox divines were furely very inaccurate in their quotations of a moft important paffage. Would a mere Englifh reader think that an author quoting thefe words: *And the three (things) one (thing)* could poffibly mean to quote this fentence: *And thefe three (perfons) are one (thing)*?

Eucherius

Eucherius indeed reads the eighth, and Etherius both the seventh and eighth verses, with *tria* in the neuter; but I know no Greek writer who has done the same in either of the verses.

Though this I think might be a sufficient objection, unless Euthymius had formally declared his quotation to be a part of scripture, I shall not think much to examine more deeply into the matter. Poor Martin, turning over the Latin translation of Euthymius, saw in the margin a reference to 1 John V. and finding it contained something like the seventh verse, triumphantly added it to his cloud of witnesses. But the most ridiculous errors find somebody or other to receive and vend them for precious truths.

Ὡς αἰεὶ τὸν ὅμοιον ἄγει θεὸς ὡς τὸν ὅμοιον.

The Latin translation is so confused, that I should have wondered if Martin, whose talent for the languages was none of the happiest, had understood it; though he might have seen cause to doubt of his own construction of the passage, if he had considered it with a little more attention or read a little farther.

A friend

A friend of mine, whofe name I fhould be happy to mention, lent me a copy of the Greek edition of this fame Euthymius Zigabenus, publifhed at Tergovifto in 1710. The place you have quoted is extant in this edition, fol. 28. col. 3—4. Here follows a literal tranflation. " The word *one* is applied, 1. to things homoufian, where there is a famenefs of nature, but a difference of perfons, as in this phrafe, *And the three are one* ; 2. to things heteroüfian, where there is a famenefs of perfons, but a difference of natures, as in this phrafe, *And both together are one, not by nature, but by conjunction.*"†

Every reader, even if I ftopped here, would fee that if the latter quotation be not in fcripture, in all probability neither is the former. But the latter certainly is not. Therefore I conclude the fame of the former. Who knows how many of the authors, now loft, from whofe works Euthymius extracted materials for his Panoply, expreffed their faith in the fame form of words? The defenders of the difputed verfe catch greedily at every place where the Fathers ufe the expreffion of " Three are one," as if fuch expreffions could

not

not but proceed from this verse, whereas the contrary supposition is infinitely more probable, that the verse proceeded from such expressions of the Fathers.

Let us resume our translation. † " As *one* is a word variously used; for we say, *one* in number, as Peter: *one* in species, as man: *one* in genus, as animal. Thus also with respect to *two*; we say, *two* in number, as Peter and Paul: *two* in species, as man and horse: *two* in genus, as essence and colour. When therefore we speak of Christ as *two*, we do not call him *two* in number, but *one* in number by the unity of person, and *two* in species, that is, in nature, by the duality of natures; for Gregory the divine says, *and both together are one, not by nature, but by conjunction.*" When I came to this sentence, I quickly conjectured (and who would not conjecture?) that since the second of these quotations bore the superscription of Gregory Nazianzen, the first too might issue from the same mint. And, to my unspeakable comfort, I found my conjecture right. The second of the passages is in Vol. I. Orat. XXXVI. p. 582. D.; the first, Orat. XXXIX. p. 630.

p. 630. B. Having been always extremely fond of Gregory, I cannot forbear transcribing as much of the context as may enlighten the reader. "But when I speak, may lightening, as it were, flash around you, from the three lights and one of God: *three*, according to their proprieties or hypostases, if any prefer that word, or persons (for we will have no quarrel about names, so long as the syllables direct us to the same sense), and *one*, according to the consideration of their essence or Godhead: for it is divided indivisibly, if I may use the expression, and connected divisibly*. For the Godhead is one in three, *and the three are one*; those [three] in which the Godhead is, or, to speak more accurately, which the Godhead is: but we will avoid excesses and defects; neither turning the unity into confusion, nor the distinction into separation. Far be from us both the conjunction of Sabellius, and the division of Arius, evils diametrically opposite, and equally

---

* Ἐν γὰρ ἐν τρισὶν ἡ θεότης ΚΑΙ ΤΑ ΤΡΙΑ ΕΝ, τὰ ἐν οἷς ἡ θεότης, ἢ τόγε ἀκριβέςερον εἰπεῖν, ἃ ἡ θεότης. See too Orat. XXXVII. p. 598. A. LI. p. 739. B.

partaking

partaking of impiety." And in the next page, " There is then one God in three [perfons], *and the three are one,* AS WE SAID."

I believe that Mr. Travis himfelf will excufe me from any farther examination of this authority. But fince I have promifed to produce every argument that to my knowledge has been or may be urged againft me, I muft not conceal that in the fame edition of Euthymius, fol. 112. col. 1. a part of the epiftle of John is thus quoted. " *And it is the Spirit that beareth witnefs, becaufe the Spirit is truth. For there are three that bear record in heaven, the Father, the Word, and the Holy Ghoft, and thefe three are one. And there are three that bear record on earth, the fpirit, and the water, and the blood, and the three agree in one. If we receive the witnefs of men, the witnefs of God is greater.*——See now again, how the preacher of truth calls the Spirit by nature God and of God, for having faid that it is the Spirit of God that witneffes, a little onward he adds, the witnefs of God is greater. How then is he a creature, &c."

Upon this paffage I obferve, firft, that an author who adopts this reafoning muft have been

been ignorant of the seventh verse. How could he otherwise have missed the opportunity of insisting upon the connumeration of the three persons, the assertion of their joint testimony and of their unity? Euthymius's reasoning at present receives all its vigour from the close conjunction of the sixth, eighth, and ninth verses, and is only clogged by the insertion of the seventh.

Secondly, I observe, that all these testimonies and arguments Euthymius professes, f. 109. c. 4. to copy from Cyril's Thesaurus. I have seen this quotation with my own eyes in Cyril's Thesaurus, but instead of the seventh and eighth verses not a word more than, *For there are three that bear record, the spirit, the water, and the blood, and the three are one.*

Thirdly, I observe, that the Latin translation (Tit. XII. near the end) thus reads the place: *Et Spiritus est qui Deum Spiritum veritatem esse testatur. Quoniam tres sunt qui testimonium afferunt, spiritus, aqua, et sanguis, et hi tres unum sunt. Si testimonium,* &c. The translator therefore had not the verse in his Greek copy. But wherever I set my steps, I stum-

I stumble upon fresh examples of forgery. This translator, though more modest than his brother the Greek editor, could not resist the pleasure of inserting the word *Deum* contrary to the text of scripture, and the scope of his author's argument. When shall we cease to give our adversaries occasion of reproaching us with pious fraud on the one hand, or childish credulity on the other?

Fourthly, I observe, that three MSS. of Euthymius, collated by Mr. Matthæi*, exactly agree with Cyril, except that one has a very slight variation. To these I add another in the Bodleian, which I myself inspected, and a fifth in the library of Trinity college, Cambridge, of which an extract is now lying before me. So far therefore is Euthymius Zigabenus from having employed this weapon against the heretics, that on the contrary it is plain he never had it to employ. It was not to be found in the shops of those artificers of faith, who furnished him with the materials for his *Panoply*.

---

* On the Catholic Epistles, p. 142—143.

From

From Euthymius to your Apostolos, that is, from one interpolation to another, is a gentle transition. Newton had said, *The Greeks received it* (1 John V. 7.) *not till this present age, when the Venetians sent it amongst them in printed books* (meaning this Apostolos). Upon this you ask two sapient questions, " Was the Apostolos not known to the Greeks till this present age ? Was the Apostolos a printed book ?" 1. You might have recollected that Newton's Dissertation was written in the last century, in the beginning of which the Apostolos was printed at Venice. 2. Yes, Sir, the Apostolos is a printed book, so far as it is an authority for the disputed verse. Newton knew that the printed book contained the verse, but he had reason to declare it an interpolation. For he tells us, from the information of some of his acquaintance, that the MSS. Lectionaries of the Greeks omitted the verse; and that the Greeks, when they were attacked on this subject, appealed to their printed copies, and affirmed that it was erased by the Arians.

Your ingenious idea that the ancient Greek church from the fifth century acknowledged this

this verse, because it is now in their Apostolos, rests upon this foundation, that the readings of the Apostolos have never been altered. But La Croze says, and with truth I believe, that ecclesiastical books are more subject to alterations than others. Your reasoning upon this assertion is so curious, that I confess myself unable to understand it. You ask, whether the church would at any time insert a reading which she did not believe to be genuine. Suppose that she would not; yet in case of various readings, the church would, sometimes from haste, sometimes from ignorance, sometimes from indolence, sometimes from a blind obedience to the dictates of a leader who pretended to superior learning or holiness, give a spurious reading the sanction of her authority.

I cannot allow the Greek church to have been so nice and critical as you would make her, because I should then cede to her the palm of learning and fidelity, to which, I firmly believe, our church has an equal right. But if we may judge from ourselves, the overseers of the Greek church gave themselves little trouble about genuine readings

in

in the public service, provided nothing heterodox was admitted. In one of the early editions of our Bible, with the Common Prayer prefixed, the text of the N.T. marks 1 John V. 7. as doubtful; in the gospel for the first Sunday after Easter it is printed in the same character, and no suspicion insinuated. To which I may add, that we have now for more than two hundred years been proving the doctrine of our XXIXth article by a spurious quotation from Augustine.

In the year 1200 the Archbishop of Lyons sent an humble petition to the chapter-general of Citeaux, praying that the gospel concerning the passion of our Lord—might be corrected. An abbot was accordingly ordered to make inquiry, and communicate the result to the next chapter. The chapter's order is thus expressed: " Scribatur in textu Matthæi Evangelistæ, ubi deest: *Diviserunt sibi vestimenta*.*"

The biographer of Lanfranc*, Archbishop of Canterbury, tells us, that his Grace cor-

---

* *Wetstein* Proleg. p. 85.

rected the Old and N. T. and the writings of the holy Fathers, *according to the orthodox faith.* Can we wonder that men thus affected, when they found a text which apparently suited their purpose, struggling into notice, but not yet generally received, should be biassed by their preconceived opinions, and endeavour to give it currency among their spiritual subjects by the stamp of their own approbation.

If our Apostolos, which the perpetual demand of the church would multiply in numberless copies, constantly retained this verse from the fifth century, by what fate or chance has every transcriber forgot to restore it to the other MSS. which were not intended for public service. The critics complain that the Evangelistaries and Lectionaries have often transfused their readings into the other MSS. But in this case the two streams of the public and private MSS. have flowed as distinct and unmingled as Alpheus and the ocean. Of the MS. Lectionaries that have been collated, none contain the three heavenly witnesses. If therefore it were certain that the copy from which the Apostolos was printed,

did

did contain them, the question would be, which authority we ought to follow?

Newton's appeal to the Greek MSS. you with your accustomed civility call, not an argument, but an assertion too extravagant for a serious refutation. For you say, p. 259. "How a Greek MS. omitting 1 John V. 7. copied out at Paris or Rome in the tenth century, can be a proof that the verse was wanting in the MSS. that Jerome used at Palestine in the fourth century, is utterly inconceivable." If you cannot conceive this, your conceptions are very narrow. This observation, however, of yours, applied to the Apostolos, will be as proper as it is now absurd. "How a Lectionary printed at Venice in the seventeenth century, fourscore years after 1 John V. 7. had been inserted in the Greek editions of the N. T. can be a proof that the same verse was extant in all the MS. Lectionaries from the fifth century downward, is utterly inconceivable!"

The Apostolos, Sir, was interpolated in printing. You will perhaps bring your old argument, which is nearly worn out, upon the stage, that if the editor inserted this verse without

without the authority of MSS. he was a cheat. But he was not a cheat, and therefore, &c. This kind concern for the morality of editors I greatly admire. But I do not accuse the editor of being a cheat. Who ever called R. Stephens a cheat, because he retains many readings in his edition, which he found in no MS.? Every editor, unless he makes actual profession to the contrary, is at liberty to follow the text of his predecessors. Common readers are ignorant what licence editors take in reforming the text of MSS. to their own notions of correctness. The Venetian overseer of the press, having been long familiar with the vulgar reading, would naturally suppose the omission to be a mere error of the copier. He would doubtless have a printed N. T. at hand, for the greater ease and quicker dispatch. When he came to this place, if he had any regard for the credit of the printed editions, or for the finest passage in scripture, he would add it to the Apostolos, and instead of thinking himself guilty of rashness or pious fraud, would plume himself on his zeal and vigilance in the cause of orthodoxy. The instances of interpolation which

which I have produced in the Syriac version, the Slavonic, and the editions of Euthymius, will infuse into any reasonable man a distrust of publishers who conceal the authority upon which they act in cautious silence. All editions, as well of scripture as of books where scripture is quoted, that give a text without notes or various readings, are by themselves incompetent witnesses. The less scandal they give to the simplicity of the vulgar, the more they excite the suspicions of the learned.

The confession of faith, though I cannot tell when it was first made, is, I am sure, too late to have any weight. The modern Greek version only serves to shew with what eagerness this verse was every where received as soon as it was known.

When I think on the miserable poverty of Greek authorities under which you labour, I am astonished that you would not accept the additional testimonies offered by Bengelius, Wetstein, and Mr. Griesbach. Bengelius wishes to draw over to his party Irenæus, Clemens Alexandrinus, Athenagoras, and Basil; but they are so shy, that he is obliged to

use

use violence; and even then they perform their work in a very aukward manner. The place from Basil looks most like our verse, *Deus, et Verbum, et Spiritus, una Deitas et sola adoranda.* If this be a quotation of 1 John V. 7. no verse has greater plenty of evidence to boast, for it is quoted by every ancient writer who has expressed his belief in three persons and one God. A scholion ascribed to Origen on Psalm CXXIII. 2. Δοῦλοι κυρίων πατρὸς καὶ υἱοῦ πνεῦμα καὶ σῶμα· παιδίσκη δὲ κυρίας τοῦ ἁγίου πνεύματος ἡ ψυχή· τὰ δὲ τρία κύριος ὁ θεὸς ἡμῶν ἐςιν, οἱ γὰρ τρεῖς τὸ ἓν εἰσιν. *The spirit and the body are servants to their masters, the Father and Son; the soul is maiden to her mistress, the Holy Ghost; the three is* (or *are*) *our Lord God;* FOR THE THREE ARE ONE. The critical chemistry that could extract the doctrine of the Trinity from this place, must have been exquisitely refining. Andreas Cretensis, καὶ τὰ τρία εἷς θεὸς, τὰ ἐν οἷς ἡ θεότης. Taken from Gregory Nazianzen above quoted. The Nomocanon published by Cotelerius, αὐτὰ τὰ τρία, πατὴρ—ἐν ταῦτα τὰ τρία.

I hardly

I hardly know whether I ought to mention the Philopatris, a dialogue written early in the fourth century, and falsely ascribed to Lucian, where the Christian Trinity is thus ridiculed: "The high-ruling God—the Son of the Father, the Spirit proceeding from the Father, one of three and three of one, think *these* to be Jupiter, believe *this* to be God." To which the other answers, "You teach me to swear in arithmetic; one three and three one; I know not what you mean." Cave* is so overjoyed at this testimony, that he undertakes to prove from it the genuineness of the three heavenly witnesses; and, having finished his task to his own satisfaction, concludes most mathematically, *Quod erat demonstrandum.* Either my eye-sight is dimmer than Cave's, or my reason less tractable, or my faith weaker; for many years since, while I had no heretical scruples about the verse in question, I read this dialogue without discovering any allusion. Bishop Eugenius too, who published Joseph Bryennius, and translated Virgil's Georgics into

* Hist. Lit. Tom. I. p. 17.

Greek

Greek hexameters, seems to be of my opinion; for after mentioning Cave's *demonstration*, he adds, * *Sed gentilem illum auctorem relinquamus, qui forsitan non ex Joannis epistola, sed ex propalato jam tunc Christianorum dogmate—unitatem naturæ—cum Trinitate—subsannare scurriliter intendebat.* But if you, Sir, think you can make any use of this authority, I beg you not to stand upon ceremony. Κοινὰ γὰρ τὰ τῶν φίλων.

I allow, however, that two Greek writers do quote this verse in full and express terms, Emanuel Calecas † and Joseph Bryennius ‡. Both eminent for antiquity and fidelity. Calecas wrote about the middle of the fourteenth century, and Bryennius at the beginning of the fifteenth. I shall have occasion hereafter to mention Calecas. At present I shall only observe, that the Acts of the Lateran council having been then long translated into Greek, it is more wonderful that so few, than that so many Greeks have quoted the disputed

* Fragm. Epist. ad Matthæi Præf. ad Epist. Cath. p. LVIII.
† P. 217. Ed. Coteler.
‡ Tom. I. p. 241. ed. Lips. 1768.

verse.

verse. As to Bryennius, he manifestly borrows from the Latin version. He reads ὁ χριϛὸς in the sixth verse, instead of τὸ πνεῦμα, and omits the clause of the eighth verse. And since he quotes Thomas Aquinas in another place*, I doubt not but that he was also indebted to him for this piece of information.

Let us now review the troops which you are leading to this dangerous battle. 1. A Synopsis of the first epistle of John, attributed to Athanasius, or Euthalius, or Sophronius, which quotes II. 23. to prove the unity of the Father with the Son. 2. A Dialogue, at least as old as the seventh century, written by Maximus or somebody else, which quotes the last words of the eighth verse, and applies them to the Trinity. 3. Euthymius Zigabenus, who quotes these words, "And the three are one," from Gregory Nazianzen's Oration on the holy Lights, and has been since compelled by his editor to quote 1 John V. 7. 4, 5. Calecas, who probably borrowed the verse from the Lateran council;

---

* Tom. I. p. 322.

and

and Bryennius, who certainly borrowed it from the Vulgate. 6. Laftly, a Lectionary printed at Venice in the year 1602, which Bengelius pronounces " to be in this place certainly interpolated from the Latin; for the leffon in the Arabic verfion, for the fame day of the fame week, knows nothing of the verfe."

Whether fo fmall, faint-hearted, and mutinous a band, can make head againft the enemy's hoft, I will endeavour to calculate, when I have concluded my account of the Latin writers.

SIR,

IF you sing Te Deum when you are most shamefully routed, what triumphs may we not expect from you when you lead your Latins into the field, whose first appearance at least, promises some shew of resistance? These Latins I shall divide into two classes, the writers before and the writers after Jerome's time: for all the evidence of your Old Italic must be given by the former set. You are sensible of the scantiness of your present allowance, and therefore wish to make all the Latins down to the end of the seventh century vouchers for this version. But this, Sir, is either ignorance or sophistry. If Jerome restored the disputed verse about the end of the fourth century, his name was neither so little known, nor his authority so little respected, that none of the succeeding writers for three hundred years would adopt

a most

a moſt important paſſage from his edition. You have only to prove (which you can do with as much eaſe as you prove moſt of your poſitions) that Jerome's ſucceſſors, though they conſtantly read and greatly eſteemed his works, reſolutely rejected all his emendations, ſlighted his new edition, and ſtuck to their ancient Vulgate. In the mean time, your Ante-Hieronymian witneſſes are Tertullian, Cyprian, and Phœbadius.

Tertullian's words are theſe: " *He ſhall take* (ſays the Son) *of mine* (John XVI. 14.) as I myſelf of the Father's. Thus the connexion of the Father in the Son, and of the Son in the Paraclete, makes three [perſons] cohering one with the other, which three are one [being, *unum*], not one [perſon, *unus*], as it is written, *I and my Father are one.*" (John X. 30.)

As often as I read this ſentence, ſo often I am aſtoniſhed that the words *tres unum ſunt* ſhould ever be urged as a quotation. On the contrary, it appears to me demonſtrable, that, inſtead of being a quotation, they are the words of Tertullian himſelf, and expreſsly diſtinguiſhed from the words of ſcripture.

1. Ter-

1. Tertullian does not declare them to be a quotation. This objection, you say, is ill-founded; and you prove, in five pages, that authors often quote without giving notice. You are sometimes, Sir, very amusing, when you prove what no man ever denied. A few pages farther, we shall find you proving that a quotation from scripture is often introduced with, *it is written*. But this, Sir, is not the whole of the objection; that Tertullian does not mark these words as a quotation, but that having been so accurate as to declare two passages to be quotations, one immediately preceding, and one immediately succeeding, he should pass over the words in question without any remark, such as, *inquit*, or *dictum est*, or *scriptum est*. If the three heavenly witnesses were in his copy of the N. T. why does he never appeal to them in the rest of this treatise, particularly in his twenty second chapter, where he insists, at length, on the expression, *Ego et Pater* UNUM *sumus*; which he quotes five times in the whole book? His argument, on this subject, takes up half a page of your Appendix: yet he is content with a slight and transient allusion to a text,

which is twice as important as the other, and by its peculiarity of expression, demanded a double share of his attention. Ought he not to have expected that the heretics would have endeavoured to elude the force of this argument, and pervert it to their own doctrine, as they had perverted John X. 30? Would he not have been equally diffuse upon the plural verb joined to the neuter singular? Let any man peruse the first page of your Appendix, and he must see that if Tertullian had then two texts before him, one asserting the unity of two of the divine persons, the other the unity of all the three, he must have been strangely forgetful, or something worse, to reason so much upon his weaker authority, and so little upon his stronger. If in the sequel a passage occurs, that might admit a doubt, whether it be a quotation or not, it is surely a circumstance of weight enough to turn the scale, that nothing was said of it three chapters before, where it might very usefully have been confronted with an unsuspected quotation.

2. In reading the Fathers, great caution is necessary. They often paraphrase what is concise;

concise; explain what is obscure; supply what is defective; *and truths divine come mended from their pen.* Often they add their own corollaries to the words of Scripture, or so mix their quotation with the web of their argument, that without a Bible at hand, it is difficult to determine, where the Scripture or the author speaks. An instance of this may be seen in this very sentence of Tertullian: *He shall take of mine, as I myself of the Father's.* If any important consequence could be drawn from these last words, no doubt but they would be defended with as much zeal, as the *tres unum sunt* which follow. Nor should I have wondered, if Cyprian, or Phœbadius had taken them for the genuine words of the Evangelist, and quoted them without scruple, upon the authority of Tertullian. And if I were disposed to assert, that Tertullian's copy of the Gospel in John XVI. 14. added, *sicut ipse de Patris,* I should have a better colour for my opinion, than you have for yours. But you say, that " Tertullian, after proving the unity of the Son with the Father, by a quotation from St. John, proceeds to prove the divinity of the Holy Ghost, by another quotation

quotation from the same St. John, *which shews a like unity of three persons in the godhead.*" I absolutely deny the truth of the latter assertion; to the rest I have no objection. I allow that Tertullian, having proved the unity of the Father and Son from St. John, proceeds to prove the divinity of the Holy Ghost from the same St. John. But he proves it from the Gospel, not from the Epistle. To avoid prolixity, I will state Tertullian's reasoning as clearly as I can; and I engage to defend my exposition, as giving the only consistent sense of which the words are capable.

" The unity of the Father and Son is frequently declared in Scripture, but most plainly in John X. 30. Praxeas makes this an unity of number; whereas, it ought to be interpreted of an unity of substance. For, if unity of person were intended, Christ would have said, *unus*, not *unum*. And the same sort of unity, that the Son has with the Father, the Holy Spirit has with the Son. For as the Son is sent by the Father, and speaks the words that he receives from the Father, so is the Spirit sent by the Son, and speaks the words that he receives from the Son; as

the

the Son himself affirms: *He shall glorify me, for he shall receive of mine.* Whatever unity, therefore, there is of the Father and Son, the same is the unity of the Son and Spirit; consequently, the same is the unity of all the three; which three are, therefore, one. When I say one, I mean not one person, but one substance. And for this reason, to avoid the subtilties of Praxeas, I use the Latin word *unum*, not *unus*; in which I conform myself to the scriptural phrase, and apply the same expression to the three persons, that the Scripture itself has applied to two."

If Tertullian had proposed to himself, to declare his belief of the Trinity, in imitation of John X. 30. he could not have invented a form of words different from the form that he has chosen. He could not say, *tres unus sunt*, much less, *tres unus est*; because, he then would, by his own confession, seem to favour the heresy of Praxeas. But, as his words now stand, the imitation is perfect; and the very order of the subject, predicate, and verb, exactly observed. I shall therefore affirm, that Tertullian, not only does not quote these magic words, *tres unum sunt*, from St. John, but that he plainly confesses them to be his own, and defends them by the analogy of Scripture.

Most of the editions of Tertullian read, *tres unum sint*, which would rather strengthen my cause. But I shall make no use of this reading, because it might easily be a mistake of the copiers, or, perhaps, of the press. Tertullian has also been thought to refer to 1 John V. 7. in two other places, de Pudicitia § 21. c. Praxeam § 30. Concerning these two places I shall say nothing; whether because I think them of too much consequence, or of too little, I leave, Sir, to your sagacious conjecture.

Eucherius, after proving the Trinity from Psalm XXXIII. 6. and other texts, concludes thus, " Ergo Pater ex quo omnia, Filius per quem omnia, Spiritus Sanctus in quo omnia, sicut et Apostolus dicit, (Rom. XI. 36.) *Quoniam ex ipso et per ipsum, et in ipso sunt omnia, ipsi gloria in secula seculorum.*" The construction of this sentence, is the same as of the passage in Tertullian. But it is clear, that the words immediately preceding *sicut*, are Eucherius's own, which he justifies by
the

the subsequent authority. In like manner, the words immediately preceding *quomodo*, are Tertullian's own, which he justifies by the subsequent authority. I request the reader to bear this place in mind, when I examine Cyprian's testimony.

Phœbadius (excuse me for violating chronology) plainly imitates Tertullian, as Bengelius observes, and therefore, is not a distinct evidence. If you object, with Bengelius, that the particle *quia* implies a quotation, I answer, 1. That this is too slender a presumption to support an argument. Or if it must be a quotation, it is a quotation from Tertullian. 2. If I allowed it to be meant for a quotation of Scripture, you could then only prove, that Phœbadius had read Cyprian, or some author who had read Cyprian. 3. The editions vary, some retaining, others omitting *quia*.

Upon Cyprian, therefore, the whole labour of supporting this verse is devolved. He seems to quote it in two places. One of these receives all its force from the other; and if Cyprian shall not appear to have quoted 1. John V. 7. in his treatise de Unitate, neither will he appear to have quoted it in his epiſtle to Jubaianus. I allow, that by ſaying, "Of the Father, Son, and Holy Ghoſt, it is written, *And theſe* (or *the*) *three are one*," Cyprian affirms, the words which follow, *it is written*, to be extant in Scripture. Why would he not quote the entire ſeventh verſe, as we have it at preſent? Alas! what unkind and perverſe mortals were theſe holy fathers! Half a minute more time, half an inch more parchment, would have cleared up all doubts, eſtabliſhed the wavering, confounded the gain-ſayers, and ſaved a multitude of ſouls. But whether through envy, or haſte, they huddled the moſt important texts into the ſhorteſt compaſs, though they are tedious and diffuſe upon others, where we could have wiſhed them to be more conciſe.

It has been made a queſtion, ever ſince the time of Simon, whether Cyprian quotes our preſent ſeventh verſe, or only applies the eighth by a myſtical interpretation to the Trinity? The ſecond ſuppoſition is ſo ſtrongly ſupported, by the authority of Facundus, that you will find ſome difficulty in ſetting aſide his teſtimony. Facundus himſelf, interpret-
ing

ing the spirit, water and blood of the Father, Son, and Holy Ghost, at last seems apprehensive that his adversaries may possibly object to his explanation; he, therefore, reserves as his strongest argument, the authority of Cyprian: " Aut si forsitan ipsi Trinitatem, quæ unus Deus est, nolunt intelligi, secundum ipsa verba, quæ posuit pro Apostolo Joanne, respondeant—Quod tamen Joannis Apostoli testimonium B. Cyprianus Carthaginensis antistes et martyr, in epistola sive libro quem de Unitate scripsit, de Patre, et Filio, et Spiritu Sancto dictum intelligit. Ait enim; *Dicit Dominus*, EGO ET PATER UNUM SUMUS; *et iterum de Patre, et Filio, et Spiritu Sancto scriptum est*, ET HI TRES UNUM SUNT." Such a thundering proof as this, left no room for objection; in the progress, therefore, of his dispute, he refers to this place again, and takes it for granted, that he has undeniably proved his point. " Nam sic ecclesia Christi, etiam cum necdum ad distinctionem Patris et Filii et Spiritus Sancti uteretur nomine personæ, tres credidit et prædicavit, P. et F. et Sp. S. sicut testimonio Joannis supra docuimus, quo dictum est; *Tres sunt qui testimonium dant in terra, spiritus, aqua et sanguis, et*

hi

hi tres unum sunt." I shall now desire the reader to consider your modest assertion, p. 40. 82. that " what Facundus or Cyprian understood, concerning the eighth verse, is immaterial to the dispute about the seventh." On the contrary, I affirm, that Facundus, urging the heretics with the distinction of persons in the Trinity, which is taught in the eighth verse, and confirming his explanation by this very passage of Cyprian, shews, first, that he himself knew nothing of the seventh verse; and, secondly, that Cyprian, in his opinion, knew no more, but extracted the doctrine of the Trinity from the eighth. Could Facundus, with a text before his eyes that would have gained him an easy victory over his enemies, labour through several pages to bend this untractable verse to his purpose? " The Spirit," says he, " signifies the Father, for *God is a spirit*, (John IV. 24.) the water, the Holy Ghost (see John VII. 37. 38.) the blood, the Son, he alone of the Holy Trinity partaking of flesh and blood." If the seventh verse was then in the generality of the Latin copies, Facundus had not only lost his wits, to use a weak reason, when he had a stronger to produce, but
his

his honesty too, in forcing an absurd interpretation of scripture upon Cyprian, which he well knew to be his own, and not Cyprian's.

Why then might not Cyprian give the sense of 1 John V. 8. in his own words, and say, *Of the Father,* Son, *and Holy Ghost, it is written,* THESE THREE ARE ONE ? To this question you answer, in Houyhnhnm language, that " Cyprian would then have *said the thing which was not* ; that he would have been guilty of an intentional falsehood; a supposition altogether monstrous and abominable." You might have a little lowered these tragical outcries, if you had considered, that the goodness, or badness, of every action may be considered in two lights; with respect to the quality of the action itself, and to the intention of the agent. That Cyprian set down his own sense of the eighth verse with an intention to mislead his readers, is an odious, and, unless it be well supported, an *abominable* accusation. But who accuses Cyprian of a deliberate falsehood ? This is your constant refuge, when argument fails you, to represent with all your pathos, the injury done to to illustrious characters, such as Cyprian, Stunica, Stephens, Beza, &c.

If Cyprian gave his own sense of a particular verse, and said, *So it is written*, though he might occasion error in others, I should not, without very strong reasons, suspect him of absolute fraud. I wish, indeed, that it were the custom to quote with more accuracy; but we know too well, that all authors (and frequently in controversy) quote, not the very words, but the sense and scope of them, or what they take to be the sense, and sometimes without warning the reader. If I had said in my III Letter, p. 42. that you profess, p. 11. 16. a willingness to believe that Mr. Gibbon, upon a certain occasion, would have acted like a knave, should I have been guilty of fraud, because I had quoted your words according to what I thought to be their true meaning? I would not be understood to defend this practice universally; I think it blameable in general, and often productive of great mistakes. All that I aver is, that it merits no harsher name, where no evil intention appears, than inaccuracy. Whatever I conceive to be the real import of a passage, I have

have a right to set down in what words I choose, so long as I believe it to be the true sense, and mean to mislead nobody. Facundus has the following sentence: " Joannes Apostolus in epistola sua *de Patre, et Filio, et Spiritu Sancto sic* † *dicit* : TRES SUNT QUI TESTIMONIUM DANT*—ET HI TRES UNUM SUNT." If Facundus had only quoted these words, and not been imprudent enough to quote and explain at length, he would have been with you a positive evidence for the authenticity of the seventh verse; but at present, unhappily, the break is filled up with * *in terra Spiritus aqua et sanguis.* I would observe, that Facundus uses the word *dicit*, and is just as peremptory in the application of the eighth verse to the Trinity, as Cyprian is in the application of his supposed seventh. A

---

† ARATOR says, A. A. II. 909. *Hic Judæa vacans, sterilis quæ* DICITUR *arbor, Exspectata tribus fructum non attulit annis,* &c. Here is Judæa said to be *called* the barren tree in scripture, as positively as, *et tres unum sunt*, is said by Cyprian, to be written of the Father, Son, and Holy Ghost. But no man in his senses, I hope, will contend that Arator's copy of Luke XIII. added a formal application of the parable to Judæa.

little

little after Facundus says, " Non ergo ait Joannes Apostolus *loquens de Patre, et Filio, et Spiritu Sancto,* TRES SUNT PERSONÆ QUÆ TESTIFICANTUR, &c." Facundus, we see, affirming that the Apostle speaks of the Trinity, affirms it in terms equally forcible with Cyprian's *scriptum est,* and yet we are certain that Facundus applies only the eighth verse; we have, therefore, a right to conclude, that Cyprian does the same. If Facundus had been as reserved as Cyprian, and only quoted a part of the eighth verse, as I have done for him ; if then the testimony of a later writer should be produced to this effect, *Quod testimonium B. Facundus de Patre, Filio, et Spiritu Sancto dictum intelligit,* you would reject it with as much contempt, and as little reason, as now you reject the same testimony given by Facundus concerning Cyprian.

Was the allegorical method of interpretation uncommon among the fathers ? No; we know that they employed it without scruple in all points, whether of doctrine or morals. Bengelius, it is true, seems to think that the primitive fathers, or at least Cyprian, were not tainted with the contagion of allegory.

allegory. " That the reader * may judge of this the better, I will transcribe the words that follow the former quotation. *The Scripture says,* OF HIS COAT, BECAUSE FROM THE UPPER PART IT WAS NOT SEWED, BUT WOVEN THROUGHOUT, THEY SAID, LET US NOT DIVIDE IT, BUT CAST LOTS FOR IT. *The coat carried unity, coming from the upper part, that is, from heaven and from the Father, which could in no wise be rent by him that received it,* &c. Again, in his treatise on the Lord's Prayer: *We find that Daniel and the three children, chose for their hours of prayer, the third, sixth and ninth, a sign of the mystery of the Trinity, which was to be revealed in after times.* What wonder, that a writer of this stamp, should forcibly apply these words, *tres unum sunt,* to the Trinity, though he were wholly ignorant of the seventh verse."

In truth, the allegorical interpretations of the scripture, given by the ancient writers, are so numerous, that it would be endless to pursue them. I shall content myself with three of the most ingenious, and most perti-

* *Griesbach,* Tom. II. p. 230.

nent to the subject. Ecclesiast. IV. 12. *A threefold cord is not quickly broken.* This is explained by Origen, Basil, Jerome, and Ambrose, of the Trinity. If any of these able divines had thus expressed himself: " Of the unity of the Trinity it is written: *A threefold cord,* &c." who would pronounce him guilty of an intentional falsehood? None, I am persuaded, except Martin and yourself, whose feelings on these subjects are painfully acute.

" When * Christ says to his disciples, that three loaves ought to be given to him that

---

* Arator Act. Apost. II. 896.

Discipulis quod Christus ait, jam nocte roganti
Tres panes debere dari: nox ista profecto est
Mundus, ut hic siquis verbi desideret escas,
Exhibeas, quæsite, dapes, doceasque volentem,
Quod Pater et Natus, quod Sanctus Spiritus unus
Sint Deus, et numerum triplicet substantia simplex.
Nec semel hoc pia jussa canunt. Angariat, inquit,
Te quicunque petens, ut pergas prævius unum,
Cetera vade simul duo millia: nonne videntur
Hoc mandata loqui? si quis te consulit errans
Ignarusque viæ, quid sit Deus, edere malis,
Prode Patrem, subjunge libens, quod Filius, et quod
Spiritus est almus, numero tres et tamen unus.

asks

asks by night (Luke XI. 5.) that night is the world, in which if any defires the meat of the word, you ought to produce your ftores, and teach him, that the Father, the Son, and the Holy Spirit, are one God, a fingle fubftance in a triple number. The facred precepts repeat this more than once. Whoever preffes you one mile, go with him alfo the other two; (Matth. V. 41.) does he not feem to fay; if any man in error afks you, what God is, tell him that he is firft the Father, next fubjoin that he is the Son and the gracious Spirit, three in number and yet one."

If one of the Fathers had written this fentence: " Our Saviour faid to the Jewifh nation, *let no fruit grow on thee henceforward for ever,*" an accufer would be ridiculous, who fhould charge him with having quoted falfely; for that thefe words are said to the fig-tree, Matth. XXI. 18. and not to the Jews. But how much more ridiculous would a defender be, who fhould maintain that the Father had certainly an additional paragraph in his copy, where our Saviour thus fpoke to the Jews, or at leaft an additional

tional verse explaining the allegory; and that to suspect the holy man of giving his own interpretation for the words of scripture, would be *monstrous and abominable!*

Lord Shaftesbury * thus blasphemously derides the language of the holy Scriptures: " I have seen in certain Christian churches an ancient piece or two affirmed on the solemn faith of priestly tradition to have been angelically and divinely wrought; but having observed the whole *style* and manner to vary from the rules of art, I presumed to assert, that if the pencil had been heaven-guided, it could never have been so lame in its performance." Would a defender of Shaftebury gravely argue that I have here been guilty of an intentional falsehood; that Shaftesbury says not a word of the Scriptures, but merely of some pictures that were shewn to him in certain churches for celestial workmanship? In such a case I should answer, if I could keep my countenance, that I had supposed Lord Shaftesbury by this allegory to

* Characteristics, vol. III. p. 230.

ridicule

ridicule the Scriptures themfelves; that the veil which covered his real meaning, was fo tranfparent, that every body might fee it, without my tearing it off; that however I was guilty of no intentional falfehood, for I firmly believed what I faid, and that the morality of fuch matters is not to be meafured by the foundnefs of our judgment, but by the ftrength of our perfuafion. I make no doubt but Facundus was as fully convinced that he and Cyprian had rightly interpreted 1 John V. 8. as I am that I have rightly interpreted Lord Shaftefbury. The only objection remaining, which can feem to have any weight, that Cyprian was not capable of fo abfurd an interpretation, I have in part anfwered already; and I fhall obferve farther, that no man ought to difpute upon any fubject where the Fathers are concerned, who either knows not, or will not own, that many interpretations of Scripture to the full as abfurd as this may be found in their works. To mention one. Many of the Fathers prove the divinity and eternal generation of the Logos from Pfalm XLV. 1. *Eructavit cor meum verbum bonum.* But the mere

mere Englilh Chriftian is defrauded of this argument for his faith by our heretical tranflation, *My heart is inditing of a good matter*.*

Cyprian is elfewhere negligent in quoting, as in Matth. VI. 13. *Suffer us not to be led into temptation.* Apoc. XIX. 10. *Worſhip thou the Lord Jeſus.* 1 John II. 17. he five times adds, *As God remains for ever.* The firſt and ſecond you defend. I ſhall therefore examine the firſt, to give a ſpecimen of your talents, for you never are more pleaſant than when you talk about criticiſm. You think, *Lead us not into temptation*, which is found in ſome MSS. the genuine reading. The note in the inner margin of the Oxford Cyprian is thus expreſſed: " Ne nos inducas, *Ar. Ebor. Pemb. Lin. Voſſ. 2. Bod. 3. 4. Vict.*" which you p. 44, 89. thus improve, as uſual. " *Lead us into temptation* are the words of the Arundelian MS. of thoſe from Pembroke College, Cambridge, of thoſe from

---

* Whoever deſires more of theſe interpretations, may ſurfeit himſelf by conſulting *Whitby's* Diſſertatio de S. Scripturarum Interpretatione ſecundum Patrum Commentarios.

York,

York, from Lincoln College, Oxford, of one belonging to Vossius, two Bodleian MSS. and one belonging to the monastery of St. Victor." Let any reader, who has not Cyprian before him, count your list; he must be wrong; he will at least make nine, and may, if he chuses, make twenty MSS. in favour of your reading, though in the edition itself it is manifest to the eye, that they are only eight. The MSS. collated to this treatise of Cyprian are in all twenty-one. If I reasoned like you, I should claim the other thirteen, as all agreeing in the common reading. However, since the collation is in general very exact, I think I shall be very generous, if I strike off four as neutrals and only suppose nine to be in my favour. To these nine I add two in the Museum, both which read, *Suffer us not to be led*, in each of the places where Cyprian quotes the clause. We have therefore a clear majority on the side of the editions.

Secondly. This majority will be greatly increased, when we learn, that the same clause is repeated again in this treatise of Cyprian,

Cyprian, and that only three MSS. defert the vulgar reading.

Thirdly. The internal evidence is in favour of this reading. For there was a plain reafon why the copiers fhould alter Cyprian's quotation to that reading of the Gofpel which was familiar to themfelves. And wherever in a quotation of Scripture, two readings are equal in other refpects, that which differs from the received text is commonly genuine.

Fourthly, Auguftine exprefsly quotes this variation from Cyprian, as you might have learned from your friend Beza. I conclude therefore that the prefent text of Cyprian is right, and that Matthew Prior was not wrong, when he faid or fung, that *Authors before they write, fhould read*, a caution to which fome of your friends, Sir, have not paid fufficient regard.

If you are curious to know how Cyprian came to adopt this glofs inftead of the genuine reading, I am almoft certain, that he was deceived by an imperfect recollection of Tertullian. We learn from Jerome, that Cyprian was a conftant reader of Tertullian, whom

whom he called his master. And from Cyprian's imitations, we might learn the same thing without Jerome's information. Tertullian then having explained De Orat. § 8. the clause *Lead us not* by *Suffer us not to be led*, his scholar, as many scholars are apt to do, took his master's interpretation for Gospel. Thus he quotes in the Council of Carthage, § 6. John III. 6. with the spurious addition, borrowed from Tertullian de Carne Christi, § 18. of which I shall take another occasion to speak.

"But though Facundus indeed tells us that Cyprian meant only to interpret the eighth verse by that sentence, *Of the Father, Son and Holy Ghost it is written*, AND THESE THREE ARE ONE, Fulgentius *directly* and *positively* represents Cyprian as quoting the seventh." Fulgentius's word is *confitetur*, which, you say, frequently means in the best writers *to declare, to shew, to profess*. And for this you refer to your trusty friend, "the dictionary of Ainsworth," of whose two examples one has been corrected from MSS. (Sueton. Aug. 4.) the other I have not been able to find, but I will venture to prophesy

prophesy that it is a mistake; a third, which " the Thesaurus of Gesner" would have supplied, is either corrupt or nothing to the purpose. Yet I shall lay no stress upon this argument, because in that barbarous age, strange liberties were sometimes taken in the use of words. I shall also grant, that Fulgentius quotes our seventh verse, and does not adopt the mystical exposition of the eighth from Cyprian, as Emlyn pretends. I shall attack Fulgentius's testimony upon a new ground. I affirm, that it is no testimony at all, except to the genuineness of the passage in Cyprian. Fulgentius fairly confesses (or if you will, *shews, declares, professes*) that he became acquainted with this verse solely by the means of Cyprian, and that he had not seen it himself in the copies of the N. T.' Else what does he mean to prove by his appeal to Cyprian? That this verse was genuine? But if it already existed in all the copies, if it were acknowledged both by orthodox and Arians, where was the use or sense of strengthening this general consent by the solitary evidence of Cyprian?

Clarke,

Clarke,* quoting Juſtin for a paſſage, which I ſhall hereafter mention, adds, that no doubt Juſtin found it in the old Greek tranſlation. Is it not clear from this appeal to Juſtin's authority, that the paſſage is not in the preſent copies of the Greek tranſlation? Would Fulgentius have ſaid, *De Patre et ſeipſo et Spiritu Sancto teſtatur ipſe Filius dicens, Ite, docete,* &c. (Matth. XXVIII. 19.) *Quod etiam beatiſſimus martyr Cyprianus confitetur,* &c. Certainly never; or if he had ſaid it, he would weaken a part of the evidence which we now have for the authenticity of that text. But Fulgentius being aware of an objection that the verſe was not then extant in St. John's Epiſtle, ſhields himſelf under the authority of Cyprian, and quotes the paſſage for genuine Scripture, upon this maxim, (which Facundus alſo adopts, though he applies it in a different way) *that Cyprian was infallible.* Nor was he ſingular in this maxim, but agreed with the general opinion that prevailed after Cyprian's martyrdom.

* Reply to Waterland, p. 135.

For,

For, as Mosheim* well observes, Cyprian's reputation was so enhanced by his fortitude in suffering a violent death, that he became the common master and oracle of the church. The merits of the martyr threw a shade over the defects of the author, and the veneration that ought to have been confined to his piety, was extended to his writings. It was therefore no wonder that Fulgentius should accept a reading which he supposed to be Cyprian's reading of a passage in Scripture; or that Facundus should accept an interpretation which he supposed to be Cyprian's interpretation of Scripture. In either case they were sure of vanquishing their enemies by an authority which it was deemed blasphemy to resist.

I think it most probable, that Cyprian in these quotations, followed, as he thought, the authority of Tertullian. Finding the

---

* Incredibile dictu est, quantam per universum orbem Christianum, post mortem pro Christo magno animo exceptam, auctoritatem adeptus sit, ut communis instar magistri et oraculi loco habereter. De Rebus Christianis ante Constantinum M. Sec. III. § XXIV. p. 597.

phrase, *tres unum sunt*, closely joined to, *quomodo dictum est*, EGO ET PATER UNUM SUMUS, he took the former part of the sentence to be a quotation from Scripture as well as the latter. " But from what part of Scripture," would Cyprian say, " could my master take it, except 1 John V. 8. I perceive his drift; he interprets the spirit, the water and the blood, of the three persons of the Trinity, and to them applies the concluding words, *the three are one*. If such an allegorical interpretation once entered Cyprian's head, it would recommend itself to his approbation equally by its own intrinsic merit and the authority of his master. I pay no compliment to De Missy, when I say that he had a clearer and more critical head than Cyprian. Yet he took Bengelius's words for a quotation from Stephens.* Tertullian proves by some curious reasons (de Jejun. § 10.) that Daniel's hours of prayer were the third, the sixth and the ninth. Cyprian lays his hands upon this piece of news as a great prize, and turns it

---

* Letter IV. p. 99.

to good account. The passage I have quoted above. He there not only asserts this as a fact of Daniel, but adds his three companions, and infers that it denoted the mystery of the Trinity, which was to be revealed in the last times. I wish you had transcribed a little more from Fulgentius in your Appendix. He has borrowed this argument from Cyprian, and I think (but I may be partial) somewhat improved it. After his first citation from Cyprian, he thus proceeds: *For in his book on the Lord's prayer, to shew that the Trinity is of one Deity, without any difference of the persons, he relates that Daniel and the children were wont to pray at intervals of three hours; where by the revolution of* THREE *hours, to the duty of* ONE *prayer, he evidently shews, that the Trinity is one God.*

I shall now request the reader once more diligently to peruse the passage of Eucherius above quoted. If Eucherius had found in any of his followers as constant a reader and zealous an admirer as Tertullian found in Cyprian, how natural would it be for such a follower, upon reading this place, to mistake the sentence, *Ergo pater ex quo omnia,*

omnia, filius per quem omnia, spiritus sanctus, in quo omnia, for a formal quotation of 1 Cor. VIII. 6. He would infer, (and he would infer with as much justice as you and others have made Tertullian's words a quotation) that by the *ficut et apostolus dicit,* Eucherius meant, not to defend his own expression by a similar passage of Scripture, but to connect two similar passages. All the difference is, that the *ficut et,* is stronger than Tertullian's *quomodo.* Or to draw up my argument in form of an abstract proposition: if an author states his own doctrine in language resembling some words of Scripture, and illustrates it by a Scriptural quotation, it is probable that some credulous reader will take the author's own words for his reading of that part of Scripture to which they bear a resemblance.

Gregory Nazianzen's father left behind him some discourses on the Trinity. In one of these, after proving his thesis from several texts, he proceeded in these words: ἐςὶν οὖν ὁ πατὴρ, ἐξ οὗ τὰ πάν]α, ὁ ὑιος, δι' οὗ τὰ πάν]α, τὸ ἅγιον πνεῦμα, ἐν ὧι τὰ πάν]α, καθὼς καὶ γέγραπ]αι, ἐξ αὐτῦ καὶ δι' αὐτῦ καὶ ἐν αὐτῶι τὰ πάν]α. *

πάν]α.* (Rom. XI. 36.) Gregory on the perusal of this passage, turned over his New Testament, and at last found in 1 Cor. VIII. 6. this sentence; *To us there is one God the Father, from whom are all things—and one Lord Jesus Christ, by whom are all things.* He therefore judiciously concluded, that his father read the whole verse thus: *To us there is one God the Father, from whom are all things, and we from him; and one Lord Jesus Christ, by whom are all things, and we by him*; AND ONE HOLY SPIRIT, IN WHOM ARE ALL THINGS, AND WE IN HIM. With this opinion, could he forget to employ his new-found text in his disputes with the heretics. Either his reverence for his father's memory, or the singular fitness of the passage for his purpose, would alone be a sufficient motive; united, they were irresistible. In his thirty-ninth oration, therefore, p. 630. C. he quotes the verse with this addition, compares it with Rom. XI. 36. and argues from it as if

---

* I have adopted the reading of the Vulgate for an obvious reason.

both

both heretics and orthodox allowed it to be genuine. His commentator, Nicetas, T. II. Orat. XXXIX. p. 1026. B. XLIV. p. 1249. A. twice follows this reading, and urges it against the Arians, adding in the latter place, *Neque enim alioqui Trinitas fuerit, nisi Spiritus quoque connumeretur*; which, as Mr. Matthæi* rightly remarks, is an unwary confession of fraud. Three MSS. Scholiasts agree in the same reading, and one has the impudence to affirm that it was erased by Arius. Ἐξελήφθη παρὰ τοῦ Ἀρείου. (read ἐξηλείφθη.) From Gregory it passed to John Damascenus, who quotes it several times, to Euthymius Zigabenus, and to Emanuel Calecas.† From Gregory or John Damascenus (for both, I believe, were early translated into Slavonic) it crept into the Slavonian version, and is in the MSS. and first editions, but omitted in the latter.

I acknowledge that I have mixed a little romance with the beginning of this story.

* Animadverf. ad 1 Cor. VIII. 6. p. 204—210.
† De Principiis Fidei, c. 3. p. 215. ed. Coteler. whom Mr. Matthæi seems to have overlooked.

But

But I was willing for once to imitate your way of setting down your own fancies for positive facts. The intelligent reader will however see that I have supposed nothing but what is probable. I take Gregory to have been deceived by finding in some eminent Greek Father a sentence similar to that which I have quoted from Eucherius. My hypothesis too is very charitable; for I was willing to bring off my favourite Gregory with the least possible loss of honour. I have pointed out the real source of the mistake, though I cannot trace its progress, nor discover through what channels it flowed into Gregory's oration.

If an admirer of Gregory, writing upon the deity of the Holy Spirit, used these words: " The blessed Apostle Paul testifies, that *to us there is one Holy Spirit, in whom are all things,* which also the most pious bishop Gregory the divine declares *(confitetur)* in his oration of the holy lights, where, to demonstrate the Trinity, he has brought the following proofs directly from Scripture: To US THERE IS ONE GOD THE FATHER, &c. *where the* FROM WHOM *and* BY WHOM *and* IN WHOM

whom *do not separate the natures—as is clear, if we attentively read in the same Apostle,* from him and by him and in him are all things, &c." would not he confess, that he was indebted for the knowledge of this text to Gregory Nazianzen, and to him only? The plain English of such an appeal would be, This sentence is wanting in our present copies, but Gregory, whose fidelity and accuracy cannot be questioned, had it in his MS. as appears from his quoting it. So Fulgentius's testimony amounts to no more than this, The verse is not now indeed in the epistle, but it was there in Cyprian's days, for he quotes it, and to suspect him either of fraud or mistake would be the height of impiety.

The implicit faith with which the Latin writers copy their predecessors often diminishes and sometimes destroys the value of their testimony. Thus a gloss crept early into some copies of John III. 6. *Et quoniam Deus Spiritus est, de Deo natus est.* I believe Tertullian to be the author of this gloss, who sometimes blends the words of scripture with his own, so that it requires much skill and pains to make the separation. From him it quickly spread through all the Latin churches, *Ceu flamma per tædas, vel Eurus Per Siculas equitavit undas.* It would be idle to recount all the writers who quote this for scripture; but some, not content with asserting it to be genuine, charge the Arians with having corrupted the copies that omitted it. Hear the holy Ambrose: " This place you Arians so expressly testify to be written of the Spirit, that you erase it from your books. And I wish you erased it only from your own, and not from the public books of the church." Observe the candour and judgment of this Saint. He acknowledges that a passage is wanting in almost all the MSS. and founds his accusation of the Arians upon the very circumstance that ought to have acquitted them. The same calumny is repeated by Bede, Fulbert and Hincmar, who *follow in the chase, not like hounds that hunt, but like those that fill up the cry.* I must not forget to add, that Grabe* defends the genuine-

---

* Not. ad *Bulli* Defenf. Fid. Nic. p. 139. *Grabius vir bonus nec indoctus fuit et in scriptis Patrum apprime versatus: criticus non fuit, neque esse potuit, ut pote neque ingenio neque judicio——satis ad eam rem instructus.* THIRLBY Dedicat. to *Justin Martyr.*

ness

ness of this interpolation, and very properly in company with 1 John V. 7.

The heifer hath calved and hath not calved. Pray, Sir, in what part of scripture may this passage be found? It is quoted by at least four of the Fathers. Tertullian * says, " We read in Ezechiel." Clemens Alexandrinus † says simply, " in scripture." Gregory Nyssen ‡ and Epiphanius § seem to quote it from Isaiah. There is some difference in the words, but they all agree in the application, which, I suppose, I need not mention.

Justin Martyr tells Trypho, that the Jews have corrupted their scripture to elude the prophecies relating to the Messiah. One of his examples is Psalm XCVI. 10. from which three words, says Justin, have been erased by the Jews, so that the true reading is, *The Lord hath reigned* FROM THE TREE. Thirlby in his note produces an host of

---

* De Carne Christi, § 23.
† Strom. VII. p. 756.
‡ In ZACAGNI's Collectan. Monument. Vet. p. 303.
§ Hæres. p. 156.

witnesses for the same reading, to whom he might have added the author against Varimadus III. 2. This reading, though manifestly false and spurious, has crept into some Psalters, and seems to have imposed upon Erasmus, who cites it without suspicion in his colloquy intitled, *Inquisitio de fide*.

These interpolations, which are well known to the learned, I have produced merely to teach the superficial reader not to place too much confidence in the citations of the Fathers. We have seen how Nicetas, though he was sensible that authority was against him, retains and defends Gregory Nazianzen's reading. We have seen how Justin Martyr and Ambrose, when they wanted to promote a passage to the rank of scripture, reproached their adversaries with having erased it.

You suppose *authenticæ literæ* in Tertullian to signify the autographs of the apostles. This construction you support by a passage from Ignatius, which I profess not to understand, but I am sure that it will not admit the sense you put upon it. You then refer

refer us to Peter* of Alexandria, who testifies, it seems, that the original Gospel of St. John was kept at Ephesus in his time. Are you really ignorant, Sir, that this Peter is an author, whose age, name and credit are totally uncertain? And Berriman † and Ernesti ‡ think that *authenticæ* means no more than *genuine, uninterpolated*. But I flatter myself that I can confirm your interpretation from Tertullian himself, § who quotes the *originale instrumentum Moysi*. Now if Tertullian had seen the *original volume of Moses*, how much more easily might he have seen the original epistle of John. Nor is it wonderful that the autograph of Moses should last to Tertullian's time, when the autograph of Esdras has lasted to the present day. For Montfaucon ‖ saw at Bologna an Hebrew MS. which, as appeared from a memorandum in the middle of the book, was written by Esdras's own proper hand.

* PETAVIUS Uranolog. p. 397.
† Dissert. on 1 Tim. III. 16. p. 13.
‡ Opusc. Philolog. et Crit. p. 308.
§ Contra Hermog. § 19.
‖ Diar. Ital. p. 400.

But to leave this solemn trifling, and return to the question. The words of Tertullian, which you have taken for a quotation from scripture, I think I have shewn to be only a deduction of his own from two texts John X. 30. XVI. 14. Phœbadius copies Tertullian. Cyprian finding two or three words, which happen to follow in the same order, 1 John V. 8. immediately succeeded by a formal quotation from scripture, thought these words also to be a quotation, and employed them without remorse in the sense, which, as he imagined, his master had affixed to them. Thus Tertullian* proves by some ingenious arguments, that Daniel's three hours of prayer were the third, the sixth and the ninth. Then comes Cyprian, takes the fact for granted, asserts the same of Daniel's three companions, and hence elicits the mystery of the Trinity. Whoever could argue at this rate, could with equal or greater ease find the same doctrine in such an expression as " *the three are one,*" though the

---

* De Jejuniis, § 10.

literal sense seemed ever so foreign to his subject.

Two or three centuries afterwards both Facundus and Fulgentius appealed to this passage of Cyprian. Neither of them could find a text of scripture, where it was expresly said of the Father, Son and Holy Ghost, "these three are one." Yet Cyprian seemed to affirm it. Facundus therefore supposed, that Cyprian mixed his own interpretation with the words of scripture. Fulgentius on the other hand, being somewhat more sanguine, supposed that he quoted literally the words of scripture. Finding therefore a kind of counterpart to Cyprian's quotation in 1 John V. 8. he would naturally conclude that the three heavenly witnesses were distinctly mentioned in Cyprian's copy, but had afterwards vanished, either by the malice of the Arians, or the negligence of the scribes, confounding the *homœoteleuta*. If you think, Sir, that it derogates from the honour of Cyprian or Fulgentius to insinuate that they could in matters of such importance, blindly follow their leaders, you ought to recollect that I pass no harsher censure

sure upon them than I have passed upon you with respect to Martin, a censure, whose justice you cannot help feeling in your mind, whether you chuse to confess it or not.

Postscript.

1. I have perhaps been much more diffuse upon this article than was necessary. But I remember, that when I was a novice in this controversy, I was very angry with the opposers of the heavenly witnesses for their obstinacy in denying Cyprian's words to be a literal quotation. My reasons for the opinion which gave birth to my indignation were chiefly two. 1. My esteem for the learning, good sense and fidelity of the fathers, which would not suffer me to believe, that they would quote negligently or interpret absurdly. 2. My reliance on the candour of the disputants in stating the adversary's arguments. But experience has instructed me to entertain more moderate and qualified sentiments of both parties.

2. Mr.

2. Mr. Travis has taken particular care not to let the reader know, that the paſſage ſo triumphantly urged, as a direct quotation of 1 John V. 7. is cited at length by Facundus, and expreſsly declared by him to be an interpretation of 1 John V. 8. But from Mr. Travis's repreſentation of the matter, you would believe that Facundus refers in general terms to Cyprian, without ſpecifying the exact place.

3. Scipio Maffei* aſſerts that Facundus alludes to the ſeventh verſe. But becauſe he makes in the ſame page ſeveral other aſſertions totally ungrounded, (ſuch as that the verſe is in Aldus's edition, that Mill allows it to be extant in other Greek MSS. not leſs ancient than the Alexandrian, &c.) I ſhall conclude that in this inſtance, as well as the others, he aſſerted what he wiſhed rather than what he knew.

4. I have written *de Unitate* in Facundus, and thus diſabled an objection which might otherwiſe be made, that Facundus cannot be

---

* Opuſcoli Eccleſiaſtici, p. 174. publiſhed with his Iſtoria Teologica.

ſafely

safely trusted, because he refers to Cyprian's treatise by a wrong title, *de Trinitate*. But learned men have long since conjectured, *de Unitate*, which might indeed have been admitted into the text, though it were not confirmed by the Verona MS. in Maffei, p. 145.

5. Mr. Travis has read Tertullian so diligently and understands him so well, that he denies, p. 233—235. Tertullian to have been a Montanist, when he wrote his treatise against Praxeas. A proper man this to confute Newton!

LETTER

LETTER XI.

SIR,

AUGUSTINE and Jerome you have thought fit to number in your own party. *Thus like an experienced officer, by a false muster-roll of authorities, you gain the pay and credit of forces you cannot produce.* * Let us therefore examine your claim to these testimonies. Augustine says of the Father, Son, and Holy Ghost, " They are one," " These three are one," which words, according to you, bespeak their derivation from this verse too clearly to require any comment. They would have been too clear to require any, if you had first quoted the passage from his treatise against Maximin, where he explains

* MIDDLETON, Farther Remarks on Bentley, vol. III. p. 456.

the spirit, the water, and the blood, into an allegory signifying the three persons of the Trinity. "If we examine," says he, "how this passage ought to be interpreted, it will not be absurd to expound it of the Trinity, of which it may be truly said, "There are three that bear witness," and, "the three are one." If you had first produced this sentence, the reader would have seen, that when Augustine elsewhere says of the Trinity, "These three are one," even allowing that the phrase is borrowed from scripture, it is only his own exposition of the eighth verse. Could Augustine, writing upon the Trinity, and quoting the very next verse to the seventh, be ignorant of it, if it were then commonly known, or refrain from using it in some part or other of his treatise? You will not object that Augustine might think the word *unum* signified unity of consent, not of essence, 1. because you affirm that he has twice quoted the seventh verse to prove the unity of essence, and, 2. because, to defend his own absurd hypothesis, that *unum* is always meant of essence, he explains away the eighth verse into an allegory.

But

But in truth, Sir, this way of quoting Augustine is a mockery of reason. We ask for a passage, where Augustine has formally appealed to scripture for the three heavenly witnesses. You produce a sentence, in which Augustine says of the Father, Son and Holy Ghost, " these three are one," in his own words, without any reference to scripture, or mark of a quotation. In the mean time you cautiously keep back the argument from Augustine's allegory, and bring scraps of quotations that can only amuse the most ignorant readers. Bengelius is much more consistent. He thinks, that the verse was withdrawn from the public copies by the *Disciplina Arcani.* Allow him his premises; and his conclusions will easily follow; 1. that no argument can be drawn from the silence of the ancient writers; and, 2. that in these short sentences they might covertly allude to the disputed text. I shall only observe, that if we suppose the first Christians to have treated the scriptures in this manner, we at once destroy the certainty and authority of our present canon. But whoever supposes, as I think every defender of the text ought

to

to suppose, that it was extant and publickly known from the beginning, cannot, with the smallest appearance of reason, pretend that it ought not to be formally and directly cited in almost every treatise on the Trinity.

Indeed the argument from Augustine's allegory is so plain and strong, that Beza fairly says, *Non legit Augustinus*; Bengelius avoids it by the *Disciplina Arcani*; and Martin himself sinks under the weight of the objection, and *only not* yields the point in his dissertation. In his Examen he makes a faint defence, but when Emlyn replied, he quitted the untenable post. And it is self-evident, that no man who had before him a clear passage for the doctrine of the Trinity, a passage where the three persons are distinctly named, would quote the adjacent sentence, and explain it mystically of the same doctrine, unless he were determined to turn the scripture into needless tautology, and weaken the force of his own reasoning.

But " in Jerome's testament this verse is read without any doubt of its authenticity." Without any doubt of its authenticity! You inform us elsewhere that all the present Latin

tin MSS. are copies of Jerome's version. But many of the oldest of these MSS. totally omit the heavenly witnesses, and many retain them in a suspicious manner. I have said enough upon this subject in my sixth letter, and shall not repeat it here. The question is, which of these copies preserves the genuine reading, and therefore, when you say, that the verse is read in Jerome's testament, you assume the very thing which you ought to prove. But to help out this lame argument you produce two quotations. The first is, *In essence therefore they are one. Itaque substantia unum sunt.* You translate it, THESE [three] ARE ONE. Why add, *these* without warrant from your original? Or why add *three*, though, I own, you distinguish it from the words of your author? Is it necessary to the sense? Or must the words *unum sunt*, whenever and wherever they are applied to the Trinity, be always meant for a direct quotation of 1 John V. 7? You are then blameably negligent in not increasing your orthodox witnesses with Marius Victorinus, whom you might have found quoted by Bengelius in the same paragraph with Marcus Celedensis.

densis. The second testimony of Jerome you produce from his explanation of faith to Cyrillus: *To us there is one Father, one Son—and one Holy Ghost—and these three are one.* But after reading a page, we find, that the quotation of which you here make a present to Jerome, belongs to Marcus Celedensis. Whether it belongs to him, I know not. It is only a conjecture of the learned from an epistle of Jerome's to Marcus Celedensis, in which he uses these words: *De fide, quam dignatus es scribere sancto Cyrillo, dedi conscriptam fidem.* Hence you argue, p. 168, that Jerome approved of Marcus's creed, and wrote another of his own. Let it be supposed, to save trouble, that Marcus is the real author of this creed, and that Jerome intends the same. How could Jerome suspect, that these words were meant for a quotation of scripture, without his friend's dropping the least hint of it? Marcus Celedensis only explains his own doctrine; which he does not profess to do in the words of scripture. Besides your argument takes for granted that Jerome examined all the quotations with scrupulous minuteness; a task to which, I believe,

believe, very few friends or readers submit. But when Jerome came to this paſſage, which bears no mark of a quotation, he muſt have been the prince of conjurers to have divined his correſpondent's intention. In ſhort, Sir, the creed addreſſed to Damaſus is univerſally acknowledged not to be Jerome's, and if it were his, our verſe is not quoted in it. The creed aſcribed to Marcus Celedenſis does not refer to the verſe, and, if it did, would ſignify nothing in the diſpute about Jerome. However you are perfectly conſiſtent in defending a ſpurious reading by ſpurious authorities.

But the weightieſt evidence remains, the Prologue to the Canonical Epiſtles. At the requeſt or command of Pope Damaſus, Jerome reviſed the Latin tranſlation, and corrected it upon the faith of the Greek MSS. Did he therefore replace the three heavenly witneſſes at this reviſion or not? If he did, why did he not then write his preface to inform the world of his recovered reading? But after Damaſus was dead, Euſtochium, it ſeems, a young lady, at once devout, handſome, and learned, requeſts him once more to revise the Catholic Epistles and correct them from the Greek. Jerome undertakes the task, and having completed it, advertises her in this prologue, that other inaccurate translators had omitted the testimony of the three heavenly witnesses, the strongest proof of the Catholic faith. Such a story as this carries its own condemnation upon its forehead. It has therefore been given up by most of the defenders of the verse; by Mill, by Abbe Roger, by Maffei, Vallarsius, Vitali, Twells, Bengelius. But you tell us, with that extent of information for which your work is notorious, that " the most disturbed imagination did not harbour any such chimeras (as that the prologue was not genuine) till the times of Martianay and Simon." You are mistaken, Sir. Sandius * had already declared the prologue to be spurious in the year 1670. We are left also to imagine from the manner in which you couple Martianay and Simon, that they were both stanch opposers of the verse. Whereas Martianay is a stanch defender of it and a furious

* Append. Interpretat. Paradox. p. 383.

antagonist

antagonist of Simon. He endeavours to disable some of Simon's arguments against this very prologue, accuses him almost of forgery in quoting a MS. and of heresy for attacking the genuineness of 1 John V. 7. Nothing, therefore, but the force of truth could make such a critic agree with his adversary in his main proposition. I must add that Kettner, who in his Dissertation * upon 1 John V. 7. and his New Vindication * had contended that the prologue was Jerome's, in a third book called the History of the text in John,* candidly acknowledges it to be spurious.

That this judgment is as true as it was impartial, will appear from many considerations. First a great majority of MSS. omits Jerome's name. You answer, that other prefaces, confessedly Jerome's, want his name in MSS. I desire you to point out a preface to any book of the Old Testament, where half as many MSS omit Jerome's name. Thirty-four of the MSS. that I collated prefix no name; six omitted the prologue; one

---

* I. Lipf. 1696. p. 57--63. II. Delitii 1702. p. 33--37. III. Francf. et Lipf. 1713. p. 134—136. 145. 172.

had loft the leaf; of two I have made no memorandum; in fhort I have only fet down eight which at once retained the prologue and attributed it to Jerome. But Jerome was fo popular, every thing that bore his name was fo eagerly fought, and fo frequently tranfcribed, that if this prologue had been generally known or thought to be his, the correctors at leaft would more generally have reftored his name, and would conftantly have fecured the infertion of the prologue in their books. But by being often abfent, and often anonymous, it betrays marks of a late birth and difhonourable extraction. It is the hard fate of celebrated authors to have a quantity of trafh fathered upon them, fometimes by defign, and fometimes by miftake. Nobody has been more freely treated in this way than Jerome. And if this has fo often happened, fince the invention of printing, how often muft it have happened before that æra?

In fome MSS. the preface is added; yet the heavenly witneffes omitted. But this you and Martin eafily folve by laying the blame upon the negligence of tranfcribers. No, Sir, it was not the negligence of the tranfcribers, transcribers, but the negligence or forgetfulness of the collators, that was the cause of this disagreement. The prologue was transcribed from a younger MS. the text of the Epistles from an older; written either before the Prologue was composed, or at least before it forced itself into a general notice.

Some of the MSS. call the Epistles *Canonical* in the title, and all in the Prologue, whereas Jerome would have called them *Catholic*. Here you tell us that Jerome has called them *Canonical* in other parts of his works, and send us for satisfaction to his catalogue of ecclesiastical writers. You ought to be told, Sir, that when correct editions are published on the faith of MSS. no critic is allowed to argue from the old and corrupt readings. The editions published by Martianay at Paris, and Vallarsius at Verona, both read *Catholicæ* in the three places of the catalogue, and produce no various reading from their MSS. I have collated ten MSS. one in the Bodleian and nine in the Museum. Two of the thirteenth and one of the fifteenth century have *canonicæ* without variation; a fourth of the fifteenth century has *canonicæ* once in the text, but *catholicæ* for a various reading between the lines from the same hand, and *catholicæ* in the text twice without any fufpicion. The remaining fix MSS. two of which are very ancient, (one at leaft a thoufand years old, MS. Cotton. Calig. A. 15.) conftantly read *catholicæ*, which I fhall therefore conclude to be the true reading. Auguftine, you add, calls the Epiftles canonical. His partiality to the Latin ufage touches not Jerome, who prided himfelf too much upon his Greek to fuffer fuch an innovation. Auguftine quotes " the Apoftle Jude in his canonical epiftle." How would you have exulted, if you had known that Jerome himfelf in his commentary on Ifaiah LXV T. III. p. 484. calls the fecond epiftle of Peter *canonical*. And to crown the whole, all the MSS. as Martianay teftifies, and two in the Bodleïan, as I teftify, concur in this reading. Martianay is afraid that this uniform confent of the MSS. fomewhat weakens the foregoing argument. But he might have been of good cheer; for there is no refemblance between the two cafes. The name *canonical* applied to feven Epiftles, four of of which were less generally received for canonical than most of St. Paul's, is the perfection of absurdity. But it is applied with propriety to a single epistle of the seven, whether doubted, or undoubted. For instance, Jerome quoting the second epistle of Peter, which many churches rejected, by this epithet fixes upon it the seal of his own opinion and authority. For the same reason Augustine calls the epistle of Jude *canonical*; as if he had said; I know that this epistle is rejected by some, but in my opinion it is the genuine composition of the Apostle. If on the other hand a writer rejecting the second epistle of Peter, the second and third of John, &c. had occasion to quote any of the other three, he might justly say, " St. Peter writes in his canonical epistle," thus distinguishing the true from the counterfeit money. This, if I mistake not, was the true reason why the Catholic epistles by degrees gained the title of *canonical*. For when the later writers saw their predecessors separately call the Epistles *canonical*, they with great judgment, gave them the same epithet in the lump. Our argument, Sir, is, not that

that Jerome never calls a single epistle *canonical*, for that he might have done by any of St. Paul's, if it had pleased him, but that he calls the whole seven *Catholic* in his genuine works, while the Prologue calls them *canonical*.

The fame of Jerome was so far extended, and his authority so great, that if a Prologue of his composition, containing such important information, had been constantly known and read from the beginning of the fifth century, it must have been quoted by some of the intermediate writers between the fifth and the ninth, a space of time in which Jerome's version triumphed over all preceding translations. If this Prologue had been universally acknowledged for Jerome's, how could Bede overlook it? Bede's silence both with respect to the disputed verse and the Prologue is a complete proof that he knew nothing of the Prologue, and a probable argument that it was not even extant in his life. The only appeals to it are made by Walafrid Strabus in the ninth, and the Sorbonne Correctorium in the tenth, century. This last author seems to have been over-
burthened

burthened with judgment, for he says, "Here some of the Greek MSS. are corrupted, as St. Jerome observes." We may therefore suppose, that the Prologue was written in some part of the time between Bede's death and the ninth century.

But if there were no other objection to this Prologue, the style alone would determine it not to be Jerome's. Whatever be his subject, his language is always spirited and perspicuous; while the Prologue is written in a barbarous and uncouth jargon. To make it the more barbarous, you have followed those editions (Append. p. 6, 13.) which read, *quod sunt* for *ut sint*, and *translatoribus ponentes*. But I shall pass by these expressions, though, if they were genuine, they would clear Jerome from all suspicion.

Next, let us consider the reasoning and connection. "*As* we formerly corrected the Evangelists to the line of truth, *so* we have by God's assistance restored these [epistles] to their proper order." The real Jerome could never have indulged himself in so silly a parallel, when he might have said, and ought to have said, *ita et has,*

Deo

Deo juvante, Græcæ fidei reddidimus. This would have been a proper subject for his joy and piety, instead of childishly commending himself for such a trifle as restoring the order of the epistles. It is also observable, that though the main drift of the author was to give currency to his favourite verse of the three heavenly witnesses, he is afraid to affirm directly that it was in the Greek MSS. and only insinuates that falsehood in cautious and perplexed language: " Which epistles, if they were faithfully *so* " turned into Latin, *as* they are arranged by " them" (the Apostles, I suppose) " neither " would create doubts in the readers, nor " would the varieties of readings impugn " one another; especially in that place of " John where we read of the unity of the " Trinity; in which we find the unfaithful " translators to have erred much from the " true faith; putting only three names,— " and omitting the witness of the Father, " the Word and the Spirit, by which the " catholic faith is chiefly strengthened, and " the one deity of the Father, Son, and Holy " Ghost proved." First, here is another ridiculous

ridiculous oppofition of *fo* and *as*. "If the tranflators had been *as* diligent in tranflating the epiftles *as* the apoftles (or the Greeks, for *ab iis* may be referred to them) have been in arranging the fame epiftles." Nor do I believe that Jerome would have ufed fuch language as this, *Neque fermonum fefe varietates impugnarent*. Befides, the author does not pofitively affirm that he has reftored the verfe upon the authority of Greek MSS. but in order to poffefs the reader with that belief, envelopes his meaning in a cloud of words. This objection will not feem of little weight to thofe who know that many perfons will infinuate a falfhood, which they dare not affert in explicit terms. If Jerome himfelf had told us fuch a piece of news as is hinted in the Prologue, he would have fpoken out and told it plainly, whether it were true or falfe. If it were true, an affected obfcurity would be as needlefs, as it was contrary to his manner. If it were falfe, he would have affirmed it no lefs boldly and called God to witnefs no lefs folemnly, than when he attefted the miracle of his being whipped by angels for reading prophane authors;

thors; or when he wrote the lives of Paul * and Hilarion, which you have so well defended,

But

* Mr. Travis says that Jerome wrote these lives, "not as positive facts, but to teach some moral or spiritual duty, and to inculcate what is useful and good." And he compares them to Pilpay and Æsop's Fables, to Homer's two poems, and to Jotham's parable. I shall therefore give the outlines of Jerome's life of Paul, that the unlearned reader may be better able to calculate the quantity of *good and useful* instruction contained in it.

" Antony thought himself the most perfect monk in
" the world, till he was told in a vision, that there was
" one much more perfect than he, and that he must set
" out on a visit to the prince of anchorets. Antony
" departed on this errand, and in his journey through the
" desert saw a centaur. Jerome modestly doubts whe-
" ther it was the natural produce of the soil, fruitful in
" monsters, or whether the devil assumed this shape to
" fright the holy man. Some time after he saw a Satyr,
" with an horned forehead and goats feet, who presented
" him with some dates as hostages of peace, and confessed
" that he was one of the false deities, whom the deluded
" Gentiles worshipped. At last Antony, quite weary
" and exhausted, found Paul, and, while they were dis-
" coursing together, who should appear on a sudden, but
" a raven with a loaf, which he laid down in their sight.
" Every day, said Paul to Antony, I receive half a loaf,
" but

But if Jerome had told us, that his Greek MSS. contained the three heavenly witnesses, he would have told a notorious falshood.

"but on your arrival Christ has given his soldiers double provision. He also told Antony, that he himself should shortly die; he therefore desired to be buried in the same cloak that Antony received from Athanasius. Antony set out full speed to fetch the cloak, but Paul was dead before his return. Here was a fresh distress; Antony could find no spade or pickax to dig a grave. But while he was in this perplexity, two lions approached with so piteous a roaring, that he perceived they were lamenting the deceased after their unpolished fashion. They then began to scratch the earth with their feet, till they had hollowed a place big enough to contain a single body. After Antony had buried his friend's carcase in this hole, the two lions came to him, and by their signs and fawning asked his blessing, which he kindly gave them, and they departed in very good humour."

Something of the same nature happened to St. Daphnis, as we learn from those Ecclesiastical Historians who *inculcate what is useful and good.* Theocritus, I. 71. Τῆνον χ'ὡκ δρύμοιο ΛΕΩΝ ΕΚΛΑΥΣΕ θανόνϊα, and Virgil, V. 27.

Daphni, tuum Pœnos etiam INGEMUISSE LEONES
Interitum montesque feros silvasque loquuntur.

All the inference that I wish to draw from this long note, is that Mr. Travis has not read Jerome's lives of the Saints which he has so manfully defended.

That

That all the Greeks before his time and all for many ages after it, should know nothing of this text, or entirely neglect it; that all the *visible* Greek MSS. which have survived to the present day, should omit it; and yet that Jerome found a cluster of Greek MSS. all of which retained it, this, according to the common course of things, is incredible and impossible. What a strange revolution, as Erasmus justly observes, that in Jerome's time the Latin copies should be defective and the Greek perfect, when at present the Latin have repaired their loss, and the Greek are become defective. You object, that the expression *infideles translatores* does not mean the generality of translators. When an expression of this kind is used without limitation, an author who wishes to be understood, as the real Jerome would wish, must be understood to mean it generally. If only a few translators were guilty, why does he not restrain his meaning by such words, as *paucis, quibusdam*, &c.? I agree with you, that *infideles* signifies no more than *inaccurate*. But if Jerome had attributed such an omission to the interpreters, he would not have dismissed

fed them with so gentle a reprimand. The softest names that he could find for them, would then be, *mid-day devils, mad dogs, blasphemous heretics, two-footed asses*, &c. If he thought it merely an error, I have so good an opinion of his critical abilities, as to believe that he would have accused the *unskilful scribes*, and not the *unfaithful translators*. And if only a few of the Latin copies were faulty, it was idle to single out this place as a specimen of the superior correctness of his own edition. In fact it is apparent that, whenever this Prologue was written, most of the Latin copies wanted 1 John V. 7. and that it was written for the express purpose of providing a remedy for this defect. I shall here take notice of a circumstance which I forgot to mention in its place. The Greek-English editor of the N. T. in 1729 appealed to an ancient Correctorium, which asserts, that this verse was wanting in the old Latin MSS. Upon which Twells says, " We call upon him to shew where," &c. intimating that the editor was a liar. However it happens that such a Correctorium did exist, and was collated by Lucas Brugensis.

genfis. He call its author Epanorthotes, and highly extols his diligence and fidelity. And his note upon 1 John V. 7. is no bad example of thofe qualities. *Epanorthotes deeffe hæc eadem Græcis libris et antiquis Latinis notat.* Who can deny that by the indefinite phrafe, *Græcis libris*, muft be meant *all the Greek MSS?* Since therefore in the time of Epanorthotes, all the Greek and the older Latin MSS. omitted the three heavenly witneffes; fince by confequence his MSS. exactly agreed with thofe which have been afterwards collated by different editors, at different times and places, this coincidence not only proves his good faith and accuracy, but the fuperior excellence of his Latin MSS. You tell us, and with great truth, I believe, that all Jerome's MSS. are loft. But how happens it, that they differed fo widely from all others? Jerome's good fortune in getting a band of thefe MSS. into his poffeffion, is exactly parallel with Stephens's in finding a large number of the fame fort. What pity that all the orthodox MSS. after being once collated, fhould immediately withdraw themfelves, and neither liften to the invitation of

their

their friends nor the challenge of their enemies!

Again, if Jerome had written this prologue, the chief aim of which is to bring into common use this *strongest proof of the Trinity*, would he never have thought of introducing it in his other works? He is very proud, in one of his epistles, of having restored *serving the Lord*, Rom. XII. 11. instead of *serving the time*. What a trifling occasion to praise himself was this compared to the other? Would he not have been in haste to tell Augustine of this grand discovery? Augustine, who looked with an evil eye upon Jerome's new edition, could not fail of being fully reconciled to it, when he had learned what an accession of strength it brought to the catholic faith. Augustine and Jerome corresponded upon biblical subjects infinitely less important. You are not insensible of the force of this argument, as appears from the miserable shifts to which you are reduced in attempting to elude it. First " he has inserted the heavenly witnesses in his version," the very point in debate. Secondly, " he has quoted them in two creeds," neither of which is written by Jerome, neither of which can be proved to quote the heavenly witnesses. But to let you into a secret, none of the prologues to the separate parts of the N. T. are Jerome's. They are all rhapsodies without method or meaning: without Jerome's learning, style or spirit; written long after his time, sometimes adorned with extracts from his catalogue or epistles. Bengelius quotes a prologue to the Acts, which is manifestly spurious, and seems, as he observes, to be the handy work of the same author, who favoured us with the prologue to the Catholic Epistles. He has inscribed it to two other friends of Jerome, to Domnion and Rogatianus. For all these reasons, I agree with Bengelius that this prologue is a forgery, but I cannot think with him that the author of it was acquainted with Greek MSS. Indeed he seems to distrust his own opinion, for he adds, at the end of the paragraph, *Qui firmos testes ex Græca antiquitate producet, gratiam ab ecclesia inibit.*

The good *Eucherius* is your next witness, in whose *Formulæ Spiritalis Intelligentiæ* Martin (Dissert.

(Differt. p. 78.) found the disputed verse and brought it forward with great parade. However, as we ought to restore every man his own, it is necessary to observe that Mill had already produced the passage, Proleg. 938. You too, Sir, in imitation of Martin, are here extremely alert. You say that Emlyn ingenuously confesses his embarrassment. Whether you have acted *ingenuously* let the public judge. Could a reader, who reads your quotation from Emlyn, guess that he spends two pages to shew that the passage is interpolated? It would truly have been, as you call it p. 40, 81, *a poor refuge to affect a doubt*, without giving any reasons. Emlyn's reasons are, 1. That Eucherius in his *Quæstiones V. et N. T.* explains the water, the blood and the spirit of the Father, Son and Holy Ghost. That in his *Formulæ* therefore he seems only to have quoted the eighth verse, because it is not likely that Eucherius or any body else, seeing the doctrine of the Trinity clearly revealed in the seventh verse, should extract it from the eighth by an unnatural interpretation. 2. That transcribers and editors often correct the citations of their authors to the current reading of their own time; particularly that the editor of Eucherius, J. Braſſicanus confeſſes that he took great pains in correcting the faults, and that " he *added* what was " wanting." It is therefore probable that this paſſage is one of thoſe additions, which, 3. is the more probable, becauſe the deſign of Eucherius, as the very title of his work imports, was to give hidden and myſtical ſenſes of ſcripture. The eighth verſe was ſufficient for this purpoſe; the ſeventh would have been ſuperfluous.

Eucherius in his *Queſtions*, after ſaying that in 1 John V. 8. there ſeems to be a reference to the Goſpel XIX. 30. thus proceeds: " *Some* therefore think that by the water " is meant baptiſm; by the blood, martyr-" dom; by the ſpirit, the perſon himſelf " who paſſes through martyrdom to the " Lord. Yet the *majority* here underſtands " the Trinity itſelf by a myſtical interpre-" tation, becauſe it bears witneſs to Chriſt; " by the water indicating the Father, for he " ſays of himſelf, Jer. II. 13. *They have* " *left me the fountain of living water*; by the
" blood

" blood demonstrating Christ, and referring
" to his passion; by the Spirit manifesting
" the Holy Ghost. Now these three thus
" bear witness of Christ. He himself says
" in the Gospel, VIII. 18. *I bear witness*
" *of myself, and the Father who sent me bears*
" *witness of me.* And again, XV. 26.
" *When the Comforter is come—he shall bear*
" *witness of me.* The Father therefore bears
" witness when he says, Matth. XVII. 5.
" *This is my beloved Son.* The Son, when
" he says, John X. 30. *I and my Father are*
" *one.* The holy Spirit; when it is said of
" him, Matth. III. 16. *And he saw the*
" *holy Spirit descending,* &c."

1. From this laboured illustration, and the pains taken to fortify it, Eucherius plainly shews, that he himself is one of the many *(plures)* who embraced the mystical interpretation. Martin (who does not easily miss any error that lies in his way) insists that *plures* means no more than *some* or *several* *(plusieurs.)* I wonder not that Emlyn was sick of disputing with so wretched a sophist. If *plures* might elsewhere admit of either sense, here it can only mean a *majority*, be-

cause it is opposed to *quidam*, and *tamen* added.

2. Lardner* rightly infers, that the author who wrote this passage, could not know any thing of the heavenly witnesses. He therefore corrects the text of Eucherius in this manner: " I. Hic numerus ad unitatem deitatis refertur, &c. II. ad duo testamenta divinæ legis referuntur, &c. III. ad Trinitatem in Joannis epistola, *Tres sunt qui testimonium dant, aqua, sanguis et spiritus.* " No. 1 is referred to the unity of God, No. 2 to the two testaments, No. 3 to the Trinity, in the epistle of John, *There are three that bear record, the water, the blood and the spirit.* I shall observe, by the way, that Martin took the sentence out of its connection, discarded the numeral, supplied *legimus* instead of *referuntur*, and so translated (in which you have followed him) *As to the Trinity, we read*, &c. When Emlyn objected, that Eucherius might only quote the eighth verse as referring to the Trinity, Martin had the assurance

* Credibility, Part II. Ch. 137. Vol. XI. p. 170—174. or Vol. V. p. 226—229.

(Exam.

(Exam. c. 8.) to maintain that the word *Trinitas* does not here signify the Trinity in a theological sense, but simply *the number three*. So that, according to him, the passage furnishes this rare sense, " *As to the number three*, we read in St. John's Epistle, *There are three*, &c.!" But he would have asserted any thing, rather than relinquish an argument or authority that he once had espoused.

3. Whoever compares the *Formulæ* with the *Questions*, will find that Lardner's emendation or something like it, must be the true reading. And I do reassert, that no writer in his perfect mind could possibly adopt this allegorical exposition of the eighth verse, if the seventh were extant in his copy. Even a madman would have method in his madness. *For sense to extasy was ne'er so thrall'd, But it reserv'd some quantity of choice, To serve in such a difference.* I appeal to any orthodox reader, whether he would force an indirect confession of his favourite doctrine, from one text by torture, when he might have a clear, full and voluntary evidence from its next neighbour. The supposition is still more ridiculous

ridiculous that Eucherius should make this quotation for no possible use.

Bengelius, though he had endeavoured to work himself up to a belief (in which however he soon faulters) that Augustine's exposition of the eighth verse was consistent with his knowledge of the seventh, Bengelius, I say, clearly saw, that if Eucherius wrote the allegory in the *Questions*, he could not possibly have the heavenly witnesses in his copy. He therefore devised an ingenious expedient to avoid the attacks of the enemy. He supposed that the author of the *Formulæ* is a different person from the author of the *Questions*. But this expedient Lardner and Mr. Griesbach spoil by telling us from Gennadius, that Eucherius dedicated his *Questions* and some of his other works to his two sons. And to heighten the distress of the scene, these *Questions* and *Formulæ* are in fact respectively dedicated to these two sons, Salonius and Veranius.

Mr. Griesbach adds, that Eucherius's first question is, " From what texts the Trinity is proved?" He answers, " From the beginning of Genesis, *Let us make man*, &c.

from

from Psalm XXXVI. 2. *By the word of the Lord*, &c. from Matth. XXVIII. 19. (the form of baptism); and from Rom. XI. 36. *From him and by him*," &c. But not a word of the disputed verse, which would been an excellent corollary, and would have presented us (as Kettner finely expresses it) with *St. John's divinity in a nut-shell*. Surely if Eucherius knew of this verse, and yet with such fair, such provoking opportunities to quote it, was still obstinately silent, he could not be a sincere Trinitarian, but either betrayed the sacred deposit which the church had entrusted in his hands, or instead of being properly and rationally orthodox, he only blundered round about orthodoxy.

Mr. Griesbach also observes, that Flacius has only inserted the earthly witnesses in his edition of the *Formulæ*. You mention this objection, p. 299. but *prudently* avoid answering it. So considerable an omission could neither be overlooked by Flacius nor his printers. He either published his edition from a MS. or another edition. Here then is reading against reading, which shall we prefer? By all the rules of criticism, the reading

ing which makes an author confiftent with himfelf. If we follow Flacius, we agree with Eucherius's quotation of fcripture in another place unfufpected of corruption or interpolation. But if we follow Brafficanus, we make Eucherius quote a text for which he had no occafion; a text which he has not quoted where it was neceffary, or at leaft where it would have been fignally ufeful; a text, which, if Eucherius could be fuppofed to know of it, would determine him to be the dulleft of mortals, and paffionately fond of nonfenfe and tautology.

Let us however review the words of Eucherius. *Tres funt qui teftimonium dant in cælo, Pater, Verbum et Spiritus Sanctus, et tres funt qui teftimonium dant in terra, fpiritus, aqua et fanguis.* How it ftrengthens the authority of our prefent vulgate that this quotation differs not from it in the fmalleft tittle! In the *Queftions* there are fome odd various readings. The eighth verfe, as there quoted, differs from the *Formulæ* four times. 1. In turning the mafculines into neuters. 2. In fubftituting *perhibent* for *dant*. 3. In omitting *in terra*. 4. In altering the order of the witneffes.

witnesses. But what is more extraordinary is, that Flacius's edition of the *Formulæ* reads as all the editions of the *Questions* read, and contains neither less nor more than these words: *Tria sunt quæ testimonium perhibent, aqua, sanguis et spiritus.* That this reading is genuine, is plain upon inspection, because, 1. It is the shorter. 2. It is the less orthodox.* 3. It differs greatly from the common editions of the Latin version. 4. It exactly agrees with Eucherius's citation of the same verse in another part of his works. 5. It transposes the witnesses so, that in the allegorical interpretation they may severally correspond with the persons of the Trinity which they typify.

If any pains-taking critic wades through these letters, as I shall be always ready to testify my admiration of his patience, so I think he cannot refuse to pay me the same compliment, when he sees me thus laboriously answering objections, which (as you

---

* By the orthodox I mean that opinion which, whether true or false, prevails in the time and country of the transcribers or editors.

falsely

falsely say of Mr. Griesbach's p. 300) *are brought forward without even the decency of an attempt to support them.* But to close the account of Eucherius. The true reading, which Lardner almost found out by conjecture, is that which I have quoted from Flacius. If it will not satisfy you, it will at least satisfy every body else, to know that there are two early editions of Eucherius, one printed at Basil, 1530, the other at Paris without any date of the year. These editions so often differ in their readings, that they were certainly derived from separate MSS. But though they vary so much in other places, they here lovingly concur in the shorter reading above mentioned. So far therefore (to use Mr. Griesbach's words) was Eucherius from quoting 1 John V. 7. that it is on the contrary most clear and evident that this verse never was in his copy.

We have now run over all the Latins down to the middle of the fifth century, without finding any express quotation of this unfortunate verse, nor even any appearance of it, except in Cyprian. But before we come to the end of the same century,
such

such a proof is produced, as must for ever strike the heretics mute. For the four hundred Catholic Bishops that Hunneric summoned to Carthage, to hear what they had to say in defence of the homoüsian doctrine, quote the three heavenly witnesses, as a proof of the Trinity *clearer than day*, and this without expressing any doubt on their own side, or meeting with any opposition from their adversaries. Martin seems to think that every one of these four hundred bishops had a bible in his pocket, and the useful places doubled down! I would gladly know by what miracle four hundred copies of St. John's epistle unanimously consented in a reading, that an hundred years before, according to the complaint which you suppose Jerome to make, was omitted by the *unfaithful translators?* How Eucherius, as I have just now proved, was ignorant of it fifty years before? How Facundus was equally ignorant of it fifty years after? This verse has been gaining ground in the Latin copies from the sixth century to the eleventh; yet, I dare say, if we should now collect four hundred Latin MSS. at a venture, we should find

find several of them omitting the heavenly witnesses; perhaps a majority of those that are not later than the tenth century. Or were these holy fathers such acute and inquisitive critics, that they would cite nothing from Scripture which was not in all the MSS? If any passage that suited their purpose occurred in some particular copies, would they not defend it for genuine, though the weight of external evidence was in the opposite scale? But not to multiply such queries, we know, if we know any thing, that an implicit faith of this kind has been the occasion of innumerable mistakes. Does not Ambrose defend a reading against the heretics, merely because it is orthodox, for he owns that it is wanting in a vast majority of the copies? In the same manner, if the Catholic bishops found in ever so few of their MSS. a text like 1 John V. 7. *clearer than the day* for their doctrine, they would doubtless presume it to be genuine. It would be in vain to urge them with the great balance of contrary testimonies. *Nihil est audacius illis Deprensis: iram atque animos a crimine sumunt.* They would argue, (falsely and absurdly furdly indeed, but still they would argue) " 1. That omissions of the verse were neither positive contradictions nor direct impeachments; only food for conjecture, and conjecture has no weight against positive facts p. 346.—2. That the omission might easily happen here, by reason of the similar beginning and ending of the two verses. 3. That the scope and connection of the Apostle's reasoning required this insertion. 4. That the Arians erased it; and that the Arians played such pranks is clear from more than one positive declaration of Ambrose." I allow that all these reasons are false and frivolous; it is enough for me, that they have frequently been employed in defence of this very passage. The unanimous testimony therefore of the four hundred bishops will by no means prove that the verse was then in all the copies, since, if it were in a very few of them, an eager disputant would seize it, and maintain it against all objections, by such arguments as I have stated above. *Qui amant, ipsi sibi somnia fingunt.* How many divines at this day quote 1 John V. 7. not only without hinting any scruple of

their

their own, but without deigning to inform their readers that it has been called in question by others. It would be a labour of Hercules to enumerate all the inferior writers who have acted in this manner, and imposed upon the simplicity of the unlearned. I shall content myself with referring to a few, and they shall be all bishops. WAKE, Exposition of the Catechism, p. 58. SECKER, Lecture XIII. PEARSON on the Creed, Art. VIII. p. 323. BEVERIDGE, Private Thoughts, Part I. p. 27. II. p. 40, 47. HUET, Demonstr. Evang. Prop. IX. Cap. 25, 82. GASTRELL, Christian Institutes, p. 132. ATTERBURY, Vol. I. Serm. X. p. 266. Here are two archbishops and five bishops, who have all applied the very verse in debate to prove the Trinity, without mentioning any argument against it, or producing any in its behalf. Yet none of them could be ignorant of the fierce disputes to which it had given rise. Some of them (Huet and Pearson) were professed critics, and ought not to have quoted it, without shewing their own reasons, or confuting their adversaries. Wake had in his possession five Greek MSS. that omitted

omitted the verse. Pearson had defended the vulgar reading of 1 Tim. III. 16. in the same book, where he has quoted the heavenly witnesses without any comment. An unlearned reader could not help concluding from this circumstance, that by defending one controverted reading, he thereby declared that none of his other quotations had ever been controverted; according to that logical rule, of which you make so judicious an use p. 302. *Exceptio probat regulam in non exceptis.* "But the four hundred bishops dared not to urge in dispute a passage that was extant only in a few copies, when they must be detected and exposed by the Arians." I have partly answered this objection, and I add, that an effectual answer to it may be found in the conduct of the greater part of divines. So many of the defenders of the Trinity have employed this text in controversy, that they appear to have thought it lawful to quote any passage which seemed to them genuine, without paying any attention to the objections of others. Thus Dr. Wallis in his first letter on the Trinity quotes our verse as a clear and decisive argument. It was not till his adverſary had diſputed its authenticity, that he condeſcended to give his reaſons (ſuch as they are) in its defence. Thus Dr. Wells in his anſwer to Dr. Clarke adopted the verſe without mentioning a ſyllable of its doubtful character. Dr. Clarke replied that the verſe was ſpurious. Dr. Wells rejoined, that in his judgment Grabe had ſufficiently proved it to be genuine in his notes on Bull's Nicene Faith. Very lately, a Mr. Barnard has written ſome letters to Dr. Prieſtly, in which he four times quotes this verſe, as one of his principal arguments, though he ought to have known that Dr. Prieſtly had publickly rejected it, long before the publication of Mr. Barnard's anſwer. A friend of yours, the author of a *Vindication of the Doctrines and Liturgy of the Church of England*, p. 32, 24. quotes Acts XX. 28. 1 Tim. III. 16. without hinting that the MSS. vary, or that the common reading has ever been diſputed. In the former quotation he prints the words, *his own blood,* in Italics. And if the author of the *Hints to the new Aſſociation*, whom this author confutes, had not expreſsly ſingled out 1 John V. 7. and declared it ſpurious,

he

he would have quoted that too with the same modesty, for it appears among his scriptural proofs of the Pseudo-Athanasian Verity, p. 26. In short, it is idle, fraudulent, contrary to reason and to fact, to argue, that, because a passage is quoted in controversy, it is therefore genuine and extant in all the copies.

If the person deputed by the Catholics to draw up their common confession of faith, had found this passage in a single MS. or even quoted by any other writer, and upon the strength of such authority admitted it into his collection of scriptural proofs, what would have been the event? They would not have staid to form their judgment of the author from his composition, but have adjusted their opinion of the composition to their previous esteem for the author. If, for instance, the *venerable* Eugenius was the composer, not a bishop present but would have subscribed heart and hand to any thing that came from his pen. Like the organist of Utrecht, * who signed the articles of the Contraremonstrants, without reading them,

Jortin's Six Dissertations, II. p. 106.

and being pressed to read them at least once, answered, *It is needless. I know well enough that you, Gentlemen, would not require me to do an ill thing.* I am sure, that if every individual bishop of the four hundred, after a diligent perusal of this confession, could subscribe sincerely to every part of it, that is to say, if he believed all the quotations apt, and all the reasonings just, it would be an imperceptible extension of his faith, to believe one of the quotations genuine, though he had never heard of it before. And if some member of the assembly for a moment had given way to any untoward suspicions, he would quickly repress them with Benedick's argument*. *I should think this a gull, but that the white-bearded fellow speaks it ; knavery cannot surely hide itself in such reverence.*

In the fourth century the controversies about the Trinity were very warmly debated, and the orthodox hastily caught at every thing that they apprehended favourable to their cause, and oftentimes made use of such texts to prove their doctrine by, as were by no means proper for their purpose.

* *Much Ado about Nothing.*

purpose. A man must be a great stranger to their writings, who has ot observed this. Their zeal for a fundamental doctrine frequently hurried them on so fast, that they did not duly weigh and consider their arguments.

Thus Dr. Bennet*. To the same purpose Dr. Horsley †. *In popular discourses and in argument* (the Fathers) *were too apt to sacrifice somewhat of the accuracy of fact to the plausibility of their rhetoric; or, which is much the same thing, they were too ready to adopt any notion, which might serve a present purpose, without nicely examining its solidity or its remote consequences.* From this frank confession of two able defenders of orthodoxy, I infer, that the orthodox Christians of the fifth century (for I suppose an hundred years had made no great improvement or alteration) would have seized any argument that might serve their purpose, and that the compiler of their creed would admit any supposed scriptural quotation, without examining the authorities on which it is founded. It is amusing to consider the dif-

---

* On the Common Prayer, Appendix, No. III. p. 288.
† Tracts, p. 355.

ferent confequences of the fame action. In defence of orthodoxy it is lawful to fet afide the teftimony of the fathers. But let any doubts be hinted, in fuch a cafe as the prefent, concerning their good faith or exactnefs, heretic and infidel are names too foft for the offender.

At vos Trojugenæ vobis ignofcitis, et quæ
Turpia cerdoni, Volefos Brutumque decebunt.

Were the Arians, upon reading this confeffion of the orthodox, fo utterly bereft of all reflection, as to give up their caufe in defpair? They muft have been aware of feveral of the texts which their adverfaries would produce. If this verfe was then received for genuine, they would be aware of that too, and provide fome anfwer, fufficient or infufficient. Would they be more diftreffed with it, than with John X. 30. *I and my Father are one?* Some of the modern divines declare that this verfe does not relate to the confubftantiality of the perfons. You yourfelf have not dared to affirm that it does. Had then none of the four hundred bifhops any objections to the ufe of fuch an argument?

ment? On the other hand, was there no Arian that so far retained his senses as to combat the Catholic interpretation? The utmost inference that can be drawn from this confession is, that the three heavenly witnesses were in the copies of the authors, or in Eugenius's copy, if he were the author. Nobody denies that they might possibly creep into some copies of that time, particularly in Africa, where Cyprian and Augustine were constantly read. But to suppose that they were in all the copies that all these bishops had seen or possessed, because they are in their confession of faith, is to assume two things equally inconsistent with reason and experience, that the MSS. of the N. T. never varied in that age, and that no disputants of any age quote any passages except such as are extant in all the copies, and acknowledged by all parties.

" But Cyrila and his confederate Arians made no objection to this verse." I cannot find that they made any objection to any other quotation or argument of the Catholics. I desire to know, whether this treatise was so vigorous a defence of orthodoxy, that none of the heretics could say a word in answer to it. If they made any answer, Victor has given us a partial and fraudulent account of the transaction. If they disputed at all, they might then object to the genuineness of the new-quoted verse, as well as to any other part of the confession. If the dispute never took place, the Catholics were in no danger of detection, and might safely quote what they liked for scripture.

If such a confession had been really presented and read; if Cyrila and his accomplices had proposed their objections in detail; if amongst these objections there had been a particular answer to this capital text, endeavouring to divert its force, and explain it away, but no suggestions tending to undermine its authenticity; if the Catholics had then resumed the dispute, reinforced their arguments with fresh aid, and at last set their own cause in so fair and strong a light, that none but the ignorant or obstinate could withstand its evidence; the catastrophe of the drama would have been natural enough, nor would it surprise us to find that Cyrila attempted to convert by force those whom he
could

could not subdue by argument. But Victor's narration, which leaves us to suppose that nothing at all was said by the heretics, carries in itself the plainest marks of fiction.

"When the day appointed for disputation came, the Catholics chose ten of their number to answer for all. Cyrila was seated on a superb throne. To this elevation the Catholics objected, and asked, Who should be the umpire and examiner? The king's notary answered, the Patriarch Cyrila. Let us know, said they, by what authority Cyrila takes that name. Whereupon the adversaries, raising a tumult, began to calumniate. And because the orthodox desired that, if an examination was not allowed, the prudent multitude at least might wait, all the sons of the Catholic church who were present are ordered to be beaten with an hundred cudgels. Eugenius exclaims against this treatment, and appeals to heaven. Then the orthodox turned to Cyrila, and said, Propose your sentiments. Cyrila said, I know no Latin. The Catholic bishops answered, We know that you have always spoken Latin; you ought not to refuse now; especially as you have kindled this flame.

flame. But he seeing that they were better prepared for the conflict, declined an audience with various pretences. Which they foreseeing, had written a decent and sufficient confession of their faith." [Here follows the confession.] " When this our book was read, they could not bear the light of truth with their blind eyes, taking it very ill that we called ourselves Catholics. And immediately they told lies to the king, that we had raised a tumult and avoided the conference." Then follows an edict of Hunneric against the Homoüsians, which charges them with endeavouring to delay the conference, to excite the people to sedition, and to disturb every thing with their clamours, that the dispute might not take place.

I appeal to the reader, whether this story be not improbable in all its circumstances. First, when the Catholics find fault with Cyrila for exalting himself to a kind of throne, he orders them to be beaten with an hundred cudgels. But upon Eugenius's uttering a short ejaculation, we hear no more of the cudgelling, and the dispute is resumed. They desire Cyrila to begin. He excuses himself,

by

by pleading ignorance of Latin. They give him the lie, and tell him they can prove that he has always fpoken Latin. This might feem a fufficient provocation to Cyrila's fiery temper to repeat his orders about the cudgelling. But he only feeks for cavils and pretences to decline the conflict. How he muft have ftared, when they pulled out a confeffion of faith, which, with proper management, would laft a modern divine three Sundays! For I prefume he would have taken fome meafures to hinder it from being read, if he had not been ftupified by aftonifhment. The Catholics read their confeffion audibly and diftinctly; when it is finifhed, the heretics have not one word to fay for themfelves, good or bad; they therefore diffolve the affembly, and by telling lies to the king perfuade him to perfecute the orthodox.

As far as I can judge by comparing Victor's narrative with Hunneric's edict, the account given in the edict is partly true. The Catholics were willing to put off the conference and prolong their ftay, in order to make converts from the Arian doctrine. This Hunneric confidered as a violation of the terms

upon

upon which he had granted them a safe conduct. In consequence of this charge, the Catholics were imprisoned, banished, doomed to hard labour, tortured, and executed. I make no objection to these wholesome severities on the score of cruelty. For if heretics had been thus served, and Hunneric's faith were pure, the regimen would have been exceedingly mild and proper. But being an heretic himself, I cannot help thinking that he carried matters a little too far. However, it appears, from Victor's own story, from the accusations of delay and tumult which each party brought against the other, that they never came to a formal conference, and that such a confession was neither read nor presented.

Again, if the confession had been presented to Cyrila, and attentively read by him, are you sure that it then contained this quotation? Does an author, when he republishes a work, never *Blot out*, *correct*, *insert*, *refine*, *Enlarge*, *diminish*, *interline*? Are the speeches published for the genuine speeches of our senators never increased or embellished in passing through the press? Did Cicero give every oration of

his

his to the public exactly as he delivered it at the bar or in the senate? When I can bring myself to believe that Thucydides and Livy copied the exact words of their heroes, then will I believe that Victor has given the precise confession of faith that put Cyrila and his impious crew into such confusion. But you say, p. 53, 113. that " Victor's narrative must be circumspect and accurate, because it was written in the face of exasperated enemies, while Arianism sat triumphant on the throne." Victor's history was not written till three years after the persecution. Hunneric was long since dead. His successor was not so violent a persecutor; and, if he was, Victor was now at Constantinople, where he wrote, free from all fears of being either contradicted or persecuted. If no Arian answer to Victor's narrative appeared, which it is impossible to tell, we must consider that in all probability his history was long in travelling to the Arian dioceses. It was written at a great distance from the scene of action, for the edification of the faithful, not for the confutation of heretics. In those days books were less easily procured, and less generally read, than in our time.

time. They were separately transcribed, and diffused with infinite slowness in comparison of the present rapid and extensive circulation.

If I were disposed to make a romance, in imitation of Victor, I should say, that when the Arians came to this text of the three heavenly witnesses quoted in the confession, they demanded in what part of St. John's works they were extant, and, upon detecting the fraud, broke off the conference. That this sacrilege of the Catholics was mentioned as a reason for increasing the severity of their punishment. But you may ask me why I call Victor's history a romance. It deserves that title for the miracles which he has stuffed into it, of which I shall give an abridgement. " The Arians tormented some Catholics who nevertheless were always recovered by the next day, and no traces of their wounds left. A virgin was fastened to a pile of wood, but on a sudden the wood rotted and fell to pieces. (So the keeper told Victor, and confirmed it with an oath.) Bishop Faustus likewise told Victor that he had seen a blind woman recover her sight. When Arbogastes's forehead was bound with cords, he broke them like cobwebs

webs by looking up to heaven. They then brought ſtronger, which he burſt only by invoking the name of Chriſt. And though he hung upon one foot, with his head downwards, he ſeemed to ſleep on the ſofteſt bed. When his friend Felix buried him in a lonely place, according to his requeſt, upon digging up the earth, he found a ſarcophagus of the fineſt marble, *ſuch as perhaps no king ever had*. Hunneric ſent ſome of the confeſſors to reap in the hot weather, at Utica. One of them excuſed himſelf, becauſe he had a withered hand; but when he came to the place, behold a miracle! his hand was reſtored to its ſtrength, and did him yeoman's ſervice. They who were baniſhed into deſarts full of ſcorpions and venomous animals, which formerly deſtroyed every paſſenger, all eſcaped alive and unhurt. Eugenius reſtored a blind man to ſight. A matron *rightly* called Victoria, after her ſhoulders were diſlocated, and ſhe was thought dead by the tormentors, was ſuddenly healed by a virgin, who ſtood by her and touched her limbs. Antony finding Eugenius in a palſy, forced the ſharpeſt vinegar down his mouth, which increaſed

his

his disease, but Christ restored him to health. Mr. Gibbon has related the miracle of the confessors who spoke after their tongues were cut out, *sermones politos sine ulla offensione locuti.* He is so copious in his relation, and so anxious in amassing authorities for it, that it seems almost to persuade him to be an Homoüsian. I cannot think this such a stupendous miracle as some would represent it. Did not St. Romanus, after his tongue was cut out*, make an elegant oration? A case in point. Besides, this miracle is lame and imperfect; for since their right hands also were cut off, to make the wonder complete, they ought to have used their maimed arm as dextrously as if an hand and fingers still belonged to it, *sermones politos sine ulla offensione scribentes.* I cannot recollect any defender of 1 John V. 7. except Kettner, who urges this miracle in behalf of the text. Even Martin, who defends most things, is half ashamed of it, and contents himself with saying, that Victor's easy belief of miracles is no impeachment of his veracity in quoting scripture. But the two circumstances

---

* PRUDENTIUS, Peristeph. X. 928.

are here very intimately connected. If Victor could relate an improbable miracle for the good of his cause, he might take a scriptural quotation that favoured his own cause, upon testimony which he ought to have rejected, and would have rejected on an indifferent subject. This reflection will be strengthened by considering that the ecclesiastical writers servilely copy their predecessors; a practice which was then more excusable from causes already mentioned. But now that the art of printing has multiplied the means of knowledge, and increased the danger of detection, does nothing of this kind happen? A single example will suffice. Feuardent, in a note upon Irenæus's silly tale about John and Cerinthus, informs us, that as soon as St. John had left the bath, it fell in and crushed Cerinthus to death. For this circumstance he quotes Jerome against the Luciferians. Not a word to this purpose in Jerome. Yet six authors, quoted by Bayle*, assert the same story, and that with as confident an air, as if

* Dictionnaire, au mot CERINTHUS.

they had good authority for the assertion. Though a common book was quoted, a book written in a language familiar to every pretender to learning, none even of those who adopted the story from Feuardent thought it worth while to verify his quotation. But, in truth, it is much easier and pleasanter to go on believing every thing that we hear or read, than to undergo the labour of enquiry or the pain of suspence.

Our next question is, Who was the author of this confession? From Victor's account we might guess it to be the joint manufacture of the four bishops who are said to have presented it. Gennadius gives Eugenius the whole honour of the composition. Some (moderns, I believe) call Victor himself the author. Bengelius ascribes it to Vigilius Tapsensis (i. e. the author of the books *de Trinitate*). My own opinion is, that it was written by that author (whoever he be), and published under the name of Eugenius. This solution comprehends both Gennadius's assertion and Bengelius's conjecture. Victor finding a book upon the subject ready to his hand, with the name of a venerable confessor prefixed,

fixed, would take it for genuine without farther enquiry, and esteem it the principal ornament of his history. But if any person thinks it more probable that Victor himself wrote the creed, to shew that he was no less able a divine than historian, I shall not dispute about so small a matter.

The books *contra Varimadum* and *de Trinitate* have been commonly attributed to Vigilius Tapsensis since Chifflet's edition. But Vigilius, in his disputation against Arius, never refers to the latter. And though he produces a long quotation from his own book against Varimadus, not a syllable of it can now be found in the treatise that bears the false title of Idacius Clarus. Nor is there any appearance that this treatise is mutilated. In short, Vigilius's claims to either of these publications are only supported by some weak and gratuitous conjectures of Chifflet*. This was what I meant, when I gave you leave to make two distinct authorities of these two treatises. But though this gracious permis-

---

* *Vigilii Tapsensis* Vindiciæ, p. 64—68.

fion of mine feems at firft fight to turn againft me, I had, I own, a malicious intention of employing it to my own advantage. Jerome, fay the heretics, would have quoted 1 John V. 7. in fome of his genuine works, if the prologue were his. No, anfwers Martin; for Vigilius, who fo often ufes this verfe in his books *de Trinitate* and *contra Varimadum*, never mentions it in the conference of Athanafius and Arius, nor in his treatife againft Eutyches, *in which it was fcarce to be conceived he could poſſibly have omitted it.* (Examen. ch. 4.) But this objection falls, if we reply that the authors of the *Altercatio*, the treatifes *de Trinitate* and *contra Varimadum*, have nothing in common, but the affumption of a falfe title. I will allow, if you infift upon it, that the difputed verfe had by this time crept into a few copies. Now, as the copies which contain more text, and are more orthodox, generally are preferred to the reft, it was natural that their readings fhould be taken for genuine, and produced againft the heretics. Some of the ancient Greek writers, in explaining the doxology, tack a new claufe to it: *For thine is the kingdom, and the power, and the glory,*

OF

OF THE FATHER, AND THE SON, AND THE HOLY GHOST. This is the reading too of an excellent MS. in the Vatican, Urb. 2. and another at Vienna, Koll. 9. And I hope, at the next revision of our translation, this verse will be corrected *secundum orthodoxam fidem.* For omissions are no argument against positive testimony; and here we have the positive testimony of twice as many Greek MSS. as retain our reading of 1 John III. 16. Let us proceed to the author *de Trinitate.* He five times quotes the verse, if we may trust some of the editions. I say, if we may trust the editions; because the quotation at the end of the first book, and another in the fifth, are neither in the old Paris nor Cologne editions. And whoever will carefully peruse the context, will perceive, that in both places the sense is much better connected, if we adopt the shorter reading, and the parts that were before separated close without leaving a scar. The same hand without doubt interpolated both the passages, as appears from the phrase with which he introduces them. I. *Jam audisti superius Evangelistam Joannem in epistola sua, tam absolute testantem.* V. *Sicut Joannes*

Evangelista in epistola sua tam absolute testatur. In the tenth book too I am almost afraid that some malicious hand has been tampering; for the words of the first book are exactly repeated, *In Christo Jesu unum sunt, non tamen unus est, quia non est eorum una persona.* However, I shall not insist upon this point, but allow both to be genuine, if you desire it. I shall only object, that the author has been inaccurate (to use no harsher word), and by substituting *in Christo Jesu unum sunt* for *tres unum sunt*, has given reasonable cause for suspicion. Perhaps, Sir, you may ask, why I think the passages above-mentioned spurious. First, for the reason already given, that in such passages additions are much more frequent than omissions; secondly, because the following subscription is added at the end of the eighth book in two MSS. one of which I have seen. *I have transcribed these eight books, which contain many things added and altered.* I should think it an affront to my reader's understanding to say another word on the subject.

I did expect that Martin would have applied another quotation from Vigilius to his argu-

argument. *Qui faciendum decernunt* (hominem) TRES SUNT, PATER, ET FILIUS, ET SPIRITUS SANCTUS; SED HI TRES UNUS EST. (Martin tranflates, *thefe three are one*, Exam. c. 4.) I think this would make as good a figure as many of your witneffes. I only mention it to fhew how eafily men writing upon the Trinity may drop expreffions, which a warm imagination might eafily miftake for a reference to the verfe of St. John.

I have already, Letter VI. p. 156. quoted 1 John V. 8, 7. as they are read in the treatife againft Varimadus, I. 5. If a citation fo manifeftly fraudulent can be of any fervice, you are heartily welcome to it. For my own part, I think it argument enough againft a fufpected text, that they who make moft ufe of it cannot agree in the reading. However, being willing to vindicate this author, I muft declare, that I believe this quotation not to have come from his hand. Firft, I obferve that the whole chapter confifts of quotations to prove the unity of the Son with the Father. This is the only quotation that he brings from the epiftle, though he brings eight from the gofpel. And fince the objection, which he professes to answer, was taken from the gospel, he seems to have made a point of conscience not to depart from the gospel in his answer. If it be objected, that he might quote this passage as an argument *a fortiori*, I answer, that he would then probably have used such a preface as he uses in his second chapter, entitled, *De unitate Patris et Filii*. Quoting Eph. IV. 3. he thus introduces it : " Et unitatem Patris et Filii et Spiritus Sancti *demonstrans*."

Secondly, the first chapter of the first book contains the positive proofs of the Trinity in Unity. These proofs are twenty-two in number, among which are Matth. XXVIII. 19. Rom. XI. 35. 2 Cor. XIII. 13. But of the three heavenly witnesses a deep silence. Surely, if he had forgotten them when he wrote his first chapter, and afterwards recollected them in the fifth, he would not have grudged turning back a few pages to insert them in a more proper place.

Thirdly, his last book is a collection of passages from scripture, where the same things are predicated of all the persons of the Trinity. The sixty-fifth chapter is entitled, *De communi*

muni testificatione, which he proves from Psalm XVIII. 8. 1 Tim. VI. 13. Rom. VIII. 16. But how much more pat would this verse have been, if he had known of it? If such a verse existed, he must have known of it, for in this very book he quotes the sixth, the tenth, the twelfth, and twentieth verses of the same fifth chapter.

I therefore make no doubt but that the heavenly and earthly witnesses were inserted in this treatise by that religious soul who forged the decretal epistle of Hyginus*. This forger has taken all the quotations preceding 1 John V. 8, 7. (except one) from our author, preserving the same order. But in return for the loan of so many quotations, he paid him with this text, which shews his scrupulous honesty. The same quotations may also be found in the decretal epistle of Pope John †. But in Pope John the present reading of the eighth and seventh verses is restored. As I shall be glad to make some

---

* HARDUIN. Concil. tom. I. p. 94. This Hyginus seems to have given Mr. *Capell Lofft* (Animadv. on Dr. *Knowles*) much trouble.

† HARDUIN. Concil. tom. II. p. 1154.

amends

amends to my author for having robbed him of so much text, and as nothing is so pleasant to a critic as correcting a classic, I shall add, that instead of *Qui me vidit, vidit et Patrem,* ought to be read, on the authority of Hyginus, *Qui me vidit, vidit et Patrem; et iterum, Qui me odit, odit et Patrem.* The omission was caused by the similar terminations. I suppose I need make no apologies to Pseudo-Hyginus. Whoever would forge a whole treatise, would hardly stick at the addition of a single sentence. Martin, in the simplicity of his heart, quotes Hyginus and John for good authorities. I know, says he, that their epistles are spurious, but they prove what was the reading of their times. I know too that the authority of forgers can never support a doubtful reading, unless it be their interest rather to reject than adopt it. However, I allow that they prove such a reading to have existed in their times, that is, in the eighth century. Nor am I quite sure that the author of Pope John's epistle did not compose the prologue attributed to Jerome. I perceive that you, Sir, have not appealed to these illustrious witnesses, Hyginus and John.

If

If this was the effect of design, I commend your *prudence*.

Of Fulgentius I have already spoken in part. If you object that, though he refers to Cyprian in one place, which may seem to hint that the state of MSS. made such a reference necessary, in another passage he quotes 1 John V. 7. without suspicion, I answer, that this will not prove that Fulgentius had better authority in one instance than in the other. I remember that Mr. Jones, in his *Full Answer to an Essay on Spirit*, Pref. p. xix. quotes 1 John V. 7. without suspicion, and from that and John X. 30. charges the author whom he is answering with blasphemy. Should we not think that for such a purpose none but certain and acknowledged texts would be quoted? Yet the same gentleman, in his *Catholic Doctrine of the Trinity*, ch. III. §. 10. confesses that there has been much dispute concerning this text, and adds his own reasons for believing it genuine. The same answer will serve for the other quotations, if they belong to Fulgentius; if not, the anonymous author would borrow them

from

from Fulgentius, the reigning polemic of the day.

Cassiodorus in the sixth century wrote his *Complexiones*, a sort of abridgement of the Acts, Epistles, and Apocalypse. These *Complexiones* were found by Maffei in the library of Verona, and by him published at Florence in 1721, and by Chandler at London in 1722. Chandler, Pref. p. ix. after observing that the contested verse was in some Latin copies at least of the sixth century, in the next page grows diffident, and says, that it is uncertain whether Cassiodorus has given us the very words of the apostle, or only his own interpretation. This scepticism provoked the gentle Maffei to treat Chandler very roughly in his *Istoria Diplomatica* and his *Opuscoli Ecclesiastici*. Let us therefore examine the words of Cassiodorus in a literal translation. "*Whosoever believeth that Jesus is the Christ, is born of God*, &c. He who believes Jesus to be God, is born of God the Father; he without doubt is faithful, and he who loves the Father, loves also the Christ who is born of him. Now we so love him, when we keep his

his commandments, which to juft minds are not heavy; but they rather overcome the world, when they believe in him who created the world. To which thing witnefs on earth three myfteries, the water, the blood, and the fpirit, which were fulfilled, we read, in the paffion of the Lord; but in heaven the Father, the Son, and the Holy Spirit; AND THESE THREE IS ONE GOD."

It is incumbent upon them who are pofitive that Caffiodorus had the heavenly witneffes in his copy, to tell us under what form they appeared. This verfe has the misfortune to be always changing fhapes. But it is all one to the defenders. So it be in the text, they care not. I would gladly learn, however, whether Caffiodorus found the eighth verfe before the feventh; whether he found the earthly witneffes in the fame order that he has followed; whether his copy had *Filius* inftead of *Verbum*; whether *tres funt in cœlo* inftead of *tres funt qui teftimonium dant i. e.*; whether it omitted the final claufe of the eighth verfe; and, laftly, whether its reading was, *hi tres unum funt*, or *hi tres unus eft Deus*. Be affured, Sir, that thefe queftions muft receive

ceive a satisfactory answer, before Cassiodorus's testimony will avail you. Where some of the ancient MSS. totally omit a passage, the change of its situation, and the variety of its readings, in others, always render it suspicious, and often demonstrate it to be spurious. Martin himself was aware of this; for in his Verité, p. 62. having occasion to mention the author against Varimadus, he quotes the eighth verse no farther than to the words *in terra*, and smothers the rest with an *etcætera*.

Omnis qui credit quoniam Jesus est Christus, &c. says St. John. *Qui Deum Jesum credit,* says Cassiodorus. If from this interpretation *Deus* had crept into the Latin copies, with what pious wrath and obstinacy would it have been defended! We should be told of Cassiodorus's diligent study of the scriptures; his taste and nicety in choosing the best readings; his painful collation of Greek MSS. and I know not what. Soon after, Cassiodorus adds, " quando in illum credunt, qui condidit mundum." Where are the last words? Not in our present copies, but in that accurate collator's Greek MSS. Let us then read in our present first verse, *Whosoever believeth that Jesus*

Jesus is God, and in the fifth, *Who conquereth the world, but he who believeth in him who created the world?* A choice voucher for a doubtful text! What you say of Greek MSS. amounts to nothing. Cassiodorus does not play the critic in his *Complexiones*, and consequently there was no need of his Greek learning. Or suppose that he sometimes followed the Greek, if one clear proof can be produced, that ever he followed the Latin in opposition to the Greek, this plea is of no weight. (See 1 Pet. III. 22.)

On a diligent examination of the *Complexiones*, I am persuaded that Cassiodorus found no more than these words in his copy, *Tres sunt qui testificantur, aqua, et sanguis, et spiritus, et hi tres unum sunt*. That he gave his own, or rather Eucherius's interpretation of these words, and applied them to the Trinity. Why else should he use the emphatic word *mysteria*, unless he intended to make some mystical application? Since he interprets *spiritus* of the human breath, what mystery, what hidden sense, do these three words contain of themselves? But let us suppose that he understood the passage in this manner:

Which

Which IS WITNESSED BY THREE THINGS *on earth*, THE WATER, BLOOD, AND SPIRIT. *These were visibly fulfilled in the passion of our Lord, but they are mysteries which spiritually represent the Father, Son, and Holy Ghost, in heaven, of whom it may be truly said,* THESE THREE ARE ONE, *that is*, *one God*. This reason will account for his keeping back the clause, *hi tres unum sunt*, and confining it to its nobler sense. This will also account for his arranging the witnesses in the same order with Eucherius, so that the water may answer to the Father, the blood to the Son, and the Spirit remain *in statu quo*. Nor is it strange that Eucherius's works, and consequently this interpretation, should visit Ravenna in the intermediate hundred and forty years that passed between the publication of the *Quæstiones* and *Complexiones*. But perhaps you will like Cassiodorus's own *positive* testimony better than my presumption. Well, Sir, I will please you if I can. In the tenth chapter of his *Divinæ Lectiones*, the title of which is *De Modis Intelligentiæ*, he expressly says that he has collected Eucherius's works. And since he collected them for the sake of their explanations

nations of scripture, he would probably adopt this allegory among other profitable remarks.

Cassiodorus thus explains 1 John II. 13, 14. *I write to you, because ye have overcome the devil, and have known God the Father, and the Son and the Holy Ghost.* Can we suppose that Cassiodorus would thus interpret the single word *God?* No, he found it in his Latin MSS. and not only in his Latin, but his Greek; and his Greek cannot be supposed later than the apostolic age. Let us therefore restore, on the uncorrupt faith of Cassiodorus and his Greek MSS. the true reading; Γράφω ὑμῖν, παιδία, ὅτι ἐγνώκατε θεὸν τὸν πατέρα καὶ τὸν υἱὸν καὶ τὸ ἅγιον πνεῦμα. There are several other places in the N. T. where the true reading has been hitherto shamefully neglected.

Matth. VI. 13. has been already mentioned.

John XVIII. 32. two MSS. in Wetstein's list have preserved the true reading, *That the word of God might be fulfilled, which he spake, signifying by what death he should die.*

John XIX. 40. the Alexandrian MS. reads, *the body of God,* which is no less true and certain, than *the blood of God,* Acts XX. 28.

A a

Acts XIII. 41. a MS. of New-college, Oxford, rightly adds, *that God is crucified, and dies.*

1 Cor. V. 7. *Christ God our passover was sacrificed for us.* So it ought to be read from Hippolytus, a MS. collated by Mr. Matthæi, and a MS. of Chrysostome, and the Lateran council, as I learn from Wetstein, on Acts XX. 28.

2 Thess. II. 16. a MS. collated by Zacagni preserves the true reading; *Now our Lord and God Jesus Christ himself,* &c. From these examples, I hope, it will appear, how falsely that infamous villain Erasmus asserted that Christ is seldom called God in the N. T.

But we need go no farther than our own fifth chapter of St. John, to shew how the text has been mutilated. The genuine reading of the twentieth verse is this: *And we know that the Son of God is come [and was incarnate for our sake, and suffered, and rose from the dead, and took us up], and hath given us an understanding,* &c. The words between brackets (or something like them) are quoted by Hilary, by Faustinus, and the author against Varimadus. They are also in the Toledo MS.

collated

collated by Blanchini, and in three others that I myself have seen. Another shameful mutilation of this chapter will occur presently.

From Cassiodorus we jump two centuries to come to your next author, Ambrose Authpert, or Ansbert, or Autpert (as I find him called in a MS.), who, in his Commentary on the Apocalypse, twice quotes the heavenly witnesses. Nobody denies that some Latin copies had this verse in the eighth century. It is then that we suppose it to have crawled into notice upon the strength of Pseudo-Jerome's recommendation. Autpert also quotes the tenth verse with a considerable various reading; " And this is the witness of God that he hath testified of his Son, [whom he hath sent a saviour upon earth*]." This addition I should not hesitate to restore to the text, unless those illustrious defenders of the faith,

Etherius and Beatus, supplied me with something better. For thus they quote a part of

* I am obliged to trust to memory.

1 John V. *Quia tres sunt qui testimonium dant in terris, aqua, sanguis, et* CARO, *et tria hæc unum sunt, et tres sunt qui testimonium dant in cœlo, Pater, Verbum, et Spiritus, et hæc tria unum sunt* IN CHRISTO JESU. *Si testimonium hominum accipimus, testimonium Dei majus est; et hoc est testimonium Dei, quod testificatus est de Filio suo,* [*quem misit salvatorem super terram, et Filius testimonium perhibuit inter scripturas proficiens, et nos testimonium perhibemus, quoniam videmus eum et annunciamus vobis, ut credatis. Et ideo*] *qui credit,* &c. What a dainty morsel of scripture had the heretics cut away, because, I suppose, it was meat too strong for their sickly stomachs. Let it be immediately restored to the rank from which it has been so long and so unjustly degraded. First, however, let us wash off a little dirt which it has contracted during its disgrace, that it may be fit to see company. *Inter scripturas proficiens* is neither Latin nor sense. To the immortal honour of true criticism, I retrieved the genuine reading by conjecture, *in terra scripturas perficiens*, which I *afterwards* found confirmed by the Toledo MS. of the Vulgate,

of

of which Blanchini has inserted a collation in his *Vindiciæ Veteris Vulgatæ**.

" Walafrid Strabo" (rather Strabus), " author of the *Glossa Ordinaria*, comments upon this verse." Since we allow this verse to have been in some copies of the eighth century, we suppose it to be in more of the ninth. Walafrid might therefore comment upon it, especially as his scruples, if he had any, would be silenced or satisfied by the fictitious Prologue. You believe that Walafrid consulted Greek MSS. and Greek MSS. too as old as the fifth century, because he says, that wherever the vulgar text of the Old Testament was faulty, the Hebrew MSS. ought to be consulted; wherever of the New, the Greek. I could prove many of the most illiterate peasants to be proficients in Greek by the same rule, for they would tell you, that where the translation is wrong or obscure, the originals ought to be examined. But if this argument proves Walafrid to have collated Greek MSS. to the N. T. it proves

---

* See both the quotations in *Wetstein*, tom. II. p. 725, 726.

him equally to have collated Hebrew MSS. to the Old. First, therefore, shew that Walafrid understood Greek and Hebrew. Next produce a competent number of examples, where Walafrid compares the various readings of the Latin, Greek, and Hebrew MSS. and sits in judgement on their merits. You say, p. 324. " Walafrid directs his readers, in all cases of difficulty, to resort to the Greek copies, *which implies* that to be his constant practice." Admirable! Theodore Beza wishes that editors would publish all the various readings of their MSS.* *which implies* that he has suppressed none of his own. Mr. Travis is very bitter against sophistry, unfair quotation, fraud, and forgery, *which implies* that he himself is perfectly free from all such peccadilloes. Many thousands of divines once a week (or oftener) teach the doctrines of religion and the duties of morality, *which implies* their stedfast belief of the one, and their constant practice of the other.

Your inference from Walafrid's advice is caught up by your friend above quoted,

* WETSTEIN, Proleg. p. 148.

p. 322.

p. 322. who says* that *Walafrid Strabo professes to have consulted the most ancient Greek MSS.* I only mention this to shew how readily men will assert the most palpable falsehoods, and how a story gains strength by travelling. Though you allow that both the Syriac and Coptic versions omit the disputed verse, this gentleman asserts that it is wanting in none but the Coptic. Another direct falsehood; which either proves that he has lost all sense of shame, or that he has not read your book with moderate attention.

The rabble of witnesses that you bring after the tenth century, deserves no attention. If you could make them ten times as many, their joint authority would be *a broken reed, on which if a man lean, it shall go into his hand, and pierce it.* I freely therefore give you Rodolph, Rupert, Bernard, Victorinus, Lombard, Aquinas, Scotus, Lyranus, and as many more as you can muster.

From Durandus you infer that the three heavenly witnesses were in the *Ordo Romanus,*

---

* Vindication of the Liturgy, &c. p. 48.

This *Ordo* was composed about the year 730. Allowing therefore that it contained this verse, it would prove little. But Durandus, by quoting the verse from the *Ordo Romanus* of his time, will not prove that it was extant there from the first compilation. None of the adversaries deny (so far as I know) that it had been in quiet possession of almost all the MSS. from the year 1000. The alterations of the liturgy would keep pace with the improvements made in the other copies, and sometimes outrun them. Or, if they did not, the heads of the church would perhaps have sent an order to this effect*: *Scribatur in textu Joannis Epistolæ ubi deest*, TRES SUNT QUI TESTIMONIUM, &c.

" The deference," say you, " yielded to the known learning and integrity of the Lateran council, caused its decrees, in matters even of a secular nature, to be received as law, not only in England," &c. Though this proves nothing in favour of the verse, it proves two other points. That the clergy then exercised dominion over the rights of

* See Letter IX. p. 229.

mankind,

mankind, and that able tithe-lawyers often make sorry critics. *Which I desire some certain gentlemen of my acquaintance to lay up in their hearts as a very seasonable innuendo.*

To your list of Latin witnesses you ought to have added three more, which Maffei found in the library of Verona. The first is a dialogue, not much differing from that which is published in Athanasius's works; the second, Athanasius's commentary on the creed; the third, a book *de divinis officiis*, which couples Matth. XXVIII. 19. 1 John V. 7. In the commentary on the creed, which Blanchini* published, or in Blanchini's notes, that passage, I doubt not, occurred, which Wetstein has quoted, and Mr. Griesbach professes himself unable to find. That author thus quotes Matth. XXVIII. 19. *Ite, baptizate gentes, ungenies eos,* &c. Here we have a scriptural precept for the use of the chrism in baptism, which has now been for ages neglected, to the utter perdition of many

---

* Ut ostendi in *Enarratione Pseudo-Athanasiana in Symbolum*, quam Veronæ edidi. *Evangeliar. Quadrupl.* Part I. p. 90.

souls. But of all writers that have quoted the verse in question, the writer of the *Sermones Dormi Secure* (V. near the end, *de conceptione Mariæ*) makes the most curious application of it. *Unde bene dicitur illud* j. *Jo.* v. *Tres sunt qui testimonium dant, scilicet Virgini Mariæ, quod sit sine originali. Et Daniel* iij. *Hii tres quasi ex uno ore laudabant Deum; scilicet quod matrem suam præservavit ab originali.* I hope you will enrich your next edition with these fresh testimonies, which will make your work complete and consistent.

Postscript.

I know that the right of Walafrid Strabus to the Preface and the *Glossa Ordinaria* is exceedingly questionable; but I have allowed it, that the dispute might be cut somewhat shorter.

SIR,

THE Greek and Latin authors that cannot be perſuaded to quote the three heavenly witneſſes, are ſo fairly enumerated by Mill, Emlyn, Wetſtein, Newton, and others, that I ſhall do little more than repeat their liſt, and add ſuch remarks as may ſeem moſt neceſſary.

GREEK AUTHORS.

Irenæus.
Clemens Alexandrinus.
Dionyſius Alexandrinus, (or the writer againſt Paul of Samoſata under his name.)
Athanaſius.
The Synopſis of Scripture.
The Synod of Sardica.
Epiphanius.
        Baſil.

Basil.
Alexander of Alexandria.
Gregory Nyssen.
Gregory Nazianzen, with his two commentators, Elias Cretensis and Nicetas.
Didymus de Spiritu sancto.
Chrysostome.
An author under his name *de sancta et consubstantiali Trinitate*.
Cyril of Alexandria.
The Exposition of Faith in Justin Martyr's works.
Cæsarius.
Proclus.
The Council of Nice, as it is represented by Gelasius Cyzicenus.
Hippolytus.
Andreas.
Six catenæ quoted by Simon.
The marginal scholia of three MSS.
Hesychius.
John Damascenus.
Germanus of Constantinople.
Oecumenius.
Euthymius Zigabenus.

LATIN

LATIN AUTHORS.

The author de Baptismo Hæreticorum among Cyprian's works.
Novatian.
Hilary.
Lucifer Calaritanus.
Jerome.
Augustine.
Ambrose.
Faustinus.
Leo Magnus.
The author de Promissis.
Eucherius.
Facundus.
Junilius.
Cerealis.
Rusticus.
Bede.
Gregory.
Philastrius.
Paschasius.
Arnobius junior.
Pope Eusebius.

This evidence, which might seem to a common understanding to form a strong negative, you waggishly call a *region of night and*

and nothing, and to guide us through this region with safety and dispatch you lay down two rules, 1. that some of these writers might have quoted the verse in other works of theirs now lost; 2. that when any of them neglect another passage confessedly genuine and equally fit for their purpose, their omission of this verse does not prove it to be spurious or unknown to them. But this accumulation of possibilities is useless and sophistical. It is indeed possible that a writer may forget or neglect to urge one of his best arguments; but that so many authors, with such repeated opportunities, should all agree in shutting their eyes against the light of this marvellous passage, is improbable, incredible, impossible.

Let any unprejudiced man conceive this verse to be generally read and admitted for genuine, and then let him conceive, if he can, that all the defenders of the Trinity could preserve an obstinate silence, and never appeal to it. But how will he bring himself to conceive such an absurdity, if he has been at all conversant with modern divinity? No text has been so often quoted, since its establishment in our printed editions; none so
readily

readily applied to the Trinity, of which it is almoſt always declared to be a compleat and formal proof. It is, in ſhort, the very ſoul of modern controverſy, *tota in toto et tota in qualibet parte.*

But you ſee clearly enough the inſufficiency of theſe two reaſons, and therefore call to your aid a third, that " ſome of the Fathers" (who have not quoted the verſe), " perhaps all of them, conceived the words of this verſe to indicate an unity of conſent only, and not an unity of nature." To make this more likely, you jocularly quote Calvin and Beza, who explain in this manner the clauſe *unum ſunt.* Dr. Horſley indeed ſays (Tracts, p. 345.) that many of the orthodox (to whom he adds himſelf) are of the ſame opinion. As far as I can judge, theſe milder and pretended orthodox are ſo few, that if the more zealous Chriſtians were divided into companies of ten, and every one of their lukewarm brethren waited upon a company, *many decads would go without a cupbearer.* I ſhall produce a few of theſe teſtimonies, as they lie before me. MARTIN earneſtly inſiſts, in the beginning of his Verité, upon the great importance of this paffage, and calls it *the ftrongeft weapon that we can employ againft the Arians.* " Were there," fays ATTERBURY, " no other text for the proof of the doctrine of the holy Trinity——but that only——where St. John fpeaks of *the three witneffes in heaven, it* would be fufficient to make that doctrine an evident part of fcripture; though in all the other paffages ufually produced for it, it fhould be allowed to be expreffed obfcurely." ALLEN, Serm. I. p. 22. fays, with infinite candour, " Very probably (the Arians) forged other MSS. and in them wilfully omitted this verfe of St. John, that fo they might in fome meafure at leaft invalidate and weaken the authority of a text, which was directly oppofite to their falfe doctrines, and which it was *utterly impoffible* to evade the force of by any artificial and unnatural conftructions." SNAPE, Serm. VIII. p. 50: " That he is one and the fame God with the Father and the Son, is declared by St. John in exprefs terms; *There are three,*" &c. FELTON, Moyer's Lectures VII. p. 368: " The doctrine cannot be expreffed in fewer or clearer words." BEVERIDGE, Private Thoughts, II. p. 40: " And yet

yet that all these three persons were but one God, St. John expressly asserts, saying, &c. which certainly are as plain and perspicuous terms, as it is possible to express so great a mystery in." If therefore we may judge from the analogy of modern times, the number of those squeamish Fathers, who would scruple to employ this text, would be trifling, compared with the bolder warriors who would draw it as the sharpest arrow from their quiver. But the mild interpretations of Calvin and Beza prove nothing concerning the Fathers. Modern expositors have deserted many passages which the ancients applied to the Trinity. Calvin's example is the less to the purpose, because he has been accused by his brethren of explaining away some of the capital texts. For instance, *I and my Father are one,* he explains of an unity of consent. But what an host of Fathers quote the same verse without fear or scruple against the heretics, to prove the deity of the Son! Let us suppose that a great number of our Greek MSS. omitted John X. 30. and that some of the most renowned, orthodox, and voluminous Fathers never quoted it, who sees not the

obvious

obvious and natural conclusion, that the verse was unknown in their age? It would be an absurd fancy to think, that they might have quoted this verse in other works; that they might omit it, because they have omitted others; or that perhaps they conceived it not to prove an unity of essence.

Besides, there was another reason for Calvin's and Beza's moderation. They knew the precarious tenure by which this verse held its place, and it would have seemed inconsistent to lay any stress upon the orthodox inferences that might be drawn from a suspected testimony. You will forgive me, too, if I hint, that some of those, who affect to adopt Calvin's exposition, imitate Æsop's fox, and call the grapes sour, because they cannot reach them.

But, Sir, if any of the Fathers thus explained away the consubstantiality of the heavenly witnesses, produce an example or two from their works. Let us have no conjectures. If you can find one ancient author, Greek or Latin, who has thus betrayed the citadel to his enemies, you will not only have a positive argument on your side, but a plausible

sible objection to that ungracious negative. But this, Sir, you cannot perform, I fear. *Your* Jerome says, that this verse is the *chief strength* of the Catholic faith. Why then does not he inculcate it perpetually, in season and out of season? Authpert twice quotes it, without any particular necessity. Such silence then in the other Fathers is unaccountable. If they had really thought that the clause *tres unum sunt* meant only unity of consent, still the passage must have claimed their attention, because it is one of the few where the three divine persons are connumerated distinctly and in order.

The greater part of mankind quotes scripture more by sound than sense. They take every detached sentence for a distinct assertion or apopthegm, and apply it according to its apparent meaning, after they have forcibly torn it from its context. Though a temperate critic might, from a diligent examination of the Apostle's argument, be induced to doubt whether the one essence of the Trinity was here intended, how few of such critics were in the primitive church, and how few are in our own! The bulk at least would lay violent hands upon the verse, and cry it up for a decisive testimony. You say, that " through the vast series of one thousand four hundred years, not a single author, whether Patripassian, Cerinthian, Ebionite, Arian, Macedonian, or Sabellian, &c. has ever taxed the various quotations of this verse with interpolation or forgery." You have read, I presume, a competent number of the works of these heretics. You have read some which were written expressly in answer to those treatises that employ the three heavenly witnesses. If you have, Sir, be so good as to inform us where they may be found. Surely, Sir, you did not believe that this argument was of any weight, even while you wrote it down. I know only of one heretic, Abbot Joachim, who has quoted the verse; and he lived when by the unanimous confession of all parties it had been long read in the Latin version. Your reasoning therefore amounts to this: Either the heretics published answers to the orthodox writers who quote 1 John V. 7. or they did not. If they published no answers, they certainly made no objection to the authenticity of that verse. If they published

lished any answers, those answers are now lost; and still, *as far as we know*, no objection has been made to the verse. What an excellent judge Mr. Travis is of a negative argument!

You perceive however, at last, that the negative argument is of some weight, and therefore you suppose that the verse was *partially lost* in some part of the interval between the years 101 and 384. You had better correct a little, and suppose that it was entirely omitted in St. John's autograph. This will solve all difficulties much better, take my word for it. I always thought that when a great number of MSS. of an ancient author omit any passage, upon which the intermediate writers, who upon other occasions freely quote that author's works, are quite silent; though the passage be very fit for their subject; though they quote other passages much less apposite; though they quote so near it that they could not help seeing it, if it were extant; though sometimes they quote the words that precede, and the words that follow; even though they extract from the next words with great labour and difficulty the very sense which this passage would furnish at a much easier and cheaper rate; I always thought, that, in such a case, the plain reason of these omissions of the Fathers was a total absence of the passage from their copies, and a total ignorance of its existence. But, according to you, omissions are no proof against a verse, where there is positive proof for it. I ask, then, how much positive proof is necessary? Is any text genuine, that may be found in the Latin version, or in a few Greek MSS. provided no actual charge of forgery be brought against it? If this be your opinion (as it seems to be), you need not be afraid of being confuted, for nobody will dispute with you. If our Greek MSS. unanimously retained this verse, while the Fathers were silent upon it, this dissent might leave us in an unpleasant state of doubt and suspence. But when the Fathers and Greek MSS. so exactly agree in rejecting a text, to adopt any other reason than the obvious fact, the spuriousness of the passage, is to set aside all evidence, for the sole end of maintaining this judicious paradox, that the worse Latin copies have preserved the genuine reading.

You

You make exceptions to some of the particular Fathers who have not quoted this verse. You say, that neither Alexander of Alexandria, nor Eusebius in his tract against the Sabellians, nor Gregory Nazianzen in his treatise on the Divinity of Christ, nor Epiphanius against Noetus, cites Matth. XXVIII. 19. But Alexander quotes John X. 30. to which 1 John V. 7. would have been an admirable parallel. If by Eusebius's tract against the Sabellians you mean the three books *de Ecclesiastica Theologia*, there is an express quotation of it in one, and a plain reference to it in another of those books. If Gregory Nazianzen does not quote the form of baptism in the oration that you have named, he quotes it as a strong proof of the Trinity in his forty-ninth oration, where he also quotes John X. 30. Now, since 1 John V. 7. unites in itself the merits of both those passages, it is strange that Gregory should never think of quoting it, he who had in his thirty-sixth oration mentioned the other three witnesses, *the spirit, the water, and the blood*. If Epiphanius does not quote Matth. XXVIII. 19. against Noetus, how often does he quote it elsewhere! You add, that the Synopsis may with great probability be ascribed to Athanasius, and that it plainly refers to the verse in question. I answer, 1. that the Synopsis is certainly spurious; and, 2. that it contains not the slightest vestige of the verse, but expressly quotes II. 23. to shew the unity of the Father with the Son. This I have proved at large, Letter IX. p. 209—213. And now let any man consider with himself, whether Athanasius, who frequently and repeatedly cites Matth. XXVIII. 19. John X. 30. and even the twentieth verse of our fifth chapter, could be so blind or negligent as to pass over such an important text. This verse would have been very commodious to prove the deity of the Son, the deity of the Holy Ghost, or the joint deity of the three persons. But neither Athanasius, nor Didymus, nor the two Gregories, nor Basil, nor Cyril, though they have all largely written upon these subjects, have paid any regard to the celestial testimony. The second person of the Trinity is here more clearly called the Logos, than even in the beginning of the gospel. How has it happened that no ancient writer whatever

ever quotes the verse for this title, though they make several fantastical applications of texts that are nothing to the purpose? You will hardly, Sir, I guess, prefer the other reading, *Filius*, which is in a few Latin and some French MSS. in Wickliffe's translation; in a MS. of Victor, and in Bernard. For if you allow that *Filius* is the genuine reading, *Verbum* must have been a most impudent forgery, and the credit of the Latin copies will be demolished at a blow. But taking *Verbum* for genuine, I can see only one reason (which I leave Mr. Travis to find out) why this verse is never quoted to shew that Christ is called *the Word*.

What a difference in value between the eighth and seventh verses! Yet the eighth is often quoted, the seventh scarcely ever. How wonderful it is that the authors who quote the eighth verse should never turn a little out of their way, allured by the charms of the seventh! We have seen the Armenian council three times quoting the seventh verse, not because the subject which they were treating required it, but merely in compliment to its extraordinary beauty and merit. If any of of the authors now extant, who quote the eighth verse, had ever quoted the seventh, in defence of the Trinity, they surely would have repeated it, if it were only for the sake of old acquaintance.

Cyril quoting the sixth, eighth, and ninth verses, argues that, because the Spirit is said to witness, and this witness is called the witness of God, therefore the Spirit is God. But insert the seventh verse, and this argument is spoiled. For the witness of God is sufficiently marked out by the witness of the Father, an heretic would answer, without extending the word God either to the Word or the Spirit.

But the strongest proof that this verse is spurious may be drawn from the Epistle of Leo the Great to Flavianus upon the Incarnation. This epistle has been translated into Greek, read in churches, sent round to the Councils both in the East and West, defended by several authors in set treatises, and consequently more generally known than most of the writings of the Fathers. In this epistle he quotes part of the fifth chapter, from the fourth to the eighth verse, and omits the

three

three heavenly witnesses. John Moschus informs us, in his *Spiritual Meadow**, that he was told by Abbot Menas, who was told by Abbot Eulogius, who was told by Archdeacon Gregory, that the Roman church had a written tradition, that Pope Leo, when he had finished his letter to Flavianus against Eutyches and Nestorius, laid it on the tomb of the foreman of the Apostles, Peter, and besought him to correct it, wherever it was erroneous or imperfect. After he had prayed, fasted, and lain on the ground, a decent time (about forty days; for the Apostle was somewhat shy, like Milton's Eve, *Who would be wooed, and not unsought be won*), Peter appeared to him, and said, " I have read and corrected ;" upon which Leo takes the letter from the tomb, opens it, and finds that the Apostle had been as good as his word. Upon this *authentic fact* I shall make a few remarks. Peter could not be ignorant of the existence of this verse, if it were genuine. We may reasonably suppose his faculties to be so far improved in heaven, that he remembered all the N. T.

---

* *Coteler.* Ecclef. Græc. Monum. tom. II. p. 416.

Or

Or if by chance he had forgotten this epistle of St. John, or this part of it, the author was at hand to set him right; *for it is impossible to suppose that St. Peter would not in such an undertaking constantly confer with such a neighbour, with such a friend, with such a man, as St. John**. He must therefore have foreseen what untoward consequences the heretics would draw, if the seventh verse were omitted in Leo's epistle, and would have certainly replaced it, if it were genuine. But by suffering the omission to pass uncorrected, we may be sure that St. Peter thought the verse spurious, or that it did not then exist. From this conclusion there is no escaping, but by a denial of the fact, and that would be to introduce an universal Pyrrhonism into history.

The only Greek evidence, earlier than the thirteenth century, that even seems to be in your favour, is the dialogue published with Athanasius. That dialogue quotes and applies to the Trinity these words, *And the three are one.* The Greek words literally agree with

---

* Mr. Travis uses these words of Crispin and Stephens, p. 58, 123.

the reading of the eighth verse in the French King's MS. No. 60. Καὶ οἱ τρεῖς τὸ ἕν εἰσιν. And since the marginal note upon that clause is in the MS. *One God, one godhead,* it need not be doubted but that the author of the dialogue meant to give the same interpretation.

You quarrel with us for urging the negative testimony of Bede and Oecumenius, while we reject Victor's for being too late. I will endeavour, Sir, to explain this matter. An important and curious passage of scripture ought to be quoted by a reasonable proportion of the writers of every succeeding age. But if either through fraud or chance, a spurious sentence is inserted into some copies of scripture, though from the general propensity of transcribers the number of interpolated MSS. may be daily increased, yet several ages must elapse before a general corruption can take place. It has however at last happened, in some places, that the corrupted copies have almost swallowed up the others. In this case, if we can find that such a passage was unknown to an author of the later ages, it is so far from being a prejudice against him,

that

that he lived so late, that he is a stronger testimony against the addition, because he shews that some uncorrupted copies remained, even after the interpolation had been making its way for so many centuries. If therefore Bede was ignorant of this verse, since Bede was a good judge of the state of Latin MSS. in his time, it will follow that the Latin copies of the eighth century generally omitted it; which is otherwise probable, because most Latin MSS. of that and the ninth centuries omit it. If Oecumenius and Euthymius Zigabenus knew nothing of the verse, it will follow that the Greek MSS. of the eleventh and twelfth centuries omitted it.

I am willing to suppose that Bede had no Greek MSS. except to the Acts. But if he had a Greek MS. of the Catholic Epistles, which wanted the three heavenly witnesses, he could not tell us of the omission of them, unless he knew of their existence in the Latin. You therefore modestly assume, that since the verse was in Jerome's version, it must have been in Bede's copy. How often shall we be favoured with this piece of sophistry? This passage was in Jerome's version; therefore Bede

Bede knew of it. I should think, Sir, this argument more agreeable to logic: The copies of Jerome's version vary; some retaining, some omitting the passage; Bede makes no mention of it; therefore Bede used a copy that omitted the passage. Next you tell us, from Martin, that Bede must have known of this text from Cyprian, Fulgentius, and the confession in Victor; all of whom he has quoted. With respect to Cyprian, he might not know to what place of scripture Cyprian referred; or he might think with Facundus that Cyprian interpreted the eighth verse. With respect to Victor and Fulgentius, if he knew nothing of the verse when he read their works, he was not obliged to record for quotations of scripture passages which he did not know to be in scripture. If he thought they were guilty of a pious fraud, was he blameable for not imitating them? This objection supposes that Bede took the trouble to examine critically every text quoted by Fulgentius and Victor. A pleasant task you would impose upon the poor man! Why, Sir, when you took upon trust, from Martin, your charges against the Syriac and

Coptic

Coptic verſions, you are conſcious that you did not examine a ſingle reference. And yet I apprehend this was a duty incumbent upon you, though Bede was bound by no tie of conſcience to hunt after the various quotations produced by his authors.

But if any perſon will read through Bede's commentary upon the fifth chapter, he muſt ſee, unleſs he be wilfully blind, that Bede was totally ignorant of the ſeventh verſe. He is ſo minute and exact, that he has tranſcribed the whole text, except two or three words at the end of one verſe, and even thoſe he inſerts in his commentary. If after all this you inſiſt, that he might know of the verſe, I can think of no proof that would ſettle the point, except an actual aſſurance of Bede's innocence under his own hand. Perhaps Bede ought to have uſed ſuch language as this: " N. B. I have never heard of an additional ſet of witneſſes, nor ever ſaw them in any copy." Let it be added, that Bede was zealouſly orthodox, as appears from his hymn on St. Edeldrida, H. E. IV. 20. *Alma Deus Trinitas, qui ſecula cuncta gubernas, Annue jam*

jam cœptis, alma Deus Trinitas*. And upon this very chapter he breaks out, *Pereat de terra memoria eorum, qui eum vel Deum vel hominem esse verum denegant.*

Newton had suspected that the words *in terra* were not written by Bede, because he so particularly explains the rest of the verse, without taking any notice of them. Erasmus had already observed that a MS. omitted these words, though a much later hand had added in the margin the three heavenly witnesses. What pity that such a copy did not come into the hands of the first editor, that Bede might have been a voucher for the verse! Emlyn tells us, upon hearsay, that the MSS. of Bede omitted *in terra*. Martin answered, that he had seen those words with his own eyes in a MS. at Utrecht. I fully believe this assertion; for I myself have seen them in a MS. at Oxford, but very modern, and of little value. All the other ten that I collated omit *in terra*, without any rasure in the text or note in the margin. Several of them boast

---

* See also his Hymn de Quatuor Temporibus, Vol. I. p. 481.

a decent

a decent antiquity, but the oldest* carries its own date, A.C. 818. I confess my rudeness to you in closely tracing your steps so often. If in revenge for this rudeness you wish to examine these MSS. and see whether I have not lied for the good of my cause (for you well know, Sir, that no credit is due to polemics), you will find two of the MSS. in our public library, two in Bennet-college library, three in the Museum, and four in the Bodleian.

In Facundus, it is true, the editions six times repeat *in terra*; but these words are so inconsistent with the interpretation which Facundus is labouring to establish, that Bengelius fairly allows them to have been added by transcribers. We ought also to consider that Facundus has been published from a single MS. The same corruption I suspect to have crept into the treatise *de duplici martyrio*, and the true reading to be: *Commemorat et Joannes Evangelista triplex testimonium, spiritus, aquæ, et sanguinis.* The same author af-

---

* Mr. ASTLE has given a Specimen in his *Origin and Progress of Writing*, Pl. XIX. Spec. 2. p. 106.

terwards

terwards says: *Quanquam* HI TRES UNUM SUNT; UNUS ENIM DEUS EST, *qui per* SPIRITUM, AQUAM, ET SANGUINEM, *declarat hominum generi virtutem et bonitatem suam.* How easily might the seventh verse grow out of such observations as these!

I shall now briefly examine the pleas that have been set up in defence of the verse. 1. " The Arians erased it." We might expect some small evidence of this accusation. What cunning fellows those Arians were to erase this testimony, not only from their own books, but from the books and memories of the Catholics. You, Sir, I perceive, will neither positively condemn nor honourably acquit these heretics. You tell us that Socrates charges them with mutilating this very epistle. Does he expressly charge the Arians? Is his charge general or particular? He complains, that *they who wished to separate the divinity and the humanity of Christ* had erased this sentence, 1 John IV. 3. *Every spirit that divides Jesus, is not from God,* " which," says Socrates, " is in the old MSS." First, I cannot see how this doctrine could give any offence to the Arians. Secondly, if Socrates had

had accused them here, his silence upon such a piece of fraud as the erasion of the three witnesses, is a strong presumption of their innocence. Thirdly, I should like to have seen a few of these *ancient MSS.* For at present every Greek MS. every version, except the Vulgate, most of the Greek Fathers (all, according to Mr. Griesbach), and some though few of the Latins, agree in the common reading. Besides, there is a quaintness, as Bengelius rightly observes, which favours more of an interpolator's genius, than an apostle's simplicity. And a scholium in one of Mr. Matthæi's MSS. very naturally accounts for the corruption. " It is the character (of Antichrist) by false prophets and spirits TO DIVIDE JESUS, *in not confessing that he is come in the flesh.*" However, if you chuse to defend Socrates, you will have the concurrence of that orthodox divine, Mr. Gibbon, Vol. IV. p. 540, or VIII. 272. For my own part, I think that his decision is very uncritical, and that the reading of the Vulgate in this place has not above twenty times as much authority as 1 John V. 7. But be that as it will, Socrates does not accuse

the

the Arians; nor is his accufation founded, if he did accufe them; nor, if the accufation could be proved, would it help, but rather hurt your argument.

The holy Fathers were very unfuccefsful in fuch accufations. I have already taken notice of Ambrofe's charge againft the Arians, that they erafed *Spiritus eft Deus* from John III. 6. What harm had this fentence done the Arians? It proves, fays Ambrofe, the Deity of the Spirit. Could not the Arians fuggeft, with fome colour of probability, that the true conftruction was, *God is a Spirit?* Or, if they cut it out here, why did the blockheads leave it in the next chapter? They had however good fuccefs, for the fentence was fcarcely to be found in any copies of that age, as Ambrofe tells us, and, I dare fay, with great truth. What dangerous impoftors! Dr. Horfley fays, that the orthodox would have poorly ferved their purpofe by forging 1 John V. 7. I fay, in like manner, that the orthodox would have poorly ferved their purpofe by forging *Spiritus eft Deus*, John III. 6. Yet I think that both places have been corrupted by orthodox copiers.

They crept into some MSS. by chance and negligence, but, as soon as they were known, were eagerly quoted and sent on every expedition against the heretics.

Another example of this laudable zeal of the Fathers against heretics may be found in Ambrose. The heretics misapplied the verse Mark XIII. 32. which seems to ascribe ignorance to the Son. Ambrose boldly denies the fact. "First," says he, "the ancient Greek MSS. have not the clause, that *neither the Son knoweth*; but no wonder, if they who have adulterated the holy scriptures, have also falsified this passage." A little after, however, conscious of the weakness of his assertion, he adds; "But grant it written by the Evangelists," and then proceeds to explain. An advocate for Ambrose will in vain suppose that he meant Matth. XXIV. 36. which will only reduce his hero from a falsehood to an equivocation. The heretics would care nothing about Matthew, if the reading in Mark were allowed to be genuine. I conclude therefore that the charges of the Fathers against the Arians shew much more valour and spirit than prudence.

2. "The

2. "This verse might be lost by the *homœoteleuton*. The eye might jump from one μαρ]υροῦντες to the other, and consequently the remaining part of the two verses would be, *For there are three that bear record on earth, the spirit, the water, and the blood, and the three agree in one.*" To which supposition I answer,

First, that this argument ought to be sparingly used. If a marginal addition be taken into the text by transcribers, it is likely to have for its beginning or ending the same words that begin or end the adjacent sentence. Thus Augustine's explanation might be turned into a marginal note, *Trinitas ipsa est, de qua recte dicitur, Tres sunt qui testimonium dant, Spiritus, id est, Pater ; sanguis, id est, Filius ; et aqua, id est, Spiritus sanctus ; et tres unum sunt.* Such a note would soon be pruned and polished into this form, *Sicut tres sunt qui testimonium dant in cœlo, Pater*, &c. which is actually the reading of several MSS. now extant. The critics generally reject the application of the prophecy in Matth. XXVII. 35. It would be ridiculous in this instance to argue from similar endings. The same

rotten

rotten buttress is used by Grabe to prop the ruinous reading, John III. 6. And the same might be used to support Cyprian's addition, 1 John II. 17. How easy it would be to say, that the words, which were in Cyprian's copy, and *consequently* in the Old Italic, and *consequently* in the Greek MSS. of the second century, and *consequently* in St. John's autograph, were swallowed up by that voracious monster, the *homœoteleuton*! *Qui autem facit voluntatem Dei, manet in æternum,* QUOMODO ET DEUS MANET IN ÆTERNUM. If any man writes glosses and explanations in the margin of a book, he will find that many of them will begin like the following or end like the foregoing sentence. This canon however will do one good thing; it will make interpolation the easiest matter in the world. A forger has nothing to do but to take care that the passage which he inserts, shall have this single requisite of a similar ending, and he will be provided with a sufficient answer to all arguments drawn from the authority of MSS. and of versions, and from the silence of intermediate writers.

Secondly,

Secondly, this argument from the *homœoteleuton* is utterly excluded by the malice of fortune. For in the leap from one μαϱ]υϱοῦντες to another, the transcriber must have left untouched those puzzling words, ἐν τῇ γῇ. But those words are in no Greek MS. in no version, in no Greek author that quotes the eighth verse; and almost all the Latin MSS. and Fathers that omit the heavenly witnesses, omit too all mention of the earth. I have referred, Letter II. p. 26, 27. to Simon's seeming assertion that a Greek MS. retained the words ἐν τῇ γῇ, but I have there given my reasons, why he is mistaken. Newton had already hinted the same suspicion; and I have since seen a manuscript note of De Missy's in the margin of Wetstein's N. T. Vol. II. p. 721, where he adopts the same opinion, though he had formerly reasoned upon the contrary supposition as an undoubted fact, Journ. Brit. XI. p. 78. I now dare boldly affirm that those words were no more in that MS. than in any other. For Abbé Roger, in his dissertation on 1 John V. 7. p. 32. transcribes the eighth verse from this very MS. and omits the words ἐν τῇ γῇ.

Bede

Bede and Facundus I have already cleared from this spurious addition. Newton also supposes, what is not improbable, that the Latin MSS. which omit the seventh verse, and retain *in terra*, were interpolated from orthodox MSS. by conscientious critics, who might not be scrupulous about so trifling an insertion, though they were afraid to add a whole sentence. But since the defenders of the seventh verse may in this case urge, with some plausibility, the *homœoteleuton*, I am content, as I have said, Letter VI. p. 152. that all such Latin MSS. be neutral.

Bengelius wishes to transpose the seventh and eighth verses. I believe that this was more frequently the position of the verses, when the heavenly witnesses first obtained admittance. But as much as this hypothesis gains in one view, it loses in the other. The allegorical interpretation will then so naturally follow the verse which it explains, particularly in the copies that announce the heavenly witnesses with a *sicut*, that the manner in which the interpolation was made will be obvious to any person acquainted with the history of MSS. Twells saw something of this

this confequence; for he reafons againft the idea of an allegory or marginal glofs upon this ground, that the oldeft and beft MSS. prefix the feventh verfe; but, fays he, if the feventh verfe were a glofs engendered by the eighth, the feventh would follow the eighth. The plain anfwer to this reafoning is, that fuch indeed was the arrangement of the two verfes, when the interpolation began, but that it was afterwards altered in compliment to the fuperior dignity and excellence of the feventh. I have declined the confideration of the *Difciplina Arcani*, nor fhall I refume it. It is a dangerous hypothefis, which, if it were admitted, inftead of ftrengthening particular paffages, would weaken the authority of the whole N. T. With equal reafon Mill believes that the marginal notes produced by Simon from Greek MSS, (the moft palpable gloffes that can be conceived), are not intended for interpretations of the eighth verfe, but are really the mangled limbs of the feventh. But while thefe learned men urge fuch frivolous arguments, they fhew more plainly than by a direct confeffion, how feverely they feel the want of evidence. So

feverely,

severely, that Bengelius at laſt *begs leave to hope, that in due time, if not St. John's own autograph, yet ſome very ancient Greek MSS. containing the verſe, may be found hidden in the ſhelves of divine Providence.* To which pious hope Wetſtein anſwers in the words of Cicero: *Hic tu tabulas deſideras Heraclienſium publicas, quas Italico bello, incenſo tabulario, interiiſſe ſcimus omnes. Eſt ridiculum ad ea quæ habemus, nihil dicere; quærere quæ habere non poſſumus.*

3. " But the tenour of the context requires us to keep the verſe." The oppoſers of the verſe ſay, on the contrary, that its inſertion confuſes the whole ſenſe, breaks the connection, and makes the moſt intricate and ambiguous ſentence that ever was ſeen. For my own part, I thought Newton's expoſition of the ſhorter reading probable and conſiſtent enough, till I was told by Dr. Horſley, Tracts, p. 346. that " it was a model of that ſort of paraphraſe by which any given ſenſe may be affixed to any given words." I ſuſpected, I confeſs, at firſt, that having before him both your expoſition and Newton's, he might have confounded them in his mind, and given to

Newton's

Newton's the character which was due to yours. But this opinion I soon abandoned. I wish therefore that Dr. Horsley had favoured us with his own paraphrase, and shewn the truth of his assertion, " that the omission of the seventh verse breaks the connection and heightens the obscurity of the apostle's discourse." Certainly the mention of the water, blood, and Spirit, in the sixth verse, is with great propriety followed by the repetition of the same terms in the genuine text; which repetition is rendered emphatic by the exaltation of the Spirit, water, and blood, into three witnesses. If the Spirit that witnesses in the sixth verse be the holy Spirit, which I think cannot be doubted, " because the Spirit is truth," why is the epithet, after being twice omitted, added in the seventh verse, to mark a distinction without a difference? If the word " holy," which is omitted in some few MSS. be spurious, why is the human spirit, without any mark or circumstance to distinguish it, repeated in the same breath? But if the Spirit in the eighth verse be the holy Spirit, what is the sense of the same Spirit witnessing both in heaven and on earth? It

will

will be to no purpose to invert the order of the words, and say, *There are three in heaven*, and *There are three on earth*, for still the Spirit is both in heaven and earth. You tell us that, without the seventh verse, the expression, *Witness of God*, in the ninth, has no due antecedent. This, Sir, is a mistake. The witness of the Spirit in the sixth and eighth verses is a proper antecedent. The Spirit may be taken in two senses. The orthodox, who understand the Spirit personally, cannot deny that the witness of the Spirit is the witness of God; nor will either the orthodox or heretics deny, that the miraculous gifts of the Spirit, which attested the divine mission of Jesus, were truly the witness of God, which he witnessed of his Son. I have diligently perused all the orthodox expositions that have fallen in my way, but without ever having the good luck to understand them. I remember one very ingenious gentleman, who, in two letters to Dr. Bentley, offers to prove that the seventh verse is essential to the context, and only assumes two self-evident propositions: 1. that the Spirit signifies the mediatorial office; and, 2. that the water

is

is the *Shechinah*. But I have dwelt longer than I intended upon this subject. Where there is no external evidence, internal evidence can never be pleaded for the necessity of so large and so important an addition. I shall therefore hasten to dismiss the subject by a brief recapitulation of the inferences which may fairly be deduced from the facts dispersed through the foregoing Letters.

The only genuine words of 1 John V. 7, 8. are these: "Ὅτι τρεῖς εἰσιν οἱ μαρτυροῦντες, τὸ πνεῦμα, καὶ τὸ ὕδωρ καὶ τὸ αἷμα καὶ οἱ τρεῖς εἰς τὸ ἕν εἰσιν. This is the reading of all the Greek MSS. above an hundred and ten; of near thirty of the oldest Latin, of the two Syriac versions, of the Coptic, Arabic, Æthiopic, and Slavonic. But Tertullian, in imitation of the phrase, *I and my Father are one**, had said of the three persons of the Trinity, *Which three are one*. Cyprian was misled by

---

* An antagonist of Beza's told him, that instead of endeavouring to wrest so stubborn a text as, *This is my body*, by vain explanations, he would do better to amend it at once, and read, *This is not my body*. The Jesuit Garasse (see *Bayle*, au mot *Beze*) soon after asserted, in print, that Beza had actually proposed this reading.

this

this paſſage of his maſter. Taking it for an alluſion to ſcripture, he wiſely inferred that it was an application of 1 John V. 8. and, as he had no doubt of Tertullian's infallibility, he adopted the ſame application, and ſaid boldly, *Of the Father, Son, and Holy Ghoſt, it is written, And the three are one.*

That Cyprian in this place interprets the eighth verſe, we are told by Facundus, who, by appealing to this very place of Cyprian to prove that the Spirit, water, and blood, are meant of the Trinity, ſhews that he knew of no ſuch text, and that in his opinion Cyprian knew of no ſuch text, as the three heavenly witneſſes. Fulgentius indeed quotes Cyprian's authority for the modern reading, but from the manner of his appeal it appears that he could not quote the verſe upon the faith of copies of his own age, and therefore relied upon the faith, as he ſuppoſed, of Cyprian's copy. In the interval of more than two centuries, when this interpretation had been expreſsly maintained by Auguſtine and Eucherius, a marginal note of this ſort crept into a few copies; *Sicut tres ſunt qui teſtimonium dant in cœlo, Pater*, &c. Such a copy

copy was used by the author of the confession which Victor has preserved. Such another was used by the author of the books *de Trinitate*, if indeed he was a different person from the other. He would miss no fair opportunity of producing his favourite text, of which he perhaps was the fonder for having newly found it. The verse however seems to have had very small success till the eighth century, when the forger or forgers of the decretals, and of the spurious prologue to the canonical epistles, recommended it to public notice. Yet still it remained a rude, unformed mass, and was not completely licked into shape before the end of the tenth century. In the twelfth and thirteenth centuries it was universally received for genuine, and therefore cited without suspicion in the Acts of the Lateran Council. These Acts were translated into Greek about the year 1300, and from them Emanuel Calecas borrowed his quotation. Joseph Bryennius, too, in the fifteenth century, quotes the same verse, but either from the Latin version, or from his friend Thomas Aquinas. In the thirteenth century, Haytho, King of Armenia, undertook to make a new edition of the Armenian scriptures, with the aid of Jerome's prologues and the Latin version. Haytho most probably inserted this verse in his edition upon the authority of his supposed Jerome; but if Haytho, which is scarcely possible, neglected it, Uscan, who improved Haytho's edition from the Vulgate, could not fail of supplying the defect. With equal accuracy and fidelity this verse has been imposed upon the modern Greeks in their printed Apostolos, upon the Indian Christians by Menezes, upon the Russians by their late editors, and upon every other Christian nation in their several translations. It has been honestly inserted in several of the Syriac editions, and in the Greek and Russian confessions of faith.

The reader, who recollects the substance of my Letters, will easily distinguish the probabilities from the positive facts. But from the facts stated in this historical deduction, it is evident, that if the text of the heavenly witnesses had been known from the beginning of Christianity, the ancients would have eagerly seized it, inserted it in their creeds,
quoted

quoted it repeatedly againſt the heretics, and ſelected it for the brighteſt ornament of every book that they wrote upon the ſubject of the Trinity.

In ſhort, if this verſe be really genuine, notwithſtanding its abſence from all the viſible Greek MSS. except two; one of which aukwardly tranſlates the verſe from the Latin, and the other tranſcribes it from a printed book; notwithſtanding its abſence from all the verſions except the Vulgate; and even from many of the beſt and oldeſt MSS. of the Vulgate; notwithſtanding the deep and dead ſilence of all the Greek writers down to the thirteenth and moſt of the Latins down to the middle of the eighth century; if, in ſpite of all theſe objections, it be ſtill genuine, no part of ſcripture whatſoever can be proved either ſpurious or genuine; and Satan has been permitted, for many centuries, miraculouſly to baniſh the fineſt paſſage in the N. T. from the eyes and memories of almoſt all the Chriſtian authors, tranſlators, and tranſcribers.

At laſt, Sir, I ſee land. I have ſo clearly explained my ſentiments concerning the authority of the diſputed verſe, and the merits of your book, in the progress of these Letters, that it will be needless to add any thing upon either of those topics. As I was persuaded that Mr. Gibbon would never condescend to answer you, I have been bold enough to trouble you with my objections to your facts and arguments. The proofs of the spuriousness of 1 John V. 7. that I have enumerated, are, in my opinion, more than sufficient to convince any reasonable man. But whatever success I may have had in the main question, there is another point, which I have proved to demonstration, that Mr. Travis is radically ignorant of the subject which he has undertaken to illustrate. You may therefore reply, Sir, or not, as shall seem good to you. If you think proper not to expose yourself again, which, to speak as a friend, I should think your wisest plan, I shall attribute your silence to a consciousness of your own weakness. You will call it contempt of your adversary, and I cannot deny the retaliation to be fair enough, considering with how small respect I have treated an author, who *has vindicated the authenticity of that important passage* (1 John V. 7.) *in a superior way,*

way, *so as to leave no room for future doubt or cavil**. But if you reply, as you half promise †, I shall not think myself bound to continue the debate, unless both your matter and style much excel your Letters to Mr. Gibbon, and still more that *Crambe recocta* ‡ which you called a defence of Stephens and Beza. Such replies will carry their own refutation with them to all readers that are not eaten up with prejudice; and others it would be folly to expect to satisfy. I shall therefore be perfectly silent, unless you can disprove the charges, that I have brought against

---

* " An Apology for the Liturgy and Clergy of the Church of England," p. 57, 58. How much stronger is this than the faint, half-faced compliment paid by the author of " Considerations on the Expediency of revising the Liturgy and Articles," p. 70. *Mr. Travis's labours on the genuineness of this text are highly meritorious!* And, as if this compliment were not cold enough, he soon damps it by adding, that many excellent critics will not admit Mr. Travis's vindication to be such as leaves no room for future doubt. From this and similar passages, our *Consistent Protestant* is, I fear, little better than an heretic.

† Gentleman's Magazine for March, 1790.

‡ Gentleman's Magazine for January, 1790.

you,

you, of ignorance and misrepresentation. In case of conviction, I dare not promise to retract publicly (for I know how frail are the vows of authors and lovers), but I promise to try. If you confess the charges, and yet maintain that the errors you have committed are venial, and consistent with a knowledge of the subject, I shall excuse myself from the controversy, and consider you as degraded from that rank of literature which entitles one writer to challenge another.

FINIS.

www.ingramcontent.com/pod-product-compliance
Lightning Source LLC
Chambersburg PA
CBHW022138300426
44115CB00006B/237